S0-FJQ-579

Special Education and Development

Perspectives on Young Children with Special Needs

Edited by

Samuel J. Meisels, Ed.D.
Associate Professor, Department of Child Study
    and
Director, LINC Outreach
    (Learning In Integrated Classrooms)
Eliot-Pearson Children's School
Tufts University

University Park Press
Baltimore

371.9
Sp 32

UNIVERSITY PARK PRESS
International Publishers in Science, Medicine, and Education
233 East Redwood Street
Baltimore, Maryland 21202

Copyright © 1979 by University Park Press

Composed by University Park Press, Typesetting Division
Manufactured in the United States of America by The Maple Press Company

Library of Congress Cataloging in Publication Data

Main entry under title:

Special education and development.

  Bibliography: p.
  Includes index.
  1. Handicapped children — Education — Addresses, essays, lectures.
2. Classroom management — Addresses, essays, lectures. 3. Open plan schools
— Addresses, essays, lectures. 4. Mainstreaming in education — Addresses,
essays, lectures. I. Meisels, Samuel J.
LC4015.S675   371.9   79-4343
ISBN O-8391-1351-X

Contents

Contributors

Nicholas J. Anastasiow, Ph.D.
Director
Institute for Child Study
Indiana University
Bloomington, Indiana 47401

Bernard Allen Banet, M.A.
Director of Planning and
  Development
High/Scope Educational Research
  Foundation
600 North River Street
Ypsilanti, Michigan 48197

Ellen B. Barnes, Ph.D.
Co-director, Jowonio: The Learning
  Place
Educational Director, The Center on
  Human Policy
Syracuse University
Syracuse, New York 13210

Anthony S. Bryk, Ed.D.
Assistant Professor
Graduate School of Education
Harvard University
Cambridge, Massachusetts 02138
and
Senior Research Associate
Huron Institute
Cambridge, Massachusetts 02138

Rebecca Brown Corwin, Ed.M.
Assistant Professor
Elementary Education
Lesley College Graduate School
Cambridge, Massachusetts 02138

David Elkind, Ph.D.
Professor and Chairman
Department of Child Study
Tufts University
Medford, Massachusetts 02155

Lane W. Gunnoe, M.Ed.
Project Coordinator, LINC Outreach
Eliot-Pearson Children's School
Tufts University
Medford, Massachusetts 02155

Frances Pockman Hawkins
Associate Director
Mountain View Center for
  Environmental Education
University of Colorado
1511 University Avenue
Boulder, Colorado 80309

George E. Hein, Ph.D.
Professor, Graduate School
  of Education
Co-director, Program Evaluation
  and Research Group
Lesley Collaborative for
  Educational Development
Lesley College
Cambridge, Massachusetts 02138

Peter Knoblock, Ph.D.
Director, Jowonio: The Learning
  Place
Professor of Special Education
Division of Special Education
  and Rehabilitation
Syracuse University
Syracuse, New York 13210

Murray Levine, Ph.D.
Professor of Psychology
State University of New York
  at Buffalo
Buffalo, New York 14226

Martha T. Markowitz, M.Ed.
Evaluation Coordinator
Eliot-Pearson Children's School
Department of Child Study
Tufts University
Medford, Massachusetts 02155

Samuel J. Meisels, Ed.D.
Associate Professor, Department
  of Child Study
and
Director, LINC Outreach
Eliot-Pearson Children's School
Tufts University
Medford, Massachusetts 02155

Anita R. Olds, Ph.D.
Lecturer
Department of Child Study
Tufts University
Medford, Massachusetts 02155
  and
Consultant, Environmental Facilities
  for Children
10 Saville Street
Cambridge, Massachusetts 02138

Lillian Weber
Professor, Elementary Education
Director, Workshop Center for
  Open Education
The City College of New York
New York, New York 10031

Preface

This book is about human development and education. Its intended audience is wide and includes special educators, general educators, students, teachers, and other educational and academic professionals.

Taken as a whole, the essays in this volume present an alternative paradigm for thinking about and working with handicapped children. It is a paradigm based on the application of the principles of developmental psychology to the education of young children with special needs.

The book serves another purpose as well. It seeks to demonstrate the relevance of open education to developmental theory and to the education of handicapped children. In the introductory chapter, the relationship between developmental theory, children with special needs, and open education is outlined and clarified. In the next chapter, Frances Hawkins focuses on the issue of children's curiosity and adults' response or lack of response to the child's initiative as a critical element in the teaching-learning process. Her chapter raises questions concerning the role that adults play in the perception of children as handicapped individuals as well as their role in the creation of disabled learners.

The next section of the book presents the reader with several concepts that are critical for understanding the application of the developmental model to special education. In his chapter, Nicholas Anastasiow reviews the work of John Dewey for the purposes of elucidating the cognitive-developmental position and of placing Dewey's work in current perspective. Dewey has long been considered a forerunner of developmental psychology and of progressive education. Anastasiow's chapter argues that Dewey's insights about development and cognitive learning and, by implication, his approach to education have been confirmed in recent years by psychologists and educators of widely differing backgrounds.

In the next chapter, David Elkind focuses on the affective and social dimensions of developmentally oriented active classrooms. In particular, Elkind discusses the active classroom's recognition of the personal curriculum, of the attachment dynamism, and of interpersonal frames as critical variables in the education and integration of children with special needs.

The third section of the book addresses issues that relate to the adaptation of learning environments that are intended to meet the needs of children with widely differing abilities and backgrounds. Lillian Weber presents an account of the Open Corridor Program that she initiated in the New York City public schools. The objective of this program has been to establish organizational modes and relationships that are responsive to the developmental path that is characteristic of each child. Her chapter serves as a compelling argument for heterogeneous grouping and for the effects of adapting teaching practice to meet the needs of individual children.

Anita Olds focuses on designing classroom environments to achieve developmentally optimal learning conditions for handicapped and nonhandicapped children. Her chapter presents a detailed rationale and practical principles for creating differentiated learning environments. The photographs and drawings that are included clearly illustrate the application of these principles of design and development.

In her chapter, Lane Gunnoe concentrates on the role of the teacher in establishing developmentally appropriate objectives and in creating individualized educational plans. She presents a model of informal classroom assessment that is designed to be responsive to the needs of individual children while still permitting the teacher to maintain a focus on the classroom as a whole.

The next section of the book presents detailed descriptions of programs that are based on developmental principles in which children with special needs are enrolled. In each of the three chapters, the programs that are described are integrated, or mainstreamed, and are consistent with the approach to open education described throughout the text. Although there is nothing about the developmental model that necessitates that handicapped children be educated in regular classrooms with their nonhandicapped peers, the emphasis in regular, developmentally oriented open classrooms on individualization and on developmental continuity renders open classrooms highly appropriate settings for the education of handicapped children. In the first chapter in this section, Murray Levine describes the integration of handicapped children in British primary schools. His descriptions of British classrooms provide insights into the type of educational practice that has so strongly influenced open education in America and into the effects of mainstreaming on handicapped children.

In the next chapter, Bernard Banet describes a preschool classroom program explicitly based on a cognitive-developmental model. Banet presents the background and basic goals and strategies of his model program, and he also notes some important longitudinal data regarding children's progress in these classrooms.

Peter Knoblock and Ellen Barnes describe a program that integrates autistic and severely emotionally disturbed children into regular classrooms. They too have explicitly designed their program to conform to a developmental model, and in their chapter they describe in detail the relevance of open education to the teaching of severely handicapped children.

The final section of the book deals explicitly with issues relating to open education. Two chapters explore recent efforts at evaluating the effects of open classrooms; the third chapter presents resources and bibliographic references.

George Hein's chapter represents a sustained critique of the standard techniques of evaluating children's educational progress and an exploration of a recent development in evaluation, namely, qualitative methodology. He examines several examples of evaluation efforts that reflect this approach and suggests their relevance to developmental issues in general and to open classrooms in particular.

In the chapter written by Anthony Bryk, Martha Markowitz, and myself, we explore the critical features of open education programs that enroll handicapped children and we attempt to focus on valid means of assessing the effectiveness of open classrooms on handicapped children. Illustrations of a mixed multiple measure approach that combines quantitative and qualitative data are drawn from a mainstreamed program based on developmental principles.

Finally, Rebecca Brown Corwin presents an annotated bibliography of books, articles, and monographs related to open education and young children with special needs. The bibliography is designed to introduce the reader to a variety of historical, theoretical, and practical resources that will extend and elaborate on some of the insights and observations included in the anthology as a whole.

As the editor of an anthology, I have the pleasant responsibility of acknowledging my indebtedness to a number of individuals. First and foremost I would like to thank the contributors to this volume. They have not only generously permitted their original work to be published in this collection; they have also tolerated the deadlines that I set and the editorial prerogatives that I have taken. My editors at University Park Press, Joan Sanow, Melissa Behm, and Janet Clocker, have been extremely helpful at every stage of the development and production of this book. Finally, I owe a special debt of gratitude to two colleagues and friends, Nick Anastasiow and Mike Guralnick, who encouraged me to begin this project, and to my wife, Alice Meisels, who encouraged me to finish it.

Samuel J. Meisels, Ed.D.

For Seth and Reba

Introduction

Special Education and Development

Samuel J. Meisels

...on a purely biological level our species is already apt for education and cannot survive without it. We are in a sense invented by education, not education by us.

David Hawkins

THE DEVELOPMENTAL MODEL

The purpose of this chapter is to apply a useful and explanatory paradigm to issues of great moment and import. The paradigm that is discussed or assumed in each of the chapters of this book is the developmental model of human growth and learning. This model is based on the premise that intellectual and affective growth takes place in children—handicapped or nonhandicapped—as a result of the *interaction between the child and the environment.*

Piaget (1970) notes that there are four critical factors in development: maturation, experience of the physical environment, the action of the social environment, and equilibration or self-regulation. According to Piaget, development is not merely a succession of learned acquisitions in which the child is systematically dependent on environmental stimuli; nor is development synonymous with the unfolding or maturation of internal or inborn sources of knowledge. Rather, development refers to a reorganization of psychological structures that results from interaction between the organism and the environment.

Fundamental to this position is the doctrine of developmental continuity and stage sequence. Piaget has articulated this doctrine most clearly in terms of cognitive growth (see Piaget, 1960). Piaget's theory of cognitive stages and intellectual advance can be summarized as follows:

3

1. Stages imply distinct or qualitative differences in children's modes of thinking or of solving the same problem at different ages.

2. These different modes of thought form an invariant sequence, order, or succession in individual development. While cultural factors may speed up, slow down, or stop development, they do not change its sequence.

3. Each of these different and sequential modes of thought forms a "structured whole." A given stage-response on a task does not just represent a specific response determined by knowledge and familiarity with that task or tasks similar to it; rather it represents an underlying thought-organization...

4. Cognitive stages are hierarchical integrations. Stages form an order of increasingly differentiated and integrated *structures* to fulfil a common function. [Kohlberg, 1972, p. 4]

The import of this theory for educational thought and planning is extensive.

First, children no longer need to be considered as members of relatively homogeneous cohorts, these groups separated principally by age, ability, and experience. In contrast, within the developmental perspective children can be seen as occupying a position on a developmental continuum. Although age and experience significantly influence development, the developmental approach admits of finer gradations of ability and hence helps to identify the similarities as well as the differences among children.

Second, the developmental approach suggests that development follows an invariant sequence or order. This implies that an educational approach that is consistent with the developmental model should focus on a child's general ability to acquire skills, rather than on externally determined, specific skill preparation.

Finally, this approach suggests a conception of development and learning that differs markedly from the model that has dominated traditional schooling and educational thought. The traditional model represents the child or learner as the passive recipient of information presented by a teacher or other source of knowledge. The developmental approach differs from this model in two critical dimensions. That is, according to the developmental approach, children are thought to learn best when they are actively exploring, manipulating, palpating, and questioning the physical and social environment. Thus, rote learning and standardized transmission of information are considered to be restrictive, at best, by the developmental educator.

Furthermore, developmental theory applied to education focuses primarily on individual children. No two children are expected to learn in the same way; therefore, individualized instruction is not merely a technique, it is a necessary condition for optimal teaching and learning.

YOUNG CHILDREN WITH SPECIAL NEEDS

The relevance of the developmental model to the education of young handicapped children is, in part, the subject matter of this book. Traditionally, children with handicaps have been treated and thought of in a holistic manner. For example, children with limited intellectual functioning and reduced adaptive skills are labeled "retarded" and are usually placed in proprietary and educational programs "designed for the retarded." They are typically expected to hold jobs in sheltered workshops with other retarded individuals and to have social interactions principally with retarded people. A similar course can be charted for individuals with other disabilities, for example, sensory disorders, such as deafness or blindness, or physical handicaps, such as cerebral palsy or spina bifida.

This approach to conceptualizing each handicapping condition as a unique and discontinuous category, plateau, or entity, distinct from "normally developing" individuals, leads inevitably to social isolation and segregation and to educational approaches based on a concept of defect, rather than difference.

This discontinuous approach to conceptualizing handicapping conditions has been severely criticized by Zigler (1967, 1969). Using mental retardation as an example, Zigler notes that handicapping conditions will never be fully understood until the fact is accepted that within the gene pool of any population

> there will always be variations in the behavioral or phenotypic expression of virtually every measurable trait or characteristic of man. From the polygenic model advanced by geneticists, we deduce that the distribution of intelligence is characterized by a bisymmetrical bell-shaped curve... [Zigler, 1967, p. 293]

He suggests that within the population of retarded individuals two groups can be identified: those with some form of retardation caused by organic or physiological factors, and the considerably larger group (approximately 75 percent) of cultural-familial retarded individuals. The critical point is that the individual with cultural-familial retardation occupies an integral place within the general distribution of intelligence that can be expected in a normal population. In Zigler's words,

> Once one adopts the position that the familial mental retardate is not defective or pathological but is essentially a normal individual of low intelligence, then the familial retardate no longer represents a mystery but, rather, is viewed as a particular manifestation of the general developmental process. [1967, p. 294]

According to this approach, rather than applying "two psychologies" or two discontinuous views of development and learning for most retarded individuals and persons of "normal intelligence," educational practice must take into account a difference in *rate* of progression through common developmental stages as well as a difference in the upper *level* of growth or development for some children and adults.

Zigler's observations about retardation can be generalized to other handicapping conditions. Children with special needs display differences in their development that distinguish them from nonhandicapped children. However, these differences need not be perceived as defects that somehow set the handicapped child on a course of development that is unrelated to that of the general population. On the contrary, the developmental model assumes a continuity in skills, ability, and knowledge. Equally, it assumes that every child will be treated in some respect as a unique learner with a particular learning history, learning style, and set of preferences and needs. In developmentally oriented classrooms, children's language, cognitive, motor, and personal social abilities are challenged and permitted to grow and take shape. Experiences that encourage such growth are as important for disabled children as they are for children without handicaps. Too frequently children with special needs are exposed principally to a deficit-oriented curriculum that focuses on a particular area of disability or handicap. In such an approach the fully functioning child is ignored for the sake of a narrowly defined area of dysfunction.

In the developmental orientation, remediation efforts are placed within the context of the whole child's needs and abilities. Thus, strengths are diagnosed, as well as weaknesses. However, few educational approaches are sufficiently individualized and differentiated to put the developmental model into practice. In this volume, informal or open education is proposed as an educational approach that is both consistent with the developmental model and appropriate for the education of children with special needs.

OPEN EDUCATION AND DEVELOPMENTAL ADVANCEMENT

Since it first achieved widespread recognition and popularity in the late 1960s, open education has suffered from what may be considered one of its chief strengths. Ironically, that strength is the powerful belief system that it represents. The implementation of any belief system is subject to extreme variation and inconsistency. Open education has had more than its share of this variability.

The Plowden Report—a prestigious British government report on primary education—captures open education's values and beliefs in the following statement.

A school is not merely a teaching shop, it must transmit values and attitudes. It is a community in which children learn to live first and foremost as children and not as future adults. . . .The school sets out deliberately to allow them to be themselves and to develop in the way and at the pace appropriate to them. It tries to equalise opportunities and to compensate for handicaps. It lays special stress on individual discovery, on first-hand experience and on opportunities for creative work. It insists that knowledge does not fall into neatly separate compartments and that work and play are not opposite but complementary. [Central Advisory Council for Education, 1967, para. 505]

During the past decade, the literature of open education has become saturated with value statements of this type. Nevertheless, the practice of open education has differed dramatically in spite of this uniformity. Hence, volumes have been written that were intended to clarify the definition of open education (Spodek and Walberg, 1975; Nyberg, 1975), to review the research concerning open education (Horwitz, 1976), to evaluate its effectiveness (Bennett, 1976), to assess teachers' understanding of it (Bussis, Chittenden, and Amarel, 1976), and to study the process of implementing it (Sussmann, 1977).

In contrast, the essays in this volume present a common approach to open education. The unifying feature of this approach is the developmental model. An open classroom that is consistent with and actually puts the developmental model into practice must satisfy a number of specific criteria. For example, such a classroom must permit children opportunities to play freely in the environment and to engage in structured manipulation of that environment. In other words, developmentally oriented open classrooms must be based on the premise that development evolves from the child's transactions with the environment as a whole, rather that from exposure to some critical or particular experience. Also, such classrooms should allow children to explore what they are interested in, and should recognize that interest is most greatly aroused and sustained when the child's action produces effects or changes in the stimulus field. A rich variety of manipulative and intrinsically rewarding materials is essential for sustaining this interest.

However, the critical feature that distinguishes open education from other educational approaches, which enables the developmental model to be translated into classroom practice, is vested in the role of the teacher. It is the teacher who has the responsibility to intervene actively in the child's learning experience. This notion was previously elaborated by John Dewey, whose work serves as a guide to developmental psychology and to open education. He wrote that:

In an *educational* scheme, the occurrence of a desire and impulse [in a child] is not the final end. It is an occasion and a demand for the formation of a plan and method of activity. . . .The teacher's business is to see that the occasion is taken advantage of. . .guidance given by the teacher to the exercise of the pupil's intelligence is an aid to freedom, not a restriction upon it. [1938, p. 71]

All too often, the open classroom teacher is erroneously described as a passive facilitator of learning. This laissez-faire view of education, in which the child is the active agent in the educational setting and the teacher subordinates himself to the child's will, is inconsistent with the developmental model. Indeed, the laissez-faire approach is most closely related to the romantic view of education. Such a view holds that the most important aspect of development comes from within the child. The impact of the environment, and hence the teacher, according to such an approach (see, for example, Rousseau, Tolstoy, A.S. Neill), is practically meaningless.

Nevertheless, the role of the teacher in the developmentally oriented open classroom is insufficiently described as "active." For example, teachers who function in programmed environments or in environments based on a behavior-oriented learning hierarchy theory actively intervene in children's learning. Yet, these classrooms differ significantly from open classrooms and, in certain respects, they are inconsistent with developmental theory.

As its name implies, hierarchy theory claims that the elements of general experience can be analyzed in terms of a multiplicity of specific learning experiences, certain of which, such as classification, seriation, and number, are critical in the acquisition of preselected concepts (Resnick, 1967). The goals in this kind of classroom are identical to the hierarchically sequenced skills. The task of the teacher is largely one of guiding children from "naivete to competence" in the use and understanding of the concepts targeted by the curricular analysis (Resnick, Wang, and Kaplan, 1973).

When implemented within the developmental model, this type of classroom approach is extremely useful for individualizing instruction and for matching curriculum experiences to the needs of specific children. However, all too often the teacher engages in curriculum or task analysis without taking into account the child's need to interact freely, concretely, and idiosyncratically with the environment. When this takes place, as is the case in many "behavioral," or environmentally based approaches, the child is assumed to acquire both specific concepts and general intellectual structures as reflections of structures that exist in the physical and social world. Hence, this approach implies that children learn best through immediate repetition and elaboration of correct responses. The teacher's role in such an approach is highly directive and noninteractive. This is particularly the case if this approach is associated with a system of rewards that are designed to modify the child's behavior but do not necessarily take into account the child's level of concept acquisition, social experience, intellectual ability, or current interests. Again, the assumption of this environmentally based approach is that development is a direct reflection of stimulus contingencies in the environment.

Missing from this approach, as from the maturationist view noted earlier, is the interaction between the child and the environment. According to Piaget and to developmental theory, it is in this interaction that cognitive and emotional growth flourishes (see Kohlberg, 1972). For open education to be consistent with the developmental model, not only must it take place in a setting where children can interact productively with their environments, but also these interactions must be extended and expanded through the activity of the teacher.

Thus, in the open classrooms described or referred to in this volume, teachers and children share a specialized type of relationship, one that is quasi experimental and is interactive in character. That is, the teacher selects an objective for the child based on the child's activity, the character of the environment, and what he knows about the child. The teacher usually chooses an implementational strategy in the same fashion. These decisions are based on extensive information concerning individual children, and they involve children's participation as much as possible. Implementational strategies are also designed to reflect the child's unique constellation of strengths and weaknesses, experiences, and desires. Such responsive and individualized educational decisions preserve and make possible interactivity and hence developmental advancement. In the chapters that follow, this interactive relationship is further clarified and elaborated and is emphasized as the critical variable in developmentally oriented open classrooms designed to serve children with special needs.

SPECIAL EDUCATION IN DEVELOPMENTAL PERSPECTIVE

Today, most children with special needs are taught in situations that do not emphasize individualization or interactivity and probably are not designed to optimize their development. The open classroom is proposed as a setting that encourages and legitimizes individual differences and that is consistent with the principles and assumptions of the developmental model.

It is possible that other educational approaches might achieve the same ends through different and more efficient means. However, the argument of this book does not stand or fall on the efficacy of open education. Rather, it rests on the notion of developmental continuity and on the significance of understanding the fundamental distinction between difference and defect. When these ideas are put into practice, all education is special education.

REFERENCES

Bennett, N. 1976. Teaching Styles and Pupil Progress. Harvard University Press, Cambridge, Mass.

Bussis, A. M., Chittenden, E. A., and Amarel, M. 1976. Beyond Surface Curriculum. Westview Press, Boulder, Colorado.

Central Advisory Council for Education (England). 1967. Children and Their Primary Schools, Vols. I and II. (The Plowden Report.) Her Majesty's Stationery Office, London.

Dewey, J. 1938. Experience and Education. Collier, New York.

Horwitz, R. A. 1976. Psychological Effects of Open Classroom Teaching on Primary School Children: A Review of the Research. North Dakota Study Group on Evaluation, Grand Forks, N.D.

Kohlberg, L. 1972. The concepts of developmental psychology as the central guide to education. In: M. C. Reynolds (ed.), Proceedings of the Conference on Psychology and the Process of Schooling in the Next Decade. Leadership Training Institute, Minneapolis.

Nyberg, D. (ed.) 1975. The Philosophy of Open Education. Routledge and Kegan Paul, London.

Piaget, J. 1960. The general problem of the psychobiological development of the child. In: J. M. Tanner and B. Inhelder (eds.), Discussions on Child Development, Vol. 9. International Universities Press, New York.

Piaget, J. 1970. Piaget's theory. In: P. H. Mussen (ed.), Carmichael's Manual of Child Psychology. 3rd Ed. John Wiley & Sons, New York.

Resnick, L. B. 1967. Design of an Early Learning Curriculum. University of Pittsburgh, Learning Research and Development Center, Pittsburgh.

Resnick, L. B., Wang, M. C. and Kaplan, J. 1973. Task analysis in curriculum design: A hierarchically sequenced introductory mathematics curriculum. J. Appl. Behav. Anal. 6:679–710.

Spodek, B., and Walberg, J. H. (eds.) 1975. Studies in Open Education. Agathon Press, New York.

Sussmann, L. 1977. Tales Out of School: Implementing Organizational Change in the Elementary Grades. Temple University Press, Philadelphia.

Zigler, E. 1967. Familial mental retardation: A continuing dilemma. Science 155:292–298.

Zigler, E. 1969. Developmental versus difference theories of mental retardation and the problem of motivation. Am. J. Ment. Defic. 73:536–556.

The Eye of the Beholder

Frances Pockman Hawkins

> Indeed, there is something like general agreement that role stereotypes, stigma, the ignorance of the able-bodied and outright discrimination often are far more important in constricting the life possibilities of even a severely handicapped individual than are the "objective" constraints placed upon an individual by the limitations of his mind or body.
>
> Gliedman and Roth, *The Unexpected Minority: Handicapped Children In America,* 1979.

A PERSONAL POINT OF VIEW

Many years ago, in the 1940s, I had the good fortune to know briefly a wise man from Denmark, Niels Bohr. I realize that at that time of crises and promise it was his fellow physicists who learned much from him in their field, but I, too, learned from him within mine. In the intervening years since my meetings with him, when a particularly serious and defiant problem stays out of focus for me, I have often recalled Bohr's soft and halting way of speaking: "Oh...some problems...some are so serious ...that...one can only joke about them." Initially, I had to wrestle with this statement and I even tried to reject such a way of gaining perspective, but the clarity of Bohr's observations, highlighted by his humor, remained and had to be reckoned with in my philosophy as a teacher.

Certainly the problem we address in these pages, the failure of a society to plan well for children at risk, is a very serious one. Each of us must address the problem with the best of his personal knowledge and style of thinking. My own approach has grown inevitably from years of working with children in classrooms and is shaped along the following lines.

First is the affirmation that, within the child, within the classroom, and within myself, seen altogether, there exists the potential and promise of new growth and development. Outside help is not excluded, and it may later be welcomed, but the starting point lies *where the action already is:* where *this* child is at this moment, in this situation, within this environment. Such an approach to children's needs has been evolved and strengthened not only by the evidence of children's thriving and learning, but also by some philosophical ammunition: George Herbert Mead's *Philosophy of the Present* (Mead, 1959) and Frederick Allen's *Psychotherapy with Children* (Allen, 1942).

With this belief in the importance of the immediate human resources, I move next with refocused attention to observe and to develop the situation — with the child's participation — in fresh, new ways. It is only after such reassessment and action have been effected that outside help, if it is needed, is sought, so that that help can be actively met, engaged, and pressed into immediate service.

I am aware of the dangers of extrapolation; yet I propose that we adopt an analagous approach when confronting the larger question to which this book is addressed. We must begin "where the action is," from which we can best learn and in consequence, to which we can best contribute. We must start with the study of the best classrooms of the present in their very real diversity, embracing a multitude of ways to meet a multitude of needs. Otherwise, we shall not be prepared to help either the able teachers who already know what help they need, or the larger number of teachers who are dissatisfied and will seek help if it exists. It is as advisors, not as supervisors, that we must be ready to give assistance. As advisors to teachers, we must be prepared to find within them, within their situations, and within ourselves the potential and the promise of those new paths waiting to be developed. I believe that if some such starting point is not accepted, the struggle to evolve better classrooms will be longer and harder, and at best, a reliving of history rather than a hopeful extension of it. The initial resources exist for developing good classrooms, but they are not yet poised for action.

If the challenge to identify classrooms where children learn is accepted, perhaps my experiences as a teacher of the young and more recently as a consultant in others' classrooms will be useful. How are good classrooms alike, how are they different? What is crucial to their being places where children thrive and learn, and what is incidental? One thing can be said categorically: classrooms will differ from each other, and they will not follow a prescribed model. In England, in Africa, and in the United States I have had the great luxury for some years of being invited to observe and to participate in classrooms other than my own. *Classrooms where children learn* — the phrase is Jay Featherstone's (Featherstone, 1971) — certainly do differ. To generalize responsibly about their likenesses, I must stay close to personal experience and watch the ways in which I think about likenesses and differences, trying to distill what is invariant from what is relative to immediate needs, situations, and talents.

Teachers of the young may rely on formulas *only* as points of departure, and reference; teachers must continuously remain aware of their own learning, and of their own ideas being formed and stretched. As professional people we have license to do this. It is also a crucial way to increase our awareness of how children's ideas are brought to life, played with, and restructured.

In this discussion, as in teaching, the fruitful path is not just one of surface observation or "treatment" and "outcome." Unless ideas guide us, we do not know how or what to observe, and unless we are conscious of this guidance we will not learn well from observation and ideas will not grow (Spitz, 1950).

By speaking of "ideas to guide us" I mean ideas in the most dignified sense of the word, referring to them as those organizing centers of knowledge and perception without which human potentials, however otherwise diverse, cannot be realized. Aristotle said that, without ideas, experience is like an army in rout; but, if at first one soldier and then another takes a stand, by their influence the whole army may come to order.

This ancient metaphor is useful, but I add to it a more pacific one, the magnet. With some children whose inner ways are clear, there are times when one can witness the magnet-like power of an idea; as if trivial or profound bits and pieces of information stored at shallow or deep levels, not yet rationally assimilated, jump together to make a new constellation. Information jumps together after being touched by an organizing force whether from the outside or from within. To young Jim, a competent and, on occasion, solemnly thoughtful 5-year-old neighbor, I informally introduced the challenge of trying to balance a variety of tinkertoy assemblies by the tip of a short rod on the tip of a finger or stand. After some preliminary awkward trials I saw Jim's manner and performance quite rapidly change to a confident assurance as his hands and eyes cooperated in placing the rods and spools *just* so. Not in words but in action, Jim showed me the organizing power of this particular new idea, bringing elements of balance that were familiar to him into the unity of a new relation, seeing a pattern among them.

After those chance talks with Bohr, I realized how certain ways of playing with ideas could allow their magnetic powers to operate. This phenomenon had occurred before in my experience, but I had not recognized it. One of Bohr's ways of unleashing those magnetic properties was through humor — turning things around or upside down, playfully contradicting the obvious, and making "little jokes." My way seems closer to Jim's — a puzzled play with the new-yet-somehow-familiar. That is why I find it necessary to state my views in tandem with case histories of children. Children are the primary individuals who have challenged and helped me clarify my thinking. (For a teacher, this is one way of staying honest.) I trust that all of us who teach and learn with our children will understand and share in my anecdotal style.

If I could give one thing to members of the younger generation who are teachers, it would be the courage to break new ground. Some children come to us at school already well on their way. These children do not demand that we teachers understand exactly how they have done it or how they are doing it; they just know *how to learn* already. Our time spent with them may accelerate or retard their learning, but our role is not crucial. That is fortunate because otherwise we would be in deep trouble with these children too.

If many children can accommodate to, or even learn in spite of, their schooling, the real test of our knowledge comes from those children who do not. The state of our generally accepted beliefs about how different or vulnerable children learn is, at best, meager. Here lies the new challenge, the new ground to be broken. This test is crucial and will become more so as we bring to our classrooms those children needing additional essential stimulation and understanding from outside their homes. Yet for *all* children there are some things that we do know about learning processes. I now want to present and illustrate some of that knowledge.

In order to speak coherently of what we *do* know about children's learning, again and again I am brought back to one central, global idea that I shall try to make explicit below. It is an idea that we all recognize, but one that is often forgotten in the pursuit of detailed new recipes, formulas, curricula, and models. Perhaps, it may seem too vague or too lacking in specificity to be useful: it is the idea of a climate, atmosphere, or ambience for learning. For me, all other ideas about learning and teaching are qualified by it, and those other ideas lose their validity when the effect of this inescapable ambience is overlooked. For example, biologists can study the chemistry of specific body cells while overlooking their interaction with the whole organism and its environment, but information gained *only* in that way is an unreliable and sometimes dangerous guide to medical practice. What takes place in one context can fail or can be reversed in others, and until we have some logical control of this dependence, we cannot generalize.

In a more practical discussion (''Jack's World,'' below) I have chosen to focus on one of the crucial characteristics of ambience — a child's curiosity — and to illustrate it by describing something from a half-morning in the life of one 5-year-old. The story of Jack, who was already in trouble in his kindergarten, is told because it so deeply underscores the meaning and the kinds of strengths certain children bring to school, strengths that are too easily labeled and treated as weaknesses. To grow and to learn in a classroom, such as the one in which we observe Jack, a child must be able to disregard atmosphere, and to ignore and be out of communication with adults. Jack could ignore the adults, but for how long and with what dangers? What about those children who need adults, who cannot ignore them?

The story of Ronald is in sharp contrast with Jack's. In linking these two utterly different children under the diagnostic heading of curiosity, I hope to develop further its meaning and promise. Jack's curiosity was manifest and focused, although unseen by the adults at his school. In contrast, Ronald might have been said to have no focus at all for whatever remained of his innate curiosity by the time he entered school.

I draw upon the experience with Ronald because it can tell us a great deal about the central power of curiosity, even as a destructive force, to survive, to rehabilitate, or to restore. Ronald leads me to consider briefly that strange phenomenon where curiosity seems both lacking and, at the same time, obsessively focused — infantile autism.

Children's curiosities are the key variable to which the balancing effects of a teacher's curiosity must respond. I do of course oversimplify. I have chosen curiosity not because it is the only human characteristic that must be well understood in bringing different children into our classrooms, but because it is a central quality that, in all its complexity is so closely related to learning.

At the end of this essay I come back to my starting point and to the need to widen further the circumference we all must travel. If my thesis is useful we can extend that route by devising criteria for further investigation and for action.

AN AMBIENCE FOR LEARNING

Classrooms where children thrive differ in methods employed, in the models they follow or ignore, and in the subject matter presented. In some respects such classrooms are similar. They have a climate that expects and encourages curiosity, and therefore which respects variety in the ways in which children communicate and learn and in the times and spaces where learning makes leaps.

I have already touched on the allegedly mysterious qualities that one senses in the ambience of certain classrooms, and now I want to unpack some of those "mysteries."

We begin by examining one crucial quality, differences, an issue often raised in terms of a conflict (or imbalance) between group needs and individual needs. This particular conflict is thought to be most pronounced in classrooms that include children with handicaps, or in classrooms where there is a wide variation in the speed or way of learning academic subject matter. Putting aside for the moment the crucial exacerbating factors of large classes and poor or no back-up services, to assume mutual interference as an inevitability is wrong. If it is seen as inevitable, it will endanger the propitious atmosphere of concern and balance *in any classroom,* regardless of the presence or absence of handicapped children. Such a formulation misses the very direction in which the transient troubles of a group of children can be resolved.

Group life can thrive where there is a delicate and resonant balance of obvious or subtle diversity. In such an ambience, learning can thrive not in spite of the mix, but because the diversity of children is necessary to the existence of learning. Necessary changes of pace and shifts of focus become possible where there are great expectations based on understanding. This is what makes a resonant balance possible. There are practical keys that make it probable, and one such key must be mentioned. That key is the power that a teacher holds to alter constellations of human beings within any group. An adult with one child, an adult with two or three children, a child with one appropriate child or adult, or a child with several appropriate others are varied mixtures that are available to match individual strengths and needs. These mixtures constitute the group's very uniqueness.

Some children can show us the ambience they seek by occasionally going off with a friend to a quiet corner with a shared game or book or silliness; but an adult's provisioning for a child who *cannot yet* indicate such a specific need requires imagination and timing as to places, materials, and likely or unlikely partnerships. Since children themselves are an integral part of this diversity, they contribute to such an atmosphere. The fact of handicap in some children becomes part of the diversity and community. It can take a very secondary place and, on occasion, a quite positive one.

To emphasize the positive aspects of diversity among children is to recognize and take seriously, for the children's experience as well as for the adult's, that human attention is never so focused on anything as to exclude a peripheral awareness of surroundings, of history, and of tomorrow. To concentrate — to zero in — we must at the same time monitor this range of things on the edge of awareness. The quality of an environment — how each fares — sensed in this way, affects the whole character of learning. Henry James writes:

> Small children have many more perceptions than they have terms to translate them; their vision is at any moment much richer, their apprehension even

constantly stronger, than their prompt, their at all producible, vocabulary. [James, 1974, p. 7].

A general prosperity for all creates its own atmosphere and a quality of environment that each child in his own time and way can sense, sometimes directly but always peripherally. As an individual difference finds expression — not repression — through achievement, the difference comes to focus and to appreciation in the eyes of other children. Children learn with each other, from each other, and about each other, as learners. It is a rare and life-enhancing thing, and some teachers and parents help create this situation. In such an atmosphere, a blind child, a child in a wheelchair, or a child who has been given to tantrums or even subtler ways of manipulating others learns to redirect his energy and strengths, and can come into and become part of the circle of those who belong and contribute.

Fear is contagious; so is confidence. To belong to a classroom in which each member develops confidence is to be personally freed. I believe it is this sense of "belongingness to a group" that Kurt Lewin was seeking to understand in some of his early work. In 1940 he wrote an essay called "Bringing up the Jewish Child" in which he notes that

> The underlying problem is not by any means exclusively a Jewish one. A member of any less privileged group has to face it. This holds true to an astonishingly high degree not only in those cases where the lack of privileges comes from social discrimination, as for example against Negroes in the United States, but also where it arises from bodily defects such as deafness. What does belongingness to a group mean to an individual, and how does that affect his behavior in certain situations? [Lewin, 1940, p. 172]

Similarly, Comer and Poussaint (1975) ask in *Black Child Care:*

> How have Black children fared since Emancipation?....They have consistently borne the devastating effects of White racism. Many have shouldered the double burden of growing up both poor and Black. Some have been damaged so severely early in life that their chances for a happy, productive adulthood have been small. [Comer and Poussaint, 1975, p. 17]

Classrooms where all children learn and are freed from ignorance and prejudice are not abundant, but they can be found and developed. Classrooms in which children fail represent one of the links in the long chain keeping us all in bondage.

Having emphasized the great potential to be found in children's individual diversity, we must ask how this diversity is to be approached, assessed, and provided for. So I come back to the key question of development and curiosity and to the way that ideas grow and grow together when curiosity is supported and thrives. In the course of observing children, as yet undamaged, such as Jack, and of being their teacher, one can find the way to see ideas rejected, sieved, changed over time, used, transposed, and finally built in.

I have an insatiable professional curiosity about all this, and, therefore, about each new child I meet and each unique pattern I perceive, but a teacher's curiosity is not enough. A teacher's curiosity and inventiveness must also seek the propitious circumstances that release and engage curiosity for a particular child. Each child brings with him enough of what is familiar to allow teachers to make sense of what is unique. What we seek is a professional curiosity and learning about that mix in a setting that both teacher and child create. It is one of the vital contributions that a teacher makes to the ambience of good classrooms. In another sense, when professional, intellectual curiosity is tuned to children's ways and is ready for surprises, it provides a safe and comfortable bridge from the teacher to the children. The propitious ambience with its resonant balance for each and for all comes from such bridges where two sorts of curiosities — the teacher's and the child's — meet. This is the context in which yet another component — communication — should be discussed.

I speak about genuine communication, not just humane manners and polite concern. The word "communication" often dangles to the point of absurdity in our talk about teaching (Spitz, 1957). If communication is to be a bridge, it must be firmly and substantially supported on both sides. On the child's side the bridge is anchored primarily by innate curiosity. Even if it is sometimes hidden, responsiveness to what is waiting in the surrounding world is there, and even a seriously damaged child has the capacity to meet that world with already accrued resources. In principle we can rely on this; it is certainly a child's primary contribution. Curiosity-responsiveness comes readily from those who are well, from those whose lives have already been supported in their expression and development, while for others it may come only after much reassurance and searching for its buried springs. I illustrate this matter of childhood curiosity in the stories of Jack and Ronald.

On the teacher's side of the bridge of communication, there must be that professional curiosity that I have been speaking of, curiosity about *this* child and this child's occupation or preoccupation of the moment and of longer. Such curiosity, together with the skill to intervene or refrain, can guide a teacher until the child develops. The resulting partnership can nourish the child, the group, and the teacher.

In addition, professional curiosity must be sustained, an undertaking that raises a basic question about the kinds of traffic the bridges are designed to support. The teacher's own understanding and enjoyment of subject matter now counts. The ability to design what will stretch or challenge a particular child's established curiosity or activate it is critical. A child will use this closed-in and intimate world as a crucial part of communication, positive or negative. A teacher who is not able to grasp what it is that the child sees or fails to see will fail to understand, will fail to recognize a potential for the growth of ideas, and will fail to perceive the structure of mind and character that the child is beginning to build. If failure is too frequent, communication is diminished and so is the ambience that it supports.

This lack of deep familiarity with child-level but adult-valued subject matter cries out for remedy among our teachers and in our research centers. It is this very lack of spark that is especially important to overcome when planning for our more vulnerable children. Their ways may not be and often cannot be those that match any existing standard curriculum guide. In progressive or open classroom settings, which are properly trying to widen choices, subject matter is sometimes unthinkingly disparaged by teachers' own inadvertent ignorance.

To emphasize further and to clarify these general statements about the bridge of communication and its support, I wish now to share in some detail the observation of a 5-year-old already in trouble with "the establishment." It is a paradigm case so negative and blind in terms of the adults involved and yet so positive in terms of the child that perhaps this contrast will allow us to see ourselves in a useful perspective, and to appreciate how inseparable the following factors must be: our knowledge of universal development, the reading of individual behavior, and the capacity to locate starting points for the growth of children's ideas, and the furtherance of their curiosity.

JACK'S WORLD

The nursery school that I visited was for children three to six years of age, described as emotionally disturbed or who have other learning problems. The children were referred by physicians, by nursery schools, and by public kindergartens. Hence, they were already considered at risk. I call this school a negative paradigm. In my experience it was in fact more typical of the current universe of nursery schools and kindergartens than its high professional auspices and its evidently large budget might suggest.

Before any children arrived on this particular morning I was shown the well-stocked classroom long enough to approve of its basic provisioning, and I was briefed about the staff and the good teacher-child ratio. By format and intent this was an "open classroom." By any formal criteria the staff was adequately educated and qualified. What seemed a possible luxury to me was that in addition to an adequate teaching staff each child was assigned a part-time therapist-teacher (TT). (Similar special assignments had been made in Anna Freud's Nursery Home for six orphans (Freud and Dann, 1951).)

After a pleasant coffee time with the senior staff members, I was invited to observe the classroom activities from an excellent observation booth where the one-way glass and the acoustics worked well and where I did not feel too cut off from the action. I settled to the pleasure of not being responsible to anyone — except myself for my own learning.

My colleague-host was just leaving the booth when he paused and pointed to a tall child who came bouncing into the classroom. I cannot remember the exact words of my host but the tone of his voice still chills me: "Oh, that one...has to be subdued in the yard...kindergarten can't handle him...impossible..." So young Jack, as I have called him, came bouncing into my focus already damned. We shall observe how incorrigible he was.

Alone and no longer being briefed, I could watch Jack. His therapist-teacher had left him near the door. He may have been subdued outside but there was now devilment on his face, liveliness in his muscles, and a "how to amuse them today" attitude was reflected by his stance and manner. I forgot the rest of the classroom, except to note that Jack's TT was for the moment occupied elsewhere, as I watched Jack go forth looking for fun or trouble, wondering where he would find it. He stopped by a low vase with golden leaves that held one brown cattail, which was fraying at the top. With speed he selected the cattail. I thought he would shake it and scatter the million winged seeds over the heads of all. It was not a dull havoc to wreak with that elegantly packed marsh plant. Then I saw Jack's attention focus on the denuded stem at the top. With care he broke off the spare stem, and I watched for what would follow. After a moment his interest seemed to shift again, not *away* from the cattail but more intently *on* the velvet-textured object that he now held protectively in his small, black hand. From that moment I was his silent partner and admirer.

Jack continued to probe very gently the looser seeds at the top, with a testing index finger, his eyes on the finger's probing. What bit lay under his private microscope? The vast numbers? The way each was attached to stem, to each other, or how each looked when partially released? I couldn't know what he was thinking, perhaps all this and more.

Only after a long examination did Jack make his selection: one seed. By such care he told me much about his concentration, dexterity, and something of what was important to this — as I now surmised — remarkable child. He held up the one seed and blew softly, matching his blowing to the delicacy of his miniature glider. The seed traveled, while Jack and I watched, until it was lost somewhere in the large classroom. Content in face and posture, he put the still-intact marsh plant gently back in its vase and moved on.

The door to my booth opened. Startled, I turned to see my host coming in. Hoping to protect the delight in the scene that I had just witnessed and to forestall another unprofessional attack on Jack, I asked for Jack's age. "Five." "He is tall," I began, "and..."

"Look at him there wandering about...can't settle down to anything...does nothing...trouble to all...."

Full of shame for such a remark, I did not respond to my host but turned away to the protection of observation and was again left mercifully alone. The intrusion had caused me to miss some of the action with Jack. When I observed again, the TT was restraining him, holding his arms against his sides, saying seriously (not angrily), "No you can't do that." Jack wriggled expertly out of the TT's grasp. I shall never know what terrible thing he had been doing.

Jack stalked away to low shelves where a large plastic hourglass caught his eye — and a hard blow from his clenched fist. So much for you, TT. The timer was well-constructed and filled with tiny colored beads, instead of sand. Colorful and intriguing, it was a thing that boys like Jack cannot resist. He must have noticed the beads jump to his bang, because the next move of this "hyperactive" child was, as I was coming to expect, logical and patient. He examined the timer with his hands and eyes, finally trying to get it open.

He was as respectful of this object's construction as he had been of the cattail's secrets. He tried to unscrew any part that could conceivably be unscrewed, but it was no go. The upright wooden posts were examined and gently tested for the possibility of being pulled apart. All efforts failing, Jack carefully put the timer back on the shelf and gave it a friendly, gentle good-bye pat. The pat was enough to cause another jump of the beads. Jack stopped. I soon realized, it was not the jump itself but the sound of the beads as they moved. In his benign mood he had heard it. With delight and evidently with some reminiscence of similar sounds, Jack grabbed the timer and immediately transformed it, as children will in their "eolithic" way, into a magnificent soft-toned maraca (Storm, 1953). Using it, he accompanied its rhythm with a playful joyous dance. I dared to hope for some adult to notice or perhaps to join Jack's dance, but for awhile Jack, in his chosen corner, was seen by no one but me. From side to side the timer-maraca was making its muted rhythm and Jack was making his soft following steps. The dance was for himself. That I could share it with him was grace.

The dance did not last. TT *had* seen, and from across the room gave evidence: "Put that thing down, Jack, and get busy putting blocks away." The dance held briefly, but TT was bigger, and in the manner of a top-sergeant insisted that Jack get started at a long task of stacking blocks left scattered by another child.

Half-heartedly, Jack began to stack the blocks, initially kept at it by the watchful eye and straw-boss manner of TT, who yelled encouragement, of a kind, from across the room: "Come on...get going...pile them neatly!" In quiet despair, but by now with no surprise, I watched the scene. *Who* was handicapped? Jack was not, yet; but how long could he or others like him survive treated *as if they were?*

Although discouraged by the previous scene, I heard soft sounds — musical, gentle, and strangely muted. Looking at Jack's mouth I realized that some of the sounds were his. I couldn't hear well or identify the other sounds until I saw Jack, still on his knees, lift a block that was already in place and drop it down again. He was matching that marimba-like sound of good wood against good wood with his voice, and matching it well.

In this quiet classroom, conversation had been scarce all morning, except for idle talk between staff, which was unprofessional in a setting where children are living and where learning demands and repays alertness to that life. There had been no encouragement or reason for Jack to talk, orders being so one-sided, so I was reassured that he did hear and responded so acutely to rhythm and tone. Jack was communicating; a responsive adult could have reciprocated through music, through making instruments, or perhaps, at first, by selecting certain blocks for tone and supporting them for better sound, thereby participating in and extending Jack's discovery. Vicariously I enjoyed the key that he had found in the room for releasing musical tones from wood.

The sounds had been a lovely byproduct of the routine of stacking, but TT, with that eagle-eye for deviance, had seen Jack's slowdown, and interfered, with his usual banter: "Stop that fooling around, Jack, and GET going." How consistently that well-meaning young man could miss Jack's perceptive action and zero in on *only* the behavior to be corrected or modified!

At home that night, going over my notes, I wondered where and how the kind of therapy/teaching, communication between patient and therapist, had been lost (see Taft, 1962). Was professional curiosity, with its skill and ability to alter its focus, also mislaid? Was some preconceived formula continually being trusted? It was as if Jack was prejudged to be incapable of innovative response (see Allen, 1942).

I tell Jack's story to learn, not to condemn. When the last blocks were in place and I had heard that inevitable "Good boy, Jack!" I turned my attention to the whole room, now as neat and seemingly untouched by children's hands as any one could desire. I thought of the untidy mid-morning array of work-in-progress, which some colleagues and I had come to expect and cherish, and when snacktime came to punctuate the day, it allowed a fresh moment for overall evaluation. I wondered if other children's buds had been nipped on this morning. There were no signs I could read as "Children at Work — Back Soon." A teacher or therapist or observer misses many clues, but here and in similar classrooms I feel that the ground rules are intentionally or unwittingly hindering any deep involvement. In numbers, this staff was luxurious to the point of over-staffing. Laissez-faire policy could certainly not be blamed, as it often can. The culprit seemed rather clear: no curious adults in communication with curious children.

Another teacher-therapist broke my reverie by announcing snack-time in a loud voice, and the ten or twelve children walked sedately to the low tables. Jack, two other children, and TT sat directly under my glass window, and I still hoped to hear a bit of conversation among the four people in this intimate setting. Here there seemed to be an easier atmo-sphere of selection and self-direction among the children, who were sit-ting on big pillows instead of chairs, and I relaxed. Children poured their own juice and took generous handfuls of an attractive nut raisin mix. Jack was the last to take the juice pitcher and he once more displayed his precocious concerns.

He stopped pouring juice just short of overflow, and I thought that he had been almost careless for the first time in judging amounts or that he was preoccupied. I did not appreciate the purpose of the near overflow until I realized that Jack had lowered his head to observe at eye-level the lovely, convex curve of the liquid surface, the meniscus. After what was a brief confirmation of this phenomenon, he carefully added a few more drops — one, two, three,... as one still can when overflow seems certain. Not breaking the delicate protective film of the liquid, he again lowered his head to check in silence and with satisfaction. From observing this brief but expert maneuver I was certain that Jack had long since filed away the existence of this phenomenon, and was thus able to retrieve it for enjoyment and curiosity. (It is one phenomenon that many of us adults, being uninformed, have never really noticed, and have had to be shown in a science class much later in life.) If TT saw or wondered at Jack's small demonstration I cannot say.

As some children will, Jack approached his three handfuls of nut mix with care and selection. All raisins, one by one, were eaten, then the slivered almonds were eaten in the same way. Did Jack have a preference? Best first? Or best last? The children ate and drank, silence reigned, and Jack, with only a few slivers left to eat, pulled a bright comfortable pillow around himself and began gently rocking from side to side. The other two children picked up the rocking rhythm and smiled at each other in the first genuine communication I had seen: shared fun. I looked at TT, still hopeful — optimist that I am — that he might smile or even accompany this new rhythm with a song, extending a beginning offered by the children, but TT had been differently programmed. He stopped the whole endeavor by expertly removing the pillow from Jack, and in a smug voice he said, "You can sit quieter without your pillow."

I have come to see the basic handicap that pervades our schools and clouds our understanding of child development as a poverty of intellectual curiosity. The *American Heritage Dictionary* lists the first meaning of curiosity as "a desire to know or learn, especially about something new or strange." Included in *Webster's* longer definition are several entries that have a negative connotation: "desire to know" is tied to "inquisitiveness" and qualified as "often implying meddlesomeness." Under obs. (obsolete) we find "careful attention, nicety, exactness, and fastidiousness." There is enough to give a sort of history of thought about this word, ending with a synonym from Hawthorne: "A prying old woman."

Whether it is intended or not, one can read in this long definition a certain developmental view of the attribute curiosity. By the time of old age, curiosity may have been corrupted to deserve equivalence with prying. For us to encourage children to give up the life-enhancing curiosity of the young is to interfere with one of the very means by which we all learn. I submit young Jack as a typical case of the positive definition given by both dictionaries. He and many others, labeled hyperactive, learning disabled, or disruptive, bring to school their weak and their strong ways — their odd ways — of unpacking the world. These children are too often met by adults who, fatigued and themselves poorly educated, cannot recognize this intact curiosity and build upon it because they themselves have had their own curiosity so dampened and damaged.

For key members of a society — the teachers of the young — to lack curiosity *is the most profound handicap of all.* It is a very rare thing for an infant to be born so damaged congenitally that he lacks that capacity totally. I select the word and concept curiosity because even with seriously retarded children, retarded genetically, congenitally, or functionally, there is enough of a spark of curiosity to ensure their humanity and to allow for some learning, if. . . . It is the *ifs* that we now address.

RONALD

A permanent inclination to trust children began in my first years of teaching in the public schools of San Francisco. Students were from varied backgrounds: children from the Dust Bowl of Oklahoma, children battered by poverty pressures in the "highest delinquency" area of San Francisco, refugee children from Germany, Russia, Czechoslovakia, and Greece, and children from a racist America. In any one class (35–40 students) I could usually count a dozen different backgrounds or cultures. It was a good time and place for *my* learning.

I remember many of these children by their effect upon my understanding of children in later experiences — sometimes less battered, or sometimes more. One child is particularly germane to the subject of this chapter and it is his story that I sketch.

Ronald, as I have called him, arrived with his mother on the first day of my first kindergarten. My education about children who are different began here. I can see his mother's tall, sturdy figure, her masklike face, and I can hear her first words: "Here is Ronald. If you have anything left in your kindergarten by the end of the morning you will be fortunate."

Before my laughter could meet such a preposterous statement, Ronald's mother had closed the door quietly behind herself and I was left looking at the palest, cleanest, saddest 4-year-old ever to focus wary eyes on me. The contrast of her words with this fragile and silent child, dressed in spotless corduroys and an immaculate, shrunken, woolen sweater, left me at a loss for what to think about the two of them — mother and child.

Ronald's mother, whom I came to know and like as we all grew over the next two years, was not only accurate in her statement that morning, but prophetic. After two weeks with Ronald in the classroom, I was defeated and ready to agree with the day care home and with his mother that he could not be contained in any ordinary classroom. It was not his daily silence that concerned me, nor the speedy chaos that he made of our room. Those incredible, depression-born children in the class managed to accept Ronald and his mischief and would assist in putting things back together in a way that showed me a side of 4- and 5-year-olds that I had not expected and have counted on ever since. Somehow we managed to work and play with Ronald as our joint baby brother, who was "wrecking everything, Miss Pockman," but who did not know any better, yet. Most troubling, however, was that sometimes he would suddenly disappear from the classroom.

We survived these disappearances, such as the time he found his way to the boys' lavatory, figured out how to remove every stitch of clothing, and was found trying to flush it all down the toilet. Ronald then learned how to open those heavy, intricate school doors and leave the building and he was finally found in the street with cable cars halting, etc. "If that happens again...." The principal was right, I knew it, and I despaired. I scolded Ronald and tried to keep two of our most stalwart children always on Ronald-duty. It was not possible.

Sometime during October, in desperation, I fastened a rope around Ronald's waist and tied the other end to me. It was the only way I could think of to protect him, and to demonstrate to his heedless, silent self that his freedom with us had boundaries and that THEY would take him away if he could not learn to honor those boundaries. After two weeks I fearfully removed the rope. Ronald stayed with us, still never speaking, never laughing, never smiling, and never crying.

Before that last particular crisis of disappearing was resolved, there were others that were equally threatening. By no means was I sure how long I could keep this child, yet my discouragement and weariness did not send me to the principal to ask that Ronald be removed. Many evenings I would plan to do so the next day, but my curiosity was too engaged, and just when I would think it was hopeless, some small thing about his persistence would give me pause. From the information I had gathered about him and from his behavior early on, I thought (correctly it developed) that he might have been treated like a caged animal and not like a child. How, I asked myself, had he managed within his small self to keep alive this endless unfocused destructive curiosity?

I now backtrack to the Friday at the end of the first two weeks of school when in desperation I was ready to give Ronald to any taker. The burden seemed too great for me and for those other 38 children.

I realized even by that time that Ronald had written off human beings, both children and adults, along his way. He treated all of us as if we were not there — except to get in his way. But then came that Friday when Mrs. M, the lady who provided day care for him when he was not in kindergarten, arrived to take him and several other children home. Something happened that made me wonder about and for the first time reconsider having Ronald removed from the class. I felt Ronald's eyes on me in an evaluative way as Mrs. M, with real and understandable frustration, spilled out the long list of Ronald's iniquities. I could easily have added to the list, but her manner and Ronald's manner kept me silent and listening. For the second time in those two frantic weeks I saw Ronald standing still and watching me, the back of his hand pressed to his mouth in a gesture I had come to expect when he was tired, which was seldom. I felt that something in his attention was different. His attention focused on me as a person who must be considered, a concept I had not been able to ascribe to him before. My intuition told me that was significant. Poor Mrs. M went on and on and finally, with too much satisfaction, summed up the verdict on this 4-year-old — that they had just been waiting for the public school to agree that he must be sent to Glen Ellen, the home for the feebleminded. It was her improper glee and the momentary intelligence that I read — or hoped that I read — in Ronald's eyes as he watched us, that cast the dice, his and mine together, for the next two years.

When I think of and meet afresh the Mrs. Ms, the abusing adults — teachers and parents of children — I find it necessary to sound a very strong note of warning about the conditions under which we should bring a wider range of children together in our classrooms. Where rigid understaffed schools and totally inadequate inservice help are the rule, the tensions are enormous. What we are learning about child abuse at home, and the tensions that contribute to it, is true for child abuse at school. The wounds to the minds of children are initially less visible, but not less crippling.

Would I take on again what I did with Ronald and with some others in my experience? Absolutely not, unless I was provided with professional assistance. The toll was too great on me, on the other children, and on my own family. The toll is too great on teachers I meet and know now. I had the good fortune to be able to leave the stifling working conditions provided by many public schools and private day care centers and to learn in my own schools — before I too became an abusing teacher.

The insupportable ingredient is a setting in which children do not thrive *and* where we adults find ourselves incapable of changing that situation. That is what parents cannot abide, what teachers cannot abide, and where children survive with only a small fraction of their potential realized. Children are psychically abused, whether physically or not, and we all know too well that with rare exceptions they grow up to abuse in turn.

During those early months with Ronald there came from him no response to words, but a dogged, messy, almost senseless exploration of everything in the room. The fishpond was never stocked during the first semester because Ronald seemed to need to handle, fondle, mouth, distribute, and smell the assorted pebbles every day.

By Thanksgiving of that first semester discouragement with Ronald's progress was great, but then the Thanksgiving party, unplanned for his destructive ways, prompted Ronald to give an unequivocal sign that he was on his way. While I rushed that morning to rearrange and prepare the old, worn room — to draw the shades, to transform the big round library table with tall red candles and decorated cookies — a visiting friend took the children down the hall. The simple magic that one can so easily give children by some modest preparations was visible when the children returned to the room and walked to their chairs. Everyone sat down except Ronald, who dropped the gently restraining hand of my friend and walked alone to the central, large table. Ronald looked at the flaming candles, turned to look at me, turned back to the candles, and then began to tremble. After what seemed a long time, the fierce trembling stopped and he turned to give me his first smile. It was crooked, it was brief, but it was enough to dispel any past doubts.

So the battle to keep Ronald continued all fall, and my early refusal to give consent to his removal had not ended the issue. His mother was desperate, often actually hungry, and had come to believe he was congenitally subnormal, so for that first year she was unable to play much of a positive part. Later with delight she could and did play a role in Ronald's development. Sometime after the fateful Friday with Mrs. M, word came from the central office that Ronald had been tested by the proper authority, had an IQ of 45, and should be removed from the normal kindergarten. With 38 other children to care for, I was tempted, but only briefly, to comply.

The fight to keep Ronald paralleled my effort to learn *how* to keep and help him while not cheating the others. In this I was not alone. My family and my friends were as indignant as I that an abused child without speech would be given a score on an intelligence test. All their delight matched mine a year later when the second test result, an IQ score of 86, confirmed what I already knew: not reliable because he seems to be learning so fast.

Slowly, Ronald began to transform that boundless undefined curiosity into the desire to learn what lay beyond the world of smells, sounds, and sights. Over the two years of much agony in depression times, years of misery and setback for his almost defeated and lonely mother, smiles continued, language came, tears were shed, and humor even surfaced. I kept Ronald in my class for two years, and one morning during the second year I remember my chagrin and delight as I stopped to quiet the children as we passed the principal's office. I had stopped the long buzzing line, turned around and whispered in my teacher's voice, "Now, who is talking?" Ronald whispered back with a broad smile and his old fight, which was now irreverence, intact, "Only you."

Such is the sketch of Ronald, its setting, and something of its context. Yes, Ronald managed to make it, although not easily and not without later setbacks. But he made it, and I gained from him a confidence in children that goes with me into every classroom. It is not a small legacy from one battered child to a new teacher.

Where such stories of success can be told, there is always a defensive way to protect the conventional categories that treat symptoms as permanent attributes. "Ah, yes, marvelous, but of course that child must have been misdiagnosed" — as having an IQ of 45, as psychopathic, as autistically inaccessible to human communication. Too often we confirm the permanence of or deepen the syndrome by our treatment of it, and that violates a canon of medicine and of teaching. Suppose that Ronald had been put on a tranquilizing drug. Recognizing that such drugs may be useful in extreme cases, I believe that the chances of children such as Ronald to remake themselves are seriously curtailed by the widespread use of drugs. I have observed the effect on abused and retarded children — it often destroys innovation and curiosity.

AUTISTIC SYMPTOMS

A special and rather carefully defined cluster of curious deficiencies and talents has come to be known as infantile autism, a syndrome I believe to be quite different from Ronald's. My experience of it has been limited, so I have had to consistently inform myself from sources in the literature. However, it belongs in this account because it represents one of the challenges in the literature that is an extreme from which teachers can learn. Any one of us has hunches and prejudices about these children, and certain parents have spoken of them with great authority. *The Seige* (Park, 1967), and a more recent book, *Son-Rise* (Kaufman, 1976) are significant accounts of different autistic children. Here I turn to Sibylle Escalona, whose formulation (with emphasis added) is concise and does not preclude further knowledge:

> If we assume that the lack of a reciprocal, affectionate animated social bond between infant and mother-person is the critical experience deficit leading to infantile autism *or other psychopathology,* all facts confirm the invariant link between this experiential variable and subsequent symptomatology. However, a lack of normal mother-baby interaction may come about largely because the infant is incapable of providing his share of the interaction (the organic view); it may occur because of the mother's inability to relate normally to the baby (the psychogenic view); or it may come about as infants vulnerable on this score are matched to mothers who have more than ordinary difficulty in responding to their babies, and cannot sufficiently accommodate to the "difficult" and relatively unresponsive baby. Regardless of how this came about, wholly inadequate human interactions in infancy lead to concurrent and subsequent childhood psychopathology. [Escalona, 1974, p. 40]

I would add one personal experience that falls into Escalona's last provision. I watched a lively, responsive, cooing, and smiling 4-month-old baby become ill with a sore throat. He was irritable and fussy, although consolable, until he was given an antibiotic and a decongestant. The pain subsided fast, his temperature went down, and he slept well. Only after some hours did I realize, with terror, that the child had ceased to be his normal, responsive self in any way. His eyes looked through me as I changed him, and his once-reaching arms lay quietly at his side. No invitation to play brought a normal response, and no words brought his former laughter or his smile. After some hours of this, when I was not alone in recognizing his strange, docile behavior, the decongestant was stopped by the doctor, and our lively, reaching, smiling infant returned to his normal self. Suppose a child is long and seriously ill, and life-saving medication is administered routinely at some developmentally critical time, with such a concomitant effect. What centers of development might be damaged? Have observers of treatment and research in hospitals been alert to such effects? (see Spitz, 1950.) What could we learn here about autism and about child development in general? What are the implications of this for schools, classrooms, and teachers?

CONCLUSION

I shall not summarize the discussion of these pages except to reiterate that the essence of good classrooms and good teaching derives from a quintessence, which is the accrued strength and curiosity-potential that teachers and diverse children bring with them. On these strengths depend crucial criteria for good classrooms and from them the ambience is derived. Once we *fully* grant that the first aim of childhood education is to help children build upon and widen their strengths, other educational concerns and constraints can be given due attention.

For a younger generation of teachers to be a small step further along than its parental one, both generations must continually attune minds and eyes to understanding and seeing, and to being innovative, especially regarding those children at risk. They give the challenge. The Ronalds *can* take a new step to look to us adults for aid. The Jacks, who maintain for awhile their curiosity to inform themselves even in a hostile ambience, can reach out to find the assistance in learning that their "disruptive behavior" is already signaling that they need. An abused child, drugged in the name of healing, can show us, by ceasing to initiate, that he is in a further kind of pathogenic trouble. Even a baby, by ceasing to reach out and play and by looking with eyes that do not see, can send out a danger signal that trouble impends.

With our self-consciousness and knowledge, we are the beholders of these young or infant initiatives. On us depends whether such clues for advancement are never seen, overlooked, modified, or destroyed; or whether the clues are seen and understood. Clues are taken, built upon, and stretched for the life-enhancing signals that they can be.

At no point in my career have I used terms, such as gifted, normal, or handicapped, to label children. My experience in public and private schools had led me to mistrust the past and prevailing use of such categories. On reflection, I realize that certain special qualifications lie in this mistrust. I have written a book about my experiences with six deaf children (Hawkins, 1973), but certainly my interest there had been in the six children, so different from each other, and in understanding and extending their extraordinary powers for communicating what was alive and important to them. In my view, the interest was not in their handicap, but in what linked them with all children, and what differentiated each one of them from all others.

We humans can be grouped and classified for many purposes, but for those children who need help in learning, we are as many in kind as we are in number. Children challenge first because every individual constellation is a novel one; and their differences, whether from weakness or strengths, can never quite be reduced to standard cases. This fact can and must make each child a microcosm for professional excitement and learning.

REFERENCES

Allen, F. H. 1942. Psychotherapy with Children. W. W. Norton & Company, Inc., New York.

Comer, J. P., and Poussaint, A. 1975. Black Child Care. Simon & Schuster, New York.

Escalona, S. K. 1969. The Roots of Individuality. Aldine Publishing Co., Chicago.

Escalona, S. K. 1974. The Child in His family. In: C. S. Anthony, and C. Koupernik (eds.), Yearbook of the International Association for Child Psychiatry and Allied Professions. Vol. III. John Wiley & Sons, Inc., New York.

Featherstone, J. 1971. Schools Where Children Learn. Liveright, New York.

Freud, A., and Dann, S. 1951. An experiment in group upbringing. In: The Psychoanalytic Study of the Child, Vol. VI. Yale University Press, New Haven.

Gliedman, J., and Roth, W. 1979. The Unexpected Minority: Handicapped Children in America. Academic Press, New York.

Hawkins, F. 1973. The Logic of Action. Pantheon Books, New York.

James, H. 1974. What Masie Knew. Penguin Books, New York.

Kaufman, B. 1976. Son-Rise. Harper & Row Publishers, New York.

Lewin, K. 1948. Resolving Social Conflicts. Harper & Row Publishers, New York.

Mead, G. H. 1959. The Philosophy of the Present. Open Court, Chicago.

Park, C. 1967. The Seige. Harcourt, Brace, Jovanovich, Inc., New York.

Spitz, R. A. 1950. Relevancy of direct infant observation. In: The Psychoanalytic Study of the Child, Vol. V. Yale University Press, New Haven.

Spitz, R. A. 1957. No & Yes: On the Genesis of Human Communication. International Universities Press, New York.

Storm, H. O. 1953. Eolithism and design. Colorado Quarterly 1.

Taft, J. 1962. The Dynamics of Therapy in a Controlled Relationship. Dover Publications, Inc., New York.

Theoretical
Foundations

John Dewey and Current Cognitive Psychology of Learning

Nicholas J. Anastasiow

No one has received more censure from the critics of contemporary education than John Dewey. Yet Dewey's philosophy of education has been developed into a psychology of learning that is more viable today than it was when it was first proposed. There were few substantive data to support his notions when he first proposed his conception of how learning takes place, how to organize knowledge so that it is consistent with how learning takes place, and how to teach so that teaching is in harmony with both of the former. Nevertheless, since Dewey's philosophical position was based on a theory, in order to concur with his notion that all theories must be tested, he organized the laboratory school of the University of Chicago as a test site. The results, which are presented in a delightful report of the experience, while supportive of his ideas, do not meet the criteria of scientific data that Dewey himself would require (Mayhew and Edwards, 1936).

Unfortunately for American education, two factors interfered with the systematic development of Dewey's educational theory. One was the overwhelming readiness of some American educators to accept his suggestions, while philosophers and psychologists were more reluctant to do so. Dworkin (1959) states that "It may be no compliment to professional educators that they so easily understood Dewey while philosophers shook their heads" (p. 14). In fact, the rush of educators to adopt Dewey's approach to schooling probably resulted from the accuracy of his critiques of traditional education and the accuracy of his descriptions of the young child 3 to 8 years of age. Schools were depressing, rigid, drill-oriented places and, in general, were stiflingly automated factories through which children were merely processed. Cremin (1961) has described these conditions at length.

The second major factor impeding the development of Dewey's theory of education was that the psychology of learning inherent in Dewey's philosophy was counter to the then dominant theme in American psychology of behaviorism and tests and measurements. The American culture, so successful in the advancement of technology, grew heady in its assurance that if a thing exists it can be measured (Thorndike, 1926), and if it can be measured it can be shaped into something desirable (Watson, 1924; Skinner, 1938). Dewey's theory was radically different. He claimed that "things" exist due to their biological determinants. Through interaction with their environment these phenomena develop into unique patterns and persons. An interactionist position is more difficult to understand than a unitary theory, and Dewey, with a writing style that has confused, bored, and enraged thousands, did not help clarify what is essentially a very straightforward position.

To the modern reader, Dewey may sound like a Piagetian or a cognitive developmental theorist, as well he should, for the foundation of modern cognitive developmental theory is identical to the fundamental assumptions of his work. For example, one major tenet that Piaget, cognitive psychology, and Dewey have in common is the emphasis on the contribution of the organism's biological base to its general development. Archambault (1964) credits Pierce's essay "The Fixation of Belief," while Kohlberg (1971) credits the work of James Mark Baldwin for the influence on Dewey of the significance of the biological roots of the organism. In either case, Dewey's philosophy is based on the biological notion of adaptation, that is, the notion that the organism seeks equilibrium and adjustment with and to its environment. To Dewey, all organisms are adaptive. Thus, by assisting (not teaching or directing) a child in the search for equilibrium and adjustment to the environment, one is arranging the environment so as to facilitate the maximum development of the child. The reader familiar with Piaget will recognize that the above statements are consistent with Piagetian theory. Piaget's theory is based in biology, which perceives man as actively selecting and interpreting environmental events and thereby constructing his own world view and cognitive structures. In Kohlberg's (1971) opinion, Piaget has developed Dewey's theory into a viable psychology. Dewey's descriptions of learning and the learner can be viewed as hypotheses for which studies in cognitive psychology (Piagetian research is one of *several*) have gathered support.

This chapter argues that one of the most viable theoretical stances that can be taken today is the cognitive-learning position. Furthermore, it will be shown that the roots and basic tenets of this position can be found in the writings of John Dewey. Dewey did not use the term *cognitive*. He used the term *thinking* or the expression, *how we think*. He did not use the term *development;* rather, he used the term *growth*. Dewey was a contemporary of Claparède, who was Piaget's teacher (Kohlberg, 1971). Both Dewey and Claparède stressed the notion of experience. It is this notion that Piaget developed and documented in his many volumes of theory and research. Both Piaget's and cognitive psychology's premises concerning experience and environment-organism transactions are to be found in Dewey. The research that has been completed in recent years can thus serve as a verification of Dewey's hypotheses and assumptions.

It is difficult to present Dewey's philosophy of education. Although it is a consistent and coherent position, Dewey presented it in a series of books and papers over a period of fifty years. Rather than quoting extensively from Dewey, what follows is synthesized from his basic work (Archambault, 1964; Dworkin, 1959; Dewey, 1900, 1902, and 1938).

An additional problem in presenting Dewey's educational position is that his philosophy covers all phases of life. His concern for the field of education includes the total range of educational problems: how humans learn, how to organize environments so that humans learn, how to teach, and how to train teachers. At the same time, Dewey's writing contains critiques of the traditional school, the progressive school, and the traditional and reform teacher training institutions.

The next sections of this chapter present some of the key premises of Dewey's writings concerning how children learn and how learning takes place. Each is discussed in detail. Following this discussion, evidence is offered to support Dewey's position. Finally, the relationship between Dewey, Piaget, and the cognitive-learning position, which has been noted throughout the chapter, is briefly summarized.

The central concern of this chapter is Dewey's conception of the learner, of the learning process, and of the learning environment. It is important to understand that labeling Dewey's position as *progressive education* is a major mistake. Dewey perceived progressive education as an improvement over traditional education in that it made major changes in the classroom by improving teacher-pupil relations and by considering pupils' needs. However, he felt progressive education was too child-centered, just as traditional education was too subject-centered. He described his desire to find a balance between the two. No specific name was coined for Deweyian education except perhaps "modern." Dewey refers to it as *"New Education"* (Dworkin, 1959, p. 24). Informal education in most respects is very close to Dewey's position, as others in this volume attest.

THE OUTCOME OF LEARNING

Dewey believed reflective thinking to be the hallmark of a free and contributing citizen and the major outcome of schooling. The scientific method of control, experience, and objective tests and reasonable proof could be applied to all areas of human activity and should be acquired through education.

To Dewey, being able to think reflectively is being able to think in the highest order. His writings are an attempt to clarify what goes on in thinking in terms that are abstractions of the processes. He divides reflective thinking into five components. To begin, the individual must be faced with a real problem, something that interferes with his ongoing activities or actions. The situation must be recognized by the individual as a problem that needs to be solved if the individual is to pursue his activity. One aspect of the "problem solution" or thought process that occurs early is the individual's generation of potential solutions. Before acting on these proposed solutions, the individual seeks clarification of the problem to identify specifically what is going on to cause the problem. He then posits tentative solutions into hypotheses that are to be tested. Reasoning about the hypotheses and selecting one to be acted upon precedes the final act of testing the selected hypothesis by acting upon it. Dewey believed that the development of each person's potential for reflective and creative thought was the end goal of education. However, when selecting problems to be solved, Dewey insisted that they represent "real" problems to the individual and that they must contribute to the pupil's growth. This growth ultimately contributes to society when the child functions as a contributing member of that society.

Dewey felt that children must learn how to select relevant data and how to form relevant hypotheses consistent with the situation, the problem, and the potential actions to solve the problem. Dewey did not believe children needed to be motivated to solve problems, provided that the problems were "real" to the student. When problems were "real" problems, the teacher need not have to draw out or activate the young child, for:

> he is already running over, spilling over, with activities of all kinds. He is not a purely latent being whom the adult has to approach with great caution to draw out some hidden germ of activity. The child is already intensely active and the question of education is the question of taking hold of his activities, of giving them direction. [Dworkin, 1959, p. 54]

For Dewey, the stipulation that the child become a contributing societal person evoked additional criteria, in terms of pupil outcomes. To think reflectively (i.e., effectively), one must have something to think about. Moreover, one has meaningful things to think about only if one is aware of man's previous knowledge (history), skills (industrial processes), and ethical base (moral values of democracy). Thus, while education is considered an end in itself, its subject matter is the sum total of what has been learned in the past. However, for education to be successful, one must carefully attend to the processes of learning, lest one merely repeat the failures of the traditional school. Being able to think clearly is paramount. Interestingly, there is evidence available today that suggests that the ability to think in terms of abstractions may be a product of systematic training, just as Dewey believed (Langer and Kuhn, 1971). In addition, Piaget and Inhelder (1969) suggest that the ability to think in abstractions may be handicapped if the person has not had sufficient experience or mastery of being able to express thought in linguistic propositions, which comes about through training. In essence, Dewey examined how man thinks effectively and then, based on that analysis, suggested the manner in which children can be engaged in learning how to think. To Dewey and to Piaget, children learn how to think through a combination of their biological inheritance and their interactions in and with an environment. Dewey does not name the capacities that children have at birth that enable them to deal with learning; he implies them when he writes about the 3- to 8-year-old. However, the cognitive psychologists do describe what is available to the infant at birth; these innate mechanisms are referred to as *schemata* (Bartlett, 1932, 1958; Neisser, 1967, 1976) or *schemes* (Piaget and Inhelder, 1969). These schemes are pre-existing structures that direct perceptual activity and are modified as the activity occurs. Dewey infers that young children actively seek to "grow" and possess capacities (schemes). His major effort is devoted to specifying how these schemes (capacities) can be maximally developed.

PROCESSES OF LEARNING

As was stated above, learning takes place through the learner's active involvement with his environment. The learner is not a passive recipient into which knowledge is poured, but an active explorer or agent in his environment. The learner is a seeker of information attempting to solve real problems. He does so by trial and error. However, the child can be aided in his learning by being helped to employ the scientific method of reflective thinking. This method can greatly assist the child in his mastery of subject matter, i.e., the world's accumulated knowledge. A person who has experienced such learning is postulated to be a person who can solve real problems by thinking, who has learned to think effectively while solving real problems, and who, in addition, desires to assist his culture in solving contemporary problems. Therefore, the process of education is the means as well as the end goal. Dewey perceives means-end dichotomies as false distinctions. Dewey wrote that, "Education must be conceived as a continuing reconstruction of experience; that the process and the goal are one and the same thing" (Dworkin, 1959, p. 27). Each is a part of a continuum of experience in which the individual engages as he "grows." That is, one learns how to think through the process of thinking about real things.

The term *growth* is ambiguous; it has been suggested that Dewey chose it to emphasize that growth has to be constantly redefined in terms of the accomplishment of the individual at the time, as well as in terms of the current state of knowledge (Dworkin, 1959). Note the similarity to Piagetian theory. As Flavell (1977) states:

> The Piagetian man actively selects and interprets environmental information in constructing his own knowledge rather than passively copying the information presented to his senses. [p. 6]

To Dewey, the need to perceive learning as dynamic was to consider both sides of the coin: the state of knowledge and the accomplishment level of the pupil. To do so is not a simple task, as he was well aware.

THE PROCESS OF EDUCATION

Effective education must consider all at once the child, the processes of education, and the subject matter to be taught. Dewey was well aware that it was far more difficult for the teacher to consider these three elements simultaneously than it was to deal with either the traditional school's concentration on subject matter or the progressive school's child-centeredness. Deweyian education requires a teacher to be a guide, helping the child in his own learning. It requires that the teacher be a skilled diagnostician, able to determine the level of a child's learning. Once the teacher diagnoses the level of the individual child's functioning, the teacher must engage in reflective thinking, observation, hypotheses-generation, testing, and verification of curricular options. Only then is instruction effective. The instructional mode recommended by Dewey is one in which the child is guided, both in learning how to solve problems as well as in learning how to select meaningful problems to solve. The teacher is a social agent who creates an environment based on the diagnoses of the pupils' current status of intellectual and skill development that will serve society. The environment must be useful, interesting, and absorbing to the child, and it must provide the information that is needed to solve problems. It must contain suggestions for problem solving, it must teach skills needed to solve problems, such as learning how to read, and it must provide clarifications for the child, usually in the form of questions and probes, when the child is in the process of hypothesis-generation and hypothesis-testing. In short, education requires planning, selection, guidance, diagnosis, instruction, and evaluation in an ongoing and synergistic process.

Thus, schooling is a deliberately contrived affair that carefully selects materials from the re-creation of cultural epochs through their cultural artifacts. The selection is guided by the criteria that these experiences lead to physical, intellectual, and moral growth and that the participating individuals obtain increased meaning or knowledge. In addition, the experiences should result in the individual's possessing an ability to explore richer channels of meaning and to inquire at a more sophisticated level. Thus, engaging the child in an inquiry about topics is a means of teaching about history, science, and how to think. It is the means of learning skills. In Dewey's terms, experience (later Dewey and Bentley, 1973, used the term *transaction*) is the basis of human learning.

HOW CHILDREN LEARN

By citing only a few anecdotes (for example, how children learn that fire burns), Dewey sets the stage for the idea that children are motivated to learn by their own activity in their own natural environment. The reader familiar with Piaget, can anticipate Piagetian notions of the child discovering (i.e., learning) the laws of conservation through his own experimentation. Dewey's and Piaget's notions, which are basic to genetic epistemology, differ on one major dimension: in general, Piaget avoids making statements concerning how to teach—he restricts his comments to how children learn. Dewey, however, interweaves both in the same discussion. For example, since the child (3- to 8-years old) is already intensely active,

> let the child first express his impulse and then through criticism, question, and suggestion bring to consciousness of what he has done, and what he needs to do. [Dewey, 1902, p. 40]

Interestingly, Kamii (1972), drawing on Piagetian theory, makes very similar suggestions on how to teach by probing and questioning. Dewey's description of learning might best be stated in modern terms as *guided discovery*. The child is curious and acts on the environment. His actions result in learning. Many of these learnings can be facilitated by the teacher, who focuses the child on the relevant dimensions and guides the

child to his own solution. However, Dewey did state a number of propositions and caveats concerning children's learning. Three of these follow:

1. Children learn through activity. Therefore, teachers should arrange
   situations that will induce activity. However, only educative activity
   will lead to appropriate learning. Activity per se does not lead to
   learning.
2. Children's interest in activity maximizes the probability of learning.
   However, Dewey makes clear his belief that children's interest alone
   is not sufficient for learning. Interest serves as a motive for learning.
3. A child learns when information is relevant to his level of growth.
   However, the information to be learned must lead to doubt or conflict in order to engage the pupil in problem solving.

Thus, the teacher, who is aware that students learn through activities
that interest them and thereby motivate them to learn, must know each
learner's characteristics as well as the subject matter to be learned. Otherwise, the teacher might engage the learner in activities that have already
been mastered or are beyond the learner's capabilities. Paraphrasing
Kant, Dewey believed "method without data is empty, data without
method are blind" (Dworkin, 1959, p. 35).

EDUCATIONAL ENVIRONMENT FOR THE YOUNG CHILD

Dewey was a skilled observer and his writing makes distinctions about
how children of different ages should be taught. To Dewey, the young
child was motorically active and he believed that this activity should be
taken advantage of rather than stifled.

One anecdote is of interest. Dewey had a great deal of difficulty finding the school furniture he desired for the laboratory school at the University of Chicago. Finally, one salesman said to Dewey, "I am afraid we do
not have what you want. You want something at which children may
work; these (desks and chairs) are for listening" (Dworkin, 1959, p. 31).
Dewey perceived that, for children 3 to 5 years of age, play was work, and
space must be arranged so that children could engage in the play-work activities that led to learning. Young children's active motoric involvement
sets the stage for the teacher's transmission of information. Children
engaged in activity demand information.

Children are at their most individual in movement; they cease to be
5-year-olds as a group and become the distinctive beings that one sees in
all other settings: home, playground, and neighborhood. To be effective,
education, must allow for the occurrence of the idiosyncratic expression
of each child (Dewey, 1902).

Dewey's description of the 3- to 5-year-old period is not a fictionalized ideal childhood but one in which the child must learn to communicate. Dewey stresses that teachers of the very young should not press instruction of academic subjects in abstract, systematic, or technical terms, but should present knowledge in a way that engages the interest and activity of the student. Poor teaching is the presentation of abstract subject matter without relevance or interest to the child. When the content is too abstract, the young child is not motivated to learn. However, when a subject matter has to be overly simplified in order for a young child to understand it, the logical character may be destroyed.

For the 3- to 5-year-old, Dewey feels that the arts and manual activities are areas to be drawn upon for subject matter. However, the child must be allowed to control his experience in order to learn from it. Thus, four major areas contribute to the 3- to 5-year-old's learning: 1) conversations and communication, 2) discoveries of how things work, 3) construction of things, and 4) artistic creations.

Dewey wrote that the child is born with a natural desire to act out and to do. The school needs to provide a social matrix in which these natural or genetic desires can be expressed. In early education, Dewey feels the child should work and study cooperatively with others in order to learn how community life is sustained.

DEWEY AND THE COGNITIVE-LEARNING POSITION

It would appear that Dewey's notions of the learner have been largely verified by Piagetian and other cognitive research. Kohlberg (1971) indicates the Piagetian theory is an extension of the basic genetic-epistemological model. As indicated earlier, Dewey's beliefs are consistent with this model. Dewey's references to the differences between the young child (before 8 years of age) and the older child (after 8 years of age) are a basic part of Piagetian theory, which postulates the transition between preoperational thought and concrete operations (5 to 7 years of age). Piaget describes in far more detail than Dewey both the earlier age-stages and the later ones.

In discussing Piagetian theory, Flavell (1977) writes that "brevity, clarity and accuracy are somewhat incompatible" (p. 6). As this chapter is focused on Dewey, references to Piaget have been chosen to highlight major similarities between Dewey and Piaget; they are not intended to imply that Dewey's theory encompasses all of Piaget. The point is that the critical basic assumptions underlying cognitive theories in general, of which Piaget's is one, are compatible with Dewey. There are many sources of evidence to draw upon. Dewey, however, emphasizes learning as much as the learner. In this respect he anticipates the current focus on cognitive-learning hypotheses. Dewey's basic premise that the organism learns through its own activity has been documented in numerous studies (for excellent summaries, see Hunt, 1961; Appleton, Clifton, and Goldberg, 1975). Dewey's conception of "the mind as essentially a process" (Dworkin, 1959, p. 102) is also current (Pribram, 1971). There is also evidence from the psychology of learning that supports Dewey's conception of the way man knows (Bartlett, 1958). It would appear that cognitive-learning psychology has found support for Dewey's major observations of how children learn and it may be prudent to examine that position in greater detail.

COGNITIVE-LEARNING POSITION

Cognition is defined as "the activity of knowing, the acquisition and use of knowledge" (Neisser, 1976, p. 1). The basic assertion for a cognitive position is that human activity is survival-oriented: the capacities that enable the individual to learn from the social environment are available at birth (Moerk, 1977). Gibson (1975) refers to the motivation for the child's learning as the need to make sense out of the environment and as the need to reduce uncertainty. Infants have available at birth natural schemata with which to act upon the environment. Infants appear to know "how to find out about their environment and how to organize the information they obtain so it can help them obtain more" (Neisser, 1976, p. 63). From birth on, individuals appear to be engaged in a question-answer search for information (Moerk, 1977). This acquisition of information does not happen purely innately. For example, in auditory reception, an external stimulation from the environment (his mother's voice) activates an infant's auditory templates. The infant responds to the stimulus by hearing (Marlen, 1977). Thus, the cognitive-learning position posits statements about innate biological trigger-mechanisms in the form of schemata, and statements about environmental events that can be acquired through learning. To Neisser, perception is the basic cognitive activity out of which all other cognitive activities must emerge. (Others suggest that language itself develops from this basic activity: see Beilen, 1975; Cromer, 1975; Bates, 1976; Moerk, 1977.) Perception, to Neisser (1976), is both a "matter of the individual discovering what the environment is really like and adapting to it" (p. 9). "Man is a social animal and it is within the social world that skills uniquely human emerge" (Lewis and Rosenblum, 1977, p. 5).

    The human infant (and adult) will act on the cognitive representation of its environment rather than on the environment per se (Mahoney,

1977). That is, "meanings are in nature but symbols are the heritage of man. The young child perceives the meaning of the object rather than the object per se" (Moerk, p. 82). These representations are related to the individual's previous learning and learning environment but are phenomenological in nature rather than direct copies of the environment (Mahoney, 1977). For example, a 7-month-old bangs a toy telephone; but at nine months, having observed or been shown or programmed, he will pick up a telephone and appear to listen to it (Zelazo, 1976). This learning of the telephone's use is seen to be cognitively mediated by the child, with thoughts, feelings, and behaviors being causally interactive (Mahoney, 1977).

Perception is a constructive process. First, the perceiver anticipates that he will perceive certain kinds of information. These anticipations are based on previous experience and the perceiver's previous schemata. The outcome of the experience will modify the original schema (Neisser, 1976).

The cognitive-learning theory posits that the primitive schemata become more complex as the individual interacts with his or her environment and that these schema become hierarchically arranged (Neisser, 1976). The process under which schema become more complex is *accommodation,* much as Piaget has described it. The development of cognitive processes is dependent on and is hypothesized to be related to neural maturations (probably by myelinization and full development of the perceptual systems and their interconnections), with major shifts correlated with environmental interactions (Epstein, 1974). Eventually, cognitive maps are developed, much like Tolman (1948) described them. Cognitive maps are not images; they are essentially perceptual anticipations, that is, preparations for picking up certain kinds of information (Neisser, 1976, p. 41). A cognitive map always includes the person *and* the environment (Neisser, 1976, p. 117). Hopefully, the earlier sections of this chapter have made it clear that Dewey made many observations about the learner that are now aspects of the cognitive position.

DEWEY AND CURRENT TRENDS IN PSYCHOLOGY

Whether Dewey laid the intellectual groundwork for the cognitive-learning theorists, as I believe, is not critical. What is important to note is that Dewey provides a philosophy for a modern psychology of learning—the cognitive-learning position. Dewey perceived learning as best enhanced when it is in answer to questions raised by the learner. Dewey believed learning (not just that occurring in schools) is a dynamic, life-long process in which the individual grows, in terms of both his personality and his intellect. In this sense, Dewey did not believe in a fixed or static intelligence as did others of his time (Terman and Thorndike, as reported in Kamin, 1975). It was only with Hunt's (1961) work that the notion of fixed intelligence was severely questioned. The role that internal states (cognition) play in human activity has become a dominant current interest in psychology, just as it was to Dewey.

Psychological theories are currently undergoing major theoretical shifts, with greater emphasis being placed on cognitive interpretations (McKeachie, 1976). In fact, Mahoney (1977) states "the most striking aspect of the cognitive 'revolution' is its pervasiveness" (p. 6). This shift in emphasis is not only in interpretations of how learning takes place, but in the fields of social, personality, psychotherapy, perception, and most other fields within psychology. The list of so-called behaviorists is being reduced as the evidence supporting a cognitive rather than a behavioral position grows. For example, such lofty principles as the law of effect and/or reinforcement have been brought under serious question (Thorndike, see McKeachie, 1976). Human behavior is being perceived as far more complex than the Watsonian or Skinnerian behavioral positions have described. Principles of learning, although still not fully conceptualized, are no longer seen as being identical to principles of conditioning (Bandura, 1976, 1977).

In the light of recent findings, many behaviorists have become more "cognitive" and have accepted some information-processing model theories. In some cases, social learning theory has been used to recast the more behavioral approaches (see Mischel, 1973). There is a growing rapprochement among cognitive and behavioral stances reminiscent of earlier cognitive-behavioral positions, such as Tolman's (1948). However, the effects are far more general. Bandura's (1969) *Principles of Behavior Modification* did much to release the behavioral position from complete dependence on environmental events by placing emphasis on the principles of observational learning, vicarious learning, imitative learning, and the internal mediators in performance.

As stated above, this interactionist position draws upon learning principles (rather than principles of conditioning). Thus, the new position has become known as cognitive-learning (Weiner and Palermo, 1974; Beck, 1976; Anastasiow, 1977 ; Mahoney, 1977). Although this theoretical shift has had a great impact on psychology in general, its impact on education has been small, with the exceptions of the informal school movement and the special cases of the preschool handicapped programs of Bricker and Guralnick (Anastasiow, 1977).

In any event, it seems clear that the trends in psychology have been recasting Dewey's ideas into a viable and modern psychology of learning.

SUMMARY

Perhaps it is just as well that Dewey's philosophy is not identified with a particular approach to education, for the emotion Dewey's name engenders has not cooled. However, Dewey's observations concerning how individuals learn, how they think, and how they should be taught seem very relevant today as new data support his contentions. His works contain the most complete statements on how children learn and how to teach that are available today. In this respect alone, they need to be examined with care.

To deal with children as if they were less than individuals is to deny them their human capacity. To arrange educational settings that do not provide for the basic requirements noted by Dewey is inexcusable anti intellectualism. Given our current knowledge of how children learn, reliance upon such outmoded and unnatural teaching strategies as drill and practice, as are found abundantly in traditional education, cannot be justified by scientific reason.

REFERENCES

Anastasiow, N. J. 1977. Strategies and models for early childhood intervention programs in integrated settings. In: M. Guralnick (ed.), Early Intervention and the Integration of Handicapped and Nonhandicapped Children. University Park Press, Baltimore.
Appleton, T., Clifton, R., and Goldberg, S. 1975. The development of behavioral competence in infancy. In: F. D. Horowitz (ed.), Review of Child Development Research. University of Chicago Press, Chicago.
Archambault, R. D. 1964 . John Dewey on Education. The University of Chicago Press, Chicago. Includes:
    Philosophy and education, pp. 3–19.
    Ethics and education, pp. 23–138.
    Aesthetics and education, pp. 141–165.
    Science and education, pp. 169–192.
    Psychology and education, pp. 195–285.
    Society and education, pp. 289–310.
    Principles of pedagogy, pp. 313–439.
Bandura, A. 1969 . Principles of Behavior Modification. Holt, Rinehart, & Winston, Inc., New York.
Bandura, A. 1976. Self-Reinforcement: Theoretical and methodological considerations. Behaviorism 4(2):135–155.
Bandura, A. 1977. Social Learning Theory. Prentice-Hall, Inc., Englewood Cliffs, N.J.
Bartlett, F. C. 1932. Remembering. Cambridge University Press, Cambridge, England.
Bartlett, F. C. 1958 . Thinking. Basic Books, Inc., New York.
Bates, E. 1976. Language and Context. Academic Press, Inc., New York.

Beck, A. T. 1976. Cognitive Therapy and the Emotional Disorders. International Universities Press, New York.

Beilin, H. 1975. Studies in the Cognitive Basis of Language Development. Academic Press, Inc., New York.

Cremin, L. 1961. The Transformation of the School. Alfred A. Knopf, Inc., New York.

Cromer, R. 1975. The development of language cognition. In: B. Foss (ed.), New Perspectives in Child Development, pp. 184–252. Penguin Books, Baltimore.

Dewey, J. 1900. The School and Society. The University of Chicago Press, Chicago.

Dewey, J. 1902. The Child and the Curriculum. The University of Chicago Press, Chicago.

Dewey, J. 1938. Experience and Education. Collier Books, New York.

Dewey, J., and Bentley, A. F. 1973. Knowing and the known. In: R. Handy and E. D. Harwood (eds.), Useful Procedures of Inquiry, pp. 89–187. Behavioral Research Council, Great Barrington, Mass.

Dworkin, M. S. 1959. Dewey on Education. Teachers College Press, Columbia University, New York. Includes:
  John Dewey: A centennial review, pp. 1–18.
  My pedagogic creed, pp. 19–32.
  The school and society, pp. 33–90.
  The child and the curriculum, pp. 91–111.
  Progressive education and the science of education, pp. 113–126.
  Introduction to the use of resources in education, pp. 127–134.

Epstein, H. T. 1974. Phrenoblysis: Special brain and mind growth periods, Part I. Human brain and skull development, pp. 207–216; Phrenoblysis: Special brain and mind growth periods, Part II. Human mental development, pp. 217–224. Dev. Psychobiol. 7(3).

Flavell, J. H. 1977. Cognitive Development. Prentice-Hall, Inc., Englewood Cliffs, N.J.

Gibson, E. J. 1975. Theory based research on reading and its implications for instruction. In: J. B. Carroll and J. S. Chall (eds.), Toward a Literate Society, pp. 288–321. McGraw-Hill Book Company, New York.

Hunt, J. 1961. Experience and Intelligence. The Ronald Press, New York.

Kamii, C. 1972. An application of Piaget's theory to the conceptualization of preschool curriculum. In: R. K. Parker (ed.), The Preschool in Action, Allyn and Bacon, Boston.

Kamin, L. F. 1975. The Science and Politics of IQ. Halsted Press, New York.

Kohlberg, L. 1971. The concepts of developmental psychology as the central guide to education: Examples from cognitive, moral, and psychological education. In: M. C. Reynolds (ed.), Proceedings of the Conference on Psychology and the Process of Schooling in the Next Decade: Alternative Conceptions, University of Minnesota, Minneapolis.

Langer, J., and Kuhn, D. 1971. Relations between logical and moral development. In: L. Kohlberg and E. Turiel (eds.), Recent Research in Moral Development. Holt, Rinehart & Winston, New York.

Lewis, M., and Rosenblum, L. A. 1977. Interaction, Conversation, and the Development of Language. John Wiley & Sons, New York.

McKeachie, W.J. 1976. Psychology in America's bicentennial year. Am. Psychol. 31(12): 819–833.

Mahoney, M.J. 1977. Reflections on the cognitive-learning trend in psychotherapy. Am. Psychol. 32(1): 5–13.

Marlen, P. 1977. Sensory templates, vocal perception and development. In: M. Lewis and L.A. Rosenblum (eds.), Interaction, Conversation, and the Development of Language, John Wiley & Sons, New York.

Mayhew, K. C., and Edwards, A. C. 1936. The Dewey School. Appleton-Century-Crofts, New York.

Mischel, W. 1973. Toward a cognitive social learning reconceptualization. Psychol. Rev. 30: 252–283.

Moerk, E. L. 1977. Pragmatic and Semantic Aspects of Early Language Development. University Park Press, Baltimore.

Neisser, U. 1967. Cognitive Psychology. Appleton-Century-Crofts, New York.

Neisser, U. 1976. Cognition and Reality. W. H. Freeman and Company, San Francisco, Cal.

Piaget, J., and Inhelder, B. 1969. The Psychology of the Child. Basic Books, Inc., New York.

Pribram, K. H. 1971. Languages of the Brain; Experimental Paradoxes and Principles of Neuropsychology. Prentice-Hall, Englewood Cliffs, N.J.

Skinner, B. F. 1938. The Behavior of Organisms: An Experimental Analysis. Appleton-Century-Crofts, New York.

Thorndike, E. L. et al. 1926. The Measurement of Intelligence. Bureau of Publications, Teachers College, Columbia University, New York.

Tolman, E. C. 1932. Purposive Behavior in Animals and Men. Appleton-Century-Crofts, New York.

Tolman, E.C. 1948. Cognitive maps in rats and men. Psychol. Rev. 55: 189–208.

Watson, J. B. 1924. Psychology: From the Standpoint of a Behaviorist. J. B. Lippincott Company, Philadelphia.

Weiner, W. B., and Palermo, D. S. (eds.) 1974. Cognition and the Symbolic Processes. Earlbaum, Hillsdale, N.J.

Zelazo, P. R. 1976. From reflexive to instrumental behavior. In: L. Lipsett (ed.), Developmental Psychology. Earlbaum, Hillsdale, N.J.

The Active Classroom and Children with Special Needs
Affective and Social Dimensions

David Elkind

An active classroom is one that is geared to the developmental level of the children it serves and is one that permits children to use the various modes of learning of which they are capable (Elkind, 1976). Children learn some things by imitation and repetition, other things by active inquiry, and still others through expressive activities, such as writing and painting. An active classroom provides the materials and the opportunities for all three kinds of learning. Although the active classroom is usually thought of in terms of its emphasis on cognition, it has some affective/social dimensions as well. This chapter discusses this "hidden side" of the active classroom, with particular reference to children with special needs.

Before proceeding it might be advisable to say something in general about children with special needs. It is important to recognize that children, regardless of their handicap or disability, are children first of all. There is a danger in thinking of a "blind child" or a "deaf child" or a "retarded child" because one tends to think of the handicap first and the child second. What must be kept in mind is that children are first and foremost children, and only secondarily are they individuals with one or another handicap.

Moreover, not every child with a special need should be mainstreamed, i.e., incorporated into a regular classroom. Although integration is a worthwhile ideal, it does not always make sense in practice. By far, the majority of classroom teachers are ill prepared to deal with children with special needs. Without adequate support services, a teacher taking in a child with special needs could well find himself overburdened and thus rendered ineffective. Nor is it clear that mainstreaming is the best experience for all children with special needs. Done well, mainstreaming could do much for the self-esteem of a child with special needs. Done poorly, it could make such a child miserable.

Accordingly, this chapter does not advocate that all children with special needs be incorporated in regular classrooms. Rather, it suggests that some children can be so incorporated and it describes how active classrooms can accommodate them. Very likely, since the active classroom is designed to respond to children's affective and cognitive abilities, it can adapt to children with special needs somewhat more readily than other types of classroom orientation. In particular, the active classroom's recognition of the personal curriculum, of the attachment dynamism, and of interpersonal frames gives it an affective/social dimension required by children in general and by children with special needs in particular.

THE PERSONAL CURRICULUM

In general, a curriculum can be regarded as a set of priorities concerning "what is to be learned when." Unfortunately, there is not one curriculum, but at least three different curricula with which the teacher must contend. First, there is the *developmental curriculum,* determined by the interaction of the child's mental abilities and his need to make sense out of the physical world in which he lives. The attainment of number, space, time, and causality concepts in a predictable sequence, as discussed by Piaget (1950), is one manifestation of this developmental curriculum. A second curriculum with which the child has to cope is the *school curriculum,* the sequence of attainments in math/science, language arts, social studies, and fine arts that is mandated by society.

In addition to the developmental and school curricula there is a third curriculum with which the teacher must deal; this is called the *personal curriculum.* The personal curriculum, the child's individual learning priorities, is determined both by the developmental curriculum and by his own individual needs, interests, abilities, and talents. As in the case of the other curricula, personal curricula are both transient, or short-range, and abiding, or long-range. An ideal educational program, one that is seldom found, occurs when the short-range as well as the long-range priorities of all three curricula coincide. For example, this occurs when children want to read and do math (coincidence of the personal and school curricula) and are allowed to do so at their level of mental ability (coincidence of the developmental and the school curricula).

Sometimes, more often that we would like, the various curricula come into conflict and one or another has to give way. Which one does the giving often cannot be decided in advance and sometimes priorities must be set as the situation demands. For example, there was a theft at the Mt.

Hope School, the laboratory school of the University of Rochester. The children did not actually witness the theft, but they were aware it had occurred. The youngsters were excited and a little frightened by the event and their feelings about the theft constituted a personal curriculum priority. The theft seemed important enough to the children that the teachers gave up their school curriculum priorities and encouraged the children to write about and draw their impressions of this critical incident.

Of course there are other situations in which personal curricula cannot be allowed to become the first priority. For example, this is true when children engage in playing games, in Eric Berne's (1964) sense of "game." Such games are frequently played by children with special needs as a way of avoiding school work. In playing a game the child puts forth a *con* (a statement) that ties into a teacher's *gimmick* (her desire to be helpful, to be successful as a teacher, and so on). Then the child pulls a *reverse,* which produces *payoffs* for both the child (the glee at having outsmarted the teacher) and the teacher (the frustration at having been taken in).

A child who plays games has personal curriculum needs that are at variance with the school curriculum priorities. He wants to engage in interpersonal games that are not constructive or helpful to himself or to others. Therefore, when a game-playing child is encountered, his personal curriculum objectives cannot be allowed to hold sway, because they are self-destructive. Once a game-playing child is detected, the games can be aborted by the teacher's not becoming hooked by the con. For example, the teacher can respond to the child who cannot find his pencil: "Sounds like you don't really want to do that right now, why don't you do reading now and come back to writing later." To the child who says, "I can't do it" when there is evidence that he can, the teacher has to say, "I believe you can do it, why don't you try?"

For children with more severe special needs, personal curriculum problems are of a somewhat different order. It is hard for adults to appreciate the emotional trauma undergone by a child who day after day must be in a situation where he cannot do what others do, or who can only do it badly. Playing a poor game of tennis, golf, or softball can temporarily elicit the same feelings in an adult. One has to multiply this feeling a hundredfold to appreciate what the child experiences in the classroom day after day. To be sure, young children lack some of the cognitive structures adults have and they are better at rationalizing and fooling themselves than adults are. Nonetheless, the experience is sufficiently traumatic to severely damage self-esteem and self-confidence.

In a sense, the child's personal curriculum can involve his need to enhance, defend, and maintain self-esteem, the sense of being a worthwhile person. At each stage of development the modes of satisfying these personal curriculum needs differ, but the basic needs remain the same. During the early years of schooling, when children have what Piaget calls concrete operations,[1] they are capable of learning adult imposed rules and they are still needful of adult approval and ratification. Indeed, the tool skills of reading, writing, and arithmetic are acquired largely to win social approval rather than because of their intrinsic interest or worth to the child. Much of the "spontaneous" learning of children is already very much socially conditioned.

Many children with special needs cannot satisfy their personal curriculum needs in a developmentally appropriate fashion, i.e., through the acquisition of these tool skills. Since they cannot enhance self-esteem through the acquisition of these skills, they seek to defend it by what often turns out to be socially disruptive and self-defeating behavior. What a child of this kind needs, first and foremost, is an interpersonal relationship in which friendship and approval are not contingent upon academic achievement. This is more easy to accomplish in an active classroom than in a traditional classroom.

In the first place, learning in the active classroom is individualized and children work at their own pace on materials adapted to their developmental level. In such circumstances it is easy for the teacher to casually put her arm around the child, say something to the effect that "you look nice today" or "thank you for helping with the clean up" without embarrassing the child. Secondly, because of the flexibility inherent in individualization, the teacher can permit the child with special needs to rearrange the day's work when he is "out of sorts." Finally, in an active classroom there is a "quiet corner," where all children, including children with special needs, can retreat to listen to records, read, or simply daydream for a bit. In short, the individualization and flexibility of the active classroom makes it easier for the teacher to accommodate the personal curriculum needs of either average or special children without disrupting the classroom as a whole.

THE ATTACHMENT DYNAMISM

There is now a good deal of evidence (Ainsworth, 1969; Bowlby, 1973) that the attachment of the infant to particular adults comes about during the last trimester of the first year of life and that this attachment increases during the second year of life, when fear of strangers and strange places is inordinate. By and large the infant remains attached to only a very small

[1]A system of mental abilities, which in their manner of operation, are similar to the basic operations of arithmetic and that permit children to engage in syllogistic reasoning and higher order classifications.

coterie of adults, usually his mother, father, and perhaps a caregiver. The adults to whom the child is attached are the child's primary source of self-esteem and hence wield considerable power over the youngster without always being aware of this fact. It is this attachment of the child to significant adults that is one of the most powerful motivations for the elaboration and utilization of mental abilities. Although the phenomenon of attachment that has just been described is quite familiar, its importance for the child's learning of the school curriculum has largely been overlooked, particularly in special education.

The importance of attachment in learning the school curriculum can be demonstrated in many different domains, but its importance can be illustrated in two practical situations. These situations are the teaching of reading to normal children and the teaching of tool subjects to youngsters with special needs. In both of these contexts the role of attachment is often ignored, and those concerned with instructing children in these situations may be primarily concerned with curriculum materials and instructional techniques rather than with interpersonal relationships. It is often assumed that the selection of the right curriculum materials and instructional techniques will release the child's "innate" curiosity and eagerness to learn. However, as has already been suggested, one cannot hope to build upon intrinsic motivation in each and every learning situation. Indeed, what appears to be intrinsic motivation is, in a good many cases, social motivation derived from the adults to whom the child is attached.

Learning to read is a case in point. Unlike walking and talking, reading is not something a child acquires spontaneously as a part of his normal, expectable adaptive apparatus. Learning to read is a difficult task and, in addition to having the requisite mental abilities and experiences, children need powerful motivation to learn to read. In the majority of cases this motivation comes from attachment to adults who encourage and reward the child's efforts at learning to read. In studies of children who read before coming to school (Briggs and Elkind, 1973, 1977), it was found that many youngsters who read early had a close friend (either an older child or adult) who spent a great deal of time helping the child to read. In the biographies of successful people who grew up amid poverty and adversity, one often reads of particular adults or teachers who recognized and encouraged their abilities and talents. Attachment to adults who encourage and reward academic achievement is probably of major significance in the lives of most individuals who succeed at schooling.

A more concrete example of the role of attachment in academic achievement helps to strengthen the argument for its importance. For the past eight years I have been supervising an undergraduate practicum wherein the college students tutor children with special needs for an entire year. Among the many things we learned in the course of running this program was that remedial work could not be introduced or used effectively until an emotional relationship, an attachment, occurred between the tutor and the child. After this occurred, the child's behavior began to change at home and at school. Once children began to feel that they were worthy of an adult's liking and respect, there was a kind of *spread of affect*[2] that made them feel good about themselves and their abilities to learn in a variety of domains.

It seems to me that this spread of affect phenomenon is of crucial importance in working with children with special needs. Whatever the child's physical, neurological, or psychological handicaps, his impaired sense of self-esteem always plays a part in his difficulties with learning. When such a youngster is made to feel better as a person, from the attention, concern, and liking of another person, he feels better about himself in general and about his capacity to cope with new learning situations in particular. We have often observed how children in our program begin to do better work at school and begin to be more tractable at home as a result of the nonacademic, but self-esteem bolstering experience, of our program.

To test the effects of attachment and spread of affect more directly, we opened a full-time school, The Mt. Hope School at the University of Rochester, in the fall of 1974. We enrolled under-achieving children of average or slightly below average intelligence. Some of the children were thought be be brain-injured, others presented behavior patterns unacceptable in traditional classroom settings. In our program we emphasized one-to-one relationships between students and children and between teachers and children. The small size of the group (2 teachers, 15 children, and 15 undergraduates) made this possible. The teachers were present full-time, the undergraduates were present a day or two a week.

During the first few months the children were quite unmanageable: they fought, destroyed materials, and seemed unable to concentrate or sit still. However, as the interpersonal relationships developed, a transformation took place. The children began to settle down and began to work at reading and math. With a lot of individualized instruction they began to have success experiences that further motivated them to continue. Where before we had trouble getting the children to read and do math, it then became almost impossible to stop them. The classrooms became bee-

---

[2]In learning theory there is a principle that is called spread of effect, referring to the generalization of reinforcement effects upon behavior. But the spread of *affect* has to do with feelings. It has to do with the fact that when we have a rewarding experience, we have an overall good feeling that colors our behavior in many different situations.

hives of children eager to read, to write, to play math games, and to verbally interact with others. Once they returned to their regular schools, 80% of the children maintained their gains over a three-year period.

The experience at the Mt. Hope School has strengthened our belief in the importance of the attachment dynamism for learning in general and for children with special needs in particular. Although our situation was somewhat ideal in that we had a large number of aides, attachment can be fostered by the organization of the active classroom even in the absence of such aides. For example, many active classrooms have vertical grouping wherein the same children stay with the same teacher for two years (usually K-1 or 1-2). This facilitates children's attachment to the teacher and makes her a more potent figure than she might otherwise be.

There are other features of the active classroom that also help foster the attachment between children and teacher. In the active classroom the teacher does not sit at the head of the room with the children behind him in rows of desks. In most active classrooms it is hard to tell where the teacher's desk is. The teacher in the active classroom is mobile in the sense that she is usually sitting with one or another child or a group of children as they work. This mobility facilitates one-to-one interactions and thus closer attachments between teacher and child are formed. In summary, the organization of the active classroom is particularly well suited to the attachment between teacher and child that is beneficial to all pupils but particularly to children with special needs.

Before closing this discussion on the attachment dynamism, it should be said that there is one type of child who may not benefit from attachment. We call such youngsters *impossible* children. Every teacher occasionally encounters a child who she does not like and who the other children do not like either. It is not unusual to discover that the child's parents also have trouble liking the youngster. Such children seem to do everything in their power to annoy, often in little ways, the adults and children with whom they interact. Often they discover and play upon the little sensitivities that each of us has and that thoughtful, caring people take pains to avoid. However, the impossible child steps on everyone's toes and always seems to know which ones are the most tender and painful.

Impossible children are difficult to teach and often have problems learning. This is true even when they have good native ability and can catch on to difficult material quickly. However, they are often so involved in their interpersonal machinations that they have little incentive or inclination to concentrate on school work. Such children are frustrating because nothing seems to work with them. If one tries to be loving they reject this effort or make a mockery of it. If one is harsh, they play the helpless victim and feel sorry for themselves. If one is indifferent, they make their presence known in obnoxious ways, and if they are punished for being too loud, they will proceed to be too soft and will not speak even when spoken to. For these children interpersonal relations present a perpetual chess game in which each move must be countered with a response determined by the previous move.

By definition, impossible children are difficult to understand. This is true because their symptoms are misleading and disguise the real issue. The situation is not unlike school phobia, wherein the child's manifest reaction, the fear of school, conceals the real fear that is quite different, namely, fear of separation from the parent. The school phobia analogy has not been chosen capriciously, because in some respects impossible children are the opposite of school phobics. Whereas the school phobic is afraid of separation, impossible children are afraid of attachment. Impossible children are afraid of love and acceptance and ward it off with all the powers at their command. Such children are impossible because they reject the dynamics of contemporary humanism, namely, love, acceptance, and freedom.

In some ways, the impossible child proves the power of the attachment dynamism. Strange as it seems, the impossible child frequently makes himself impossible in order to please or satisfy the parents' often unconscious wish. If the parents need an objectionable child that they can reject without social disapproval (no one else likes the child either), the child will unconsciously comply to satisfy the parental need. To be sure, something in a particular child will provoke rejection on the part of the parents, but the child's objectionable behavior reflects the power of the attachment dynamism and how easily it can become perverted.

In line with these unconscious dynamics, the conscious assumptive realities of impossible children, that is, the hypotheses that the child formulates and assumes to be part of reality rather than assumptions about it, can take many different forms. Some children believe that if they like someone else it will hurt or destroy them. These children have to avoid liking other people in order to protect them. Other children just assume that everyone is evil and that if you look hard enough or long enough you can find the evil in everyone. Still other impossible children seem to believe that the world owes them a living and that they do not need to do anything in return because everyone has it so good while they have it so bad. These fantasies account for some of the varieties among impossible children, but the basic dynamic, fear of attachment, is common to them all.

In dealing with impossible children it is important to be accepting but not overly loving and friendly. As in the case of school phobics who, although they are afraid of separation, generally want to be more independent, impossible children really want to be liked and to like others, but their anxieties get in the way. Sometimes these anxieties have to be verbalized to help the child deal with them realistically: "I think you are working very hard not to like me and for me not to like you, but it's okay to like people." While some impossible children can be helped in the classroom, some may benefit from the help of mental health professionals. For our purposes, the main point about impossible children is that the attachment dynamism operates in them as it does in all children, albeit in a somewhat different form. Even in an active classroom, which takes heed of the importance of attachment in learning, some children cannot be helped and additional professional assistance is required.

Still a third affective social dimension of the active classroom is its recognition of the importance of situational "frames" that are different from social roles and that children need to learn if they are to be successful at school. The next section discusses these frames.

THE COGNITIVE FRAME

As it is employed in contemporary sociology (Bernstein, 1971; Goffman, 1974), a frame is a repetitive social situation that embodies a set of implicit rules, expectancies, and understandings, which govern behavior in those situations. When people follow the constraints of the frame an emotional equilibrium is maintained. However, if someone breaks the rules of the frame, the equilibrium is disrupted and some sort of remedial work has to be done to restore the equilibrium. The disruption of a frame is not catastrophic but it is uncomfortable, and that is why individuals work hard to restore breaches in frame behavior.

A familiar frame situation is the waiting room, whether this be a doctor's office, a busy bakery where one takes numbers, or an airport gate waiting area. In such situations one is expected to take one's turn, not to push into line, not to attend too closely to other people's dress or conversation, not to speak too loudly, and to follow the instructions of whoever is vested with authority in that situation. Anyone who violates these rules immediately becomes a focus of attention and sometimes the object of a cutting remark. Thus, the man who pushes into line while other passengers are waiting patiently to board an aircraft is looked upon with distaste and may be asked, "What's your damn hurry?"

In educational settings there are many different frames, each with its own set of rules, understandings, and expectancies. For example, there is a group reading frame in which children come together as a group to read. Each child may read a part of the story and then is expected to read along silently while other children take turns reading aloud. Ordinarily, children learn the frame rules of the educational setting quite easily and these are more or less background to their foreground learning activities. Nonetheless, the rules are there and constitute what can be called *learning frames*.

What often happens in the case of many children with special needs is that the learning frame becomes the foreground, the center of attention, and the learning activity moves into the background. That is to say, a child who is having difficulty in school begins to break frame rules. The child may get up and noisily roam about when other children are at work. When such behavior occurs, it is wrong to assume that the child does not understand the frame rules that are in play—that you do not disturb other children who are at work. Indeed, the "misbehavior" is a reflection of the fact that the young person is now attending to the frame rules in order to avoid the learning task. He has effectively reversed figure and ground, and wants to do battle on frame rules rather than upon learning tasks.

Accordingly, when a child deliberately breaks frame rules, there is little point to reiterating them since he knows them very well already or he would not be breaking them. In effect, the child is saying that the social disapproval of breaking frame rules is to be preferred to the social ridicule for displaying school failure. The proof of this analysis is given by the fact that when such a child finds something interesting to do, and is permitted to do it, he obeys the frame rules very nicely indeed. (To be sure, there are some hyperkinetic youngsters who cannot, for organic reasons, obey frame rules, but such children may be fewer than we suppose. Also, some retarded children may not understand the frame rules and may need to be instructed in them.)

Another difficulty children with special needs encounter with frames has to do with discriminating between child-child and child-adult frames. For most children the rules for dealing with children are different from the rules for dealing with adults. For example, even young children shift verbal "registers" and use different grammatical forms when they switch from talking to children to talking to adults (Gelman and Schatz, 1977). More generally, among young children communication by pushing, shoving, pulling, pinching, etc., is regarded as an appropriate means of getting one's message across. However, such communication is generally not permitted in child-adult frames. Or, more exactly, expressive adults may communicate to children by touching, patting, or caressing, but children are not expected to return these actions in kind. Between children, physical communication is a symmetrical relation, whereas between children and adults physical communication is asymmetrical.

One consequence of the experience of continuous failure of the child with special needs is that there is a blurring of the child-child and child-adult frame rules. For example, such a child may poke, shove, and pull at the teacher to get his attention, much as the child might behave toward other children. In the same way, an emotionally troubled child may use words with the teacher that most children would reserve for child-child frames. Moreover, sometimes troubled children become excessively angry at other children for pushing and shoving them as if they were the adult and as if the other child were breaking the child-adult frame rules.

It should be noted that the situation here is just the reverse of that wherein the child is violating the rules of the learning frame. In that situation the youngster knows the rules and that is why he is breaking them; but in the case of the disturbed child's violation of child-child and child-adult frame rules, the young person fails to discriminate which rules are appropriately in operation. Interestingly, when children break child-child or child-adult frame rules, it is generally assumed that they understand the rules and are deliberately breaking them. In this situation the child's violation of frame rules is attributed to personal traits, such as need for attention, immaturity, and the like. In fact, when a child breaks adult-child or child-child frame rules, what he needs is help in discriminating which rules apply where. To such children it is appropriate to say, "You and your friends can push and shove one another, but it is not okay to push and shove me. I am a grown-up."

Unfortunately, a troubled child's difficulty in discriminating child-child and child-adult frame rules is compounded by a negative spread of affect. The anxiety, fear, and frustration that such a child experiences in the classroom becomes associated with all aspects of the school setting. Classrooms, desks, and workbooks all become signs of unhappy experience and produce emotional states that make appropriate frame discrimination difficult. These negative associations can be mitigated to some degree by the spread of positive affect that proceeds from the attachment dynamism, but other things can be done as well. Recognition of these frames and frame difficulties in an active classroom facilities helping children to deal with the frames more effectively.

In an active classroom it is recognized that children with problems occasionally need to be removed from the learning environment, to go for walks, to play ball with a tutor, or to visit a local craftsperson. The active classroom itself is set up so as to suggest a more informal, relaxed setting. Plants and animals, large comfortable pillows on the floor, and really good art work all add to the sense of a rich, interesting evironment that has much to offer besides academic failure. By creating a comfortable and interesting environment, the emotional "feel" of the place will inhibit the negative spread of affect that the troubled child experiences in more traditional classroom settings. In the informal setting of the active classroom, with some of the negative affect reduced, it is easier for the child to discriminate between child-child and child-adult frame behaviors.

SUMMARY AND CONCLUSION

The affective and social dimensions of the active classroom that facilitate the assimilation of children with special needs has been reviewed in this chapter. Basically, an active classroom is one geared to the children's level of development and is a setting that facilitates a variety of learning modes. In addition, an active classroom pays particular attention to each child's, as well as the group's, personal curriculum needs. It also recognizes the importance of emotional attachment in academic achievement and fosters such attachment by its organization. Finally, in an active classroom there is recognition of the implicit rules, understanding, and expectancies, that is, frames, that form the background of all learning situations. A recognition of the difficulty children with special needs have with frame rules helps the teacher in the active classroom to ease such children's learning problems. In particular it makes such classrooms particularly well suited for assimilating children with special needs.

REFERENCES

Ainsworth, M.D.S. 1969. Object relations, dependency and attachment: A theoretical review of the infant-mother relationship. Child Dev. 40: 969–1025.
Berne, E. 1964. Games People Play. Ballantine, New York.
Bernstein, B. B. 1971. Class, Codes and Control. Routledge and Kegan Paul, London.
Bowlby, J. 1973. Separation. Basic Books, Inc., New York.
Briggs, C., and Elkind, D. 1973. Cognitive development in early readers. Dev. Psychol. 9: 279–280.
Briggs, C., and Elkind, D. 1977. Characteristics of early readers. Percept. Mot. Skills 44: 1231–1237.
Elkind, D. 1976. Child Development and Education. Oxford University Press, New York.
Gelman, R., and Schatz, M. 1977. Appropriate speech adjustment: The operation of conversational constraints on talk to two year olds. In: M. Lewis and L. A. Rosenblum (eds.), Interaction, Conversation and Development of Language. John Wiley & Sons, Inc., New York.
Goffman, E. 1974. Frame Analysis. Harvard University Press, Cambridge.
Piaget, J. 1950. The Psychology of Intelligence. Routledge and Kegan Paul, London.

Adapting Learning
Environments

Adapting Classrooms for *All* the Children

Lillian Weber

OPEN CORRIDOR CLASSROOMS

The classrooms that the City College Advisory Service has been developing in the New York City public schools since 1967 have been named Open Corridor classrooms. In each classroom an effort has been made to develop organizational modes and relationships that are more responsive to each child's learning and to the developmental path characteristic of each child. From the very beginning we were aware of the enormous teacher supports that would be needed in making these changes; therefore, the focus was on the *community* of classrooms linked in this effort, not solely on each solitary classroom. Thus, in contrast to the massing of population in city schools, which renders teachers and children anonymous, and in contrast to the solitary isolation of teachers behind closed doors, the Open Corridor tried to set up a frame for the growth of intimate communities stressing interactive and supportive relationships between teachers of like mind in different areas of schools. The Open Corridor tried to set the frame for the growth of a community based on heterogeneity and inclusion, in which difference could be seen as positive contribution. From its very inception the Open Corridor included parents as a requisite to its existence. Indeed, in some situations parents were active in its initiation. Open Corridor development was dependent on administrative understanding and support, which, over the ten years of Open Corridor growth, in many instances became administrative leadership of corridor development.

The plan was that the corridor—the common space for teachers and children—would be the physical link and the communications link between the teachers. Although each classroom could continue its function as a subcommunity, the corridor would identify the new community, thereby eliminating the isolation of teacher from teacher, class from class, and children from children. It could de-emphasize the sharp separation of grade and ability levels. Teachers in the Open Corridor would begin to organize their rooms so that children could work independently or in small groups. Teachers could be guided to provide the materials that would not only reinforce skills, but also arouse a child's interest, stimulate his thinking, and generate problem-solving. In this way, teachers could be open to each other's efforts. Children in this space would be open to what was happening in other classrooms. By the arrangement of mixed grade levels on the corridor, children would continue to have access to experiences that they had before their present placement and to experiences they might anticipate in the future. In this corridor, materials and experiences could be shared, and activities that were hard to manage in the classroom could be readily accommodated. Teachers worked to develop environments in their own classrooms that ensured access to materials and learning experiences and that were thus more open to a child's active learning process. Within this institutional frame it was hoped that teachers could begin to develop the adaptations they needed in order to function with responsibility for *all* children.

OUR FOCUS—THE ORDINARY CLASSROOM POPULATION

When the City College Advisory Service began its work in 1967, the question for us was not the relationship of open education to special education. Certainly, many of us came to open education with experiences in other settings that supported an individual child's development and strengths, and gave time and space for the restabilization or reconstruction that the child needed to contend with the unevenness of his development. Many of us had worked in early childhood settings, where it was very rare for a child to be excluded. Some of us even had experiences adapting classroom arrangements to accommodate blind or orthopedically impaired children. We were accustomed to the inclusion of ranges of emotional behavior and general development; our conception of the continuum of the norm was broad rather than narrow. With this background as the frame for our vision, the continuum of the norm as it confronted us in the public school classrooms of 1967 seemed to be a narrow one.

It was the normal classroom that we confronted in our effort to broaden the continuum. We were looking at the so-called ordinary student population and the question we proposed was how to help teachers work more individually with children. In the existing situations the focus was not on the individual child. Instead, a rough categorization of children was made, determined by the results of testing children on how much information they had taken in from the prescribed syllabus, which was taught to the whole class. From this categorization the students were arranged in homogeneous groupings based on test scores: "bright," "middle," and "low-range" classes—reflecting clusters on the bell-curve of test results. To avoid the stigma of labeling, these clusters were often numbered by an exponential refinement of grade listing: 1^1, 1^2, 1^3, etc. (*Of course* everyone knew what the exponent meant.) For the most part, the curriculum focused on what the tests covered. No other approach to reach the child's potential was sought. The result was a situation in which upward mobility between groups became minimal. This central fact about homogeneous grouping seemed to spell the failure of this approach to educating children.

FAILURE OF HOMOGENEOUS GROUPING

We did not come lightly to the decision that heterogeneous grouping had to be the first condition for the changes we sought. At the outset, although we were looking at the ordinary, so-called normal population in the schools, questions were raised about the accuracy of placements in CRMD classes.[1] We were also concerned about the distortion of normal societal relations in this closed educational organization that allowed no interaction between the children in any of the classes. Our concentration was on the homogeneous grouping pattern of placement that was presumed to be the economical and efficient response to the differences revealed in the bell-curve graphs of children's performance. It was thought that teachers could better organize their work to meet the level of children's ability in homogeneous classes since teachers could then justify whole-class presentations. Under the umbrella of assumed homogeneity, teachers were responsible not only for *coverage* of a pre-assigned plan of work for the whole class but also for *control* of the whole class, which becomes necessary when the presentation is to the whole class and in the same mode. It seemed to us that this school structure was deficient in its response to human differences. Large numbers of children were reported to be failures. Organizing a teacher's work around the presumed homogeneity actually prevented the teacher from providing for those children who were not responding. Clearly, organizing the schools in these ways made differences a problem, rather than an aspect of humanness with positive potential.

[1]Classes of *Children with Retarded Mental Development* are named after the New York City Board of Education special education division, the Bureau for Children with Retarded Mental Development.

Criteria for Placement

Although remediation in reading was usually provided, in order to raise the scores that were the major criterion for group placement, it was only provided for those children already defined as failures. Even if this was a reasonable and promising approach to raising scores, the sparse allocation of time (twenty minutes once or twice a week) that the remedial reading teacher gave to each child had little effect on scores. The equation of "slow" with "poor" placed the reader in such groupings, which in themselves seemed to be fixed. Children not responding either to the whole-class presentation or to remediation were eliminated, regrouped, or retained. Any unusual variations in the learning curve provoked still further refinement of the "homogeneous" classifications. To complicate matters further, some placements were inevitably questionable even within the context of the approved criteria. As is the problem in any system of classification, judgments had to be made, and, of course, some children were judged "borderline" according to the criteria used. Such children tended to become fixed in the lower class of placement. If children created problems for the teacher who used whole-class methods, the children exhibited *downward* mobility when reassigned to classes with lower exponents. How often has such downward mobility ended in CRMD or other kinds of special placement? How often has such placement resulted from difficulties of response to whole-class presentation?

The criteria for placement either ignored or blurred the issues that related to a child's development, such as the uneven progression of his "putting it together," or his own ways of organizing his experiences. Whatever the original intent, such grouping obscured the issue of providing for differences in children, as it was based on the single dimension of scores for achievement within a prescribed curriculum, within the prescribed time of a school grade, and justified by the supposed necessity of whole-class teaching and grade progression. Any differences provided for in those groupings reflected a dimension that was considered relevant to that school structure, described in the bell curve, and recorded in widespread failure. If such fixed grouping is descriptive, then for many children compulsory education was custodial not educative. Upon closer examination, it seemed that school had become a custodial arrangement predominantly for the poor and for minorities.

Thus, to raise questions about failure, about compulsory education, and about whether schools could be made to support the continuity of each child's growth was to challenge many aspects of the school structure as well as of the society. For those of us with our focus on schools, the central question was the issue of grouping. Our questions about school structure necessarily led us away from the deficit approach that criticized the child or his background and led us instead to criticize the deficient response of the school structure to human difference. Obviously we also had to turn away from a tendency to focus on *irreversible* deficit.[2] If teachers' energies were to be mobilized for questioning, and certainly if they were to be mobilized for active participation in change, the enormously pervasive erosion of the belief in educability would have to be halted and reversed.

BEHAVIOR AND DISCIPLINE

How rarely teachers found homogeneous organization "easy," and how often they faced failure in their work were revealed in their numerous expressions of hopelessness about being able to teach *anything* to many of the children. Teachers spoke about poor discipline, behavior problems, and "problem" children. They were quite aware that the traditional structure of schooling—homogeneous and whole-class—did not "work" for many children. Locked into fixed placement and unsuccessful in their school progression, these "problem" children led school lives that were scarred by behavior difficulties and combatant relationships with the teacher, other children, and themselves. The hopelessness in teacher-child relationships was further reflected in exclusions and suspensions from schools—an issue that was brought to public attention in newspaper stories on the recalcitrant pupil. In more minor ways, exclusions from whatever learning environment had been provided were widespread. In a situation in which a teacher related to a whole class, trying to bring everyone in the class to the same close focus, anything that disturbed the close focus became annoying.

Exclusion

The experience of the teacher working within whole-class, prescribed expectations was that discipline was very difficult to enforce. Some children were placed in the front of the room, at the blackboard, or in the

---

[2]Educability assumes growth and operates on the premise of the nonfixed nature of descriptive characteristics. It is basic to all practice in education. One can refer to longitudinal studies (for example, the work of Lois Barclay Murphy (1976) and Patricia Carini (1975)) and to the whole genre of autobiography for support of this view of possibility in human growth. In the 1960s doubt was cast on the premise of educability. Compensatory programs and programs with special focus on deficits were developed. Evaluations of compensatory programs in the 1970s, e.g., the Westinghouse evaluation of Head Start programs (see Cicirelli et al., 1969), had the effect in many instances of further weakening the teacher's commitment to educability. Methodology in many of the programs offering compensation presumed fixed qualities of failing children and developed approaches especially for such children in the context of these (fixed) qualities.

back of the room. For everyone else, time was wasted while the teacher waited for or scolded those children into taking their assigned places. A child might then be left alone, even for long periods of time, staring out into space, doing nothing. So many children were told to stand outside the door that the procedure could constitute a use of the hallway! (This use of the hallway for purposes of separation or exclusion from classroom obviously existed long before our corridor use for activity overflow.) Children were sent to sit in the principal's office or, if they were not that delinquent, they were used as monitors. It was reported that such children were hardly ever in the classroom. No one contended that the children who were difficult in the classroom were outside the range of normal development or outside the realm of participation in normal experience. Nevertheless, if the difficulties continued long enough, the teacher sometimes stopped thinking of the exclusion as temporary. A visitor to those homogeneously grouped classrooms would sometimes see a child not working at all, messing about in the back of the room, or wandering around the room while everyone else worked. The teacher had apparently given up on efforts to control the child via temporary exclusion, and, if asked, would say, "I've referred him," or "I've asked for testing." What seemed to be the case, and what was observed repeatedly, was that the teacher, having "referred" the child, had transferred the burden of thinking about the child to that process called "referral."

I am convinced from conversations with teachers that they were persuaded that the child really needed referral and that help would result. I am also sure that teachers often visualized that help would be imminent, that somebody would presently whisk the child away to a helping setting. However, what was the truth? The truth was that testing and referral often took ages. The truth was that saying "I've referred him" did not end the teacher's responsibility, because the child was *still* in the classroom. The referral process was often inactive for six months or longer after referral. During that period in which the teacher had "referred him," the child was not being taught; worse than that, he was being ignored. The teacher sometimes seemed unaware not only of the fact that referral might take a long time, but also that in many cases the recommendation of the referral process would be for supportive activity *in* as well as *outside* the classroom. The frustrations, the delays, and the combatant relationship inherent in such situations could result in suspensions. It was exactly these situations—filled with problems resulting from the poor fit of the whole-class homogeneous structure to the patterns of some children's function—that were central to the discussion when we began our work.

At that time we concluded from our analysis of grouping patterns that homogeneous grouping and whole-class teaching were poor structures with which to meet human differences. Obscuring the issue of providing for differences, homogeneous grouping produced problems for which the solutions inevitably became further segregation, more refined classifications of homogeneous groupings, or even exclusion. Thus, our decision in favor of heterogeneous grouping was initially a recognition of the failure of homogeneous grouping. Children were heterogeneous and diverse and needed to be provided for. Our analysis indicated that provision had to be made not only for the academic heterogeneity and diversity of ability that might underline the records on performance but for the diversity of children's physical and emotional development. The teacher's preoccupation could not be solely with content because there was no way of dealing only with a child's intake of content. A child could not be disconnected from his body, his behavior, his selective focus, his interest, his individual way of organizing, and his adapting to experiences. Indeed, he used his body, exhibited his behavior, and expressed his interests in his intake of content. This complexity could be convenient or inconvenient. At various times, the same child could either "fit" within what was planned or be a poor "fit," but those of us in primary education could not ask that the child's body, interests, and emotions be left outside the classroom door while we dealt with the child's cognition.

If we were to relate to what we knew about children—that they were different and that they assimilated things differently—a way had to be found to work with individually different children or with small groups that shared a need or interest for some brief period. A way had to be found to mesh the various aspects of a child's development and his potential for further development—in other words, to find the path of educability in each and every child.

THE OPEN CLASSROOM

Our commitment to support each child's developmental potential was based on a challenge to homogeneous grouping, and our work was based on the assumption of educability. Our presence in the classroom could be justified in no other way. We consider the assumption of educability to be the true meaning of compulsory education, for unless the compulsory situation serves to support a child's development, it has no excuse for being. We felt that we had to engage teachers in a continuing discussion about the meaning of their commitment to educability, so that they could understand that the decision to institute heterogeneous grouping was inevitable.

In addition, we had to support the teacher in meeting the classroom problems inherent in the task set by the commitment to support each child's developmental potential. We have assisted teachers by helping them exchange accounts of what they had done, helping them assess how far they have met a child's needs, and examining their work with children in order to guide them in further attempts. As we studied the successful responsive environments created by some teachers, we extended our own understanding of what is implied by provision for the individual. We shared some of the insights gained in the course of difficult implementation and we shared the reasoning that preceded our commitment to heterogeneous grouping, with the hope that teachers would see the pertinence of the experience to their present situations.

Everything about our concept of the organization of the open classroom follows from our analysis of the particular kind of help that teachers needed. In the new context of acceptance of *all* the children and with a commitment to their educability, the teacher faced the problem of how to set up the room so that she would have time and freedom to relate to those who had been problems and failures in the single-dimensional context of whole-class teaching. The problem was how to relate to children who had not been and could not be reached when the teacher functioned under the compulsions of prescribed content "coverage." Certainly, if the teacher was to work with a small group, provision had to be made for other children. According to our analysis, decentralization of the room into interest areas was the appropriate response, but we recognized that many questions would have to be answered before a teacher could take that step. Classroom changes and teachers' understandings of needed change were often uneven and slow. Before taking the big step to interest areas, which are based on the assumption that children will actively select their own points of focus, the teacher usually took many smaller steps.

The Small-group Focus

We helped teachers assume an active role in providing special small-group focus for certain children without any implication that these children would learn forever in this way and no other. The teacher needed reassurance that we were not pushing her into confrontation with the achievement goals of the unchanged system. Indeed, with small-group and individual provision, she could at least maintain her efforts in ways that were impossible for her under the old whole-class organization. No longer forced to pass over her failure in her own need to "get on" with coverage, she could find ways to foster the child's continuous progress toward these achievement goals. We emphasized that such small groupings must not represent fixed groupings or any diagnosis of irreversibility. The teacher arranged for *periods* of specific focus. These first arrangements were assessed and reassessed by teachers seeking further refinement for the individual. From such assessment, new views of the importance of interaction and interest and of the teacher as a responsive and adaptive facilitator have been emerging. Such assessment made it possible for the teacher to step beyond first arrangements to a long-range view, in which she searched for more positive relationships to the child's growth. Observation of the child's growth was essential in this search. Observation had to extend beyond the child's use of what the teacher had prepared and valued to observation of the child in other settings, so that other dimensions of possibility to which she as teacher could relate supportively might be defined. New ways of planning and recording followed inevitably from these new conceptions of a teacher's obligation to the individual and to small groups instead of to prescribed curriculum and whole-class coverage. It also became clear that new conceptions of curriculum construction were inherent in the view that a teacher's obligation is to adapt offerings so that *each* child may learn.

In our view, provision for differences could not be a permanent provision based on the assumption of fixed differences. It could not put all responsibility for "use" on the child. When faced with what seemed to be a child's dysfunction, the teacher, believing in the developmental thrust of *all* human beings, was obligated to further observe and to relate responsively, adaptively, and flexibly to the child as educable. To believe in a child's developmental thrust and his educability was to believe that in spite of all differences in putting together an understanding of the world, each and every child did do so. Simply *allowing* the child's presence in the classroom is not enough; simply *exposing* him to use of the classroom's setting — if indeed the child's response is nonuse — is not enough. At the least, the teacher's role is to make an effort to understand his way, to support his path of understanding, and to pull him into hard work on his own learning. Only in this way can we hope to find a way to help the child. Obviously the teacher's role in *adapting* the classroom in response to children's use assumes more than just single possibilities for response.

We helped teachers to use the time of waiting after "referral" for trying out some special adaptations of the environment with the child. These adaptations might serve to buy time for the child's own stabilization processes. After connection to the referral resources was finally made, we helped the teacher to use the suggestions made by the referral resource for even more sensitive adaptations of her own provision and to use the supplementary help given by these external-to-the-classroom resources for a new supportive context of classroom effort. We have witnessed many instances of a child stabilizing and regaining his learning thrust as a result of short intensive periods of special provision, special teacher attention, and special structure, all of which supported the child's own coping mechanisms.[3]

Teachers faced many difficulties in making changes that would be supportive of children's growth. Some of these difficulties resulted from children's different personal histories; others resulted from the constriction of the institutional framework within which the teachers worked. In addition to the general pressures on the teachers, in the current context of pressure for accountability, of supposed teacher surplus, and of budget cuts, teachers fear for their jobs, thus exacerbating their perception of difficulties and limiting their willingness to risk change.

STUMBLING BLOCKS TO IMPLEMENTATION — THE TEACHER

The different resources each teacher brought to the classroom resulted in different understandings of what was implicit in changed practice. Within the differences of their understandings, teachers who believed in each child's potential for further growth developed different classrooms with different degrees of success. In these classrooms, teachers could interact responsively with each child and assist each child in growing through interaction with others. As we worked with teachers, we discovered that some were inhibited in making provision even for temporary supportive structures. Certainly some of the teachers, inheriting the thin relationships and single focus of the past, have had a shallow base of observation feeding their knowledge of children. They have not recognized quickly enough the need for temporary special provision and focus.

We stressed the importance of the teacher's role as observer of all children, but observation of the children who require special provision was essential. It was for these that the search for positive connotation of difference was necessary.

The fact that some teachers may still try to cover prescribed content is another impediment to specific provisions. They may still think of *a* curriculum. While many teachers are not working totally in whole-class ways, they are nevertheless teaching whole groups part of the time, so that they feel interrupted by any child not well-provided for by this format. Many of them feel the pressure to reach a standard, the class norm, or whatever the school district demands. In their anxiety, teachers re-create for themselves, at least in part, a feeling that any deviation from pinpoint focus is interruption.

---

[3]These instances are reported in teacher records and taped accounts collected at the Workshop Center for Open Education. Excerpts are published from time to time in *Notes From Workshop Center For Open Education* (City College of New York).

Global statements about interruption are characteristic. For example, teachers often say that a child "blows up all the time." This is almost never the case. Any teacher, in her despair about being tired that day and because for the past week the child has been a nuisance, tends at times to make global statements. The teacher should be taken up on her statement. Is there anything that a child can work on so that his concentration can be observed? Let's do a time check on the lengths of the child's period of involvement. Is it really true that his focus shifts every thirty seconds? Let's figure out a contained situation, such as a busy-work situation, to protect the class for a short time and to help the teacher pull herself together while some of the possible positives are figured out.

Special Provisions

What is normal responsibility? The professional expectation (formal or informal) of planning specifically for four or five children is unfamiliar to many teachers. Many teachers are unfamiliar with the use of specific although temporary structures to contain and limit intrusive behavior while searching for positive relationships. They insufficiently use the flexible possibilities in open classrooms for such temporary arrangements. They may be horrified, thinking that such arrangements violate unrestricted choice, which they consider abstractly as inherent in open education. Many teachers may not understand or accept the temporary nature or the purpose of the arrangements that give them the chance to catch their breath or to prevent hurt. Unable to deal with the reality of the intrusions and unable to contain or limit them, teachers may have nothing to suggest except extreme treatment, such as exclusion.

Another source of the difficulty some teachers experience in making adaptive arrangements lies in the fact that they can become intrigued or even fascinated with their own curricular ideas. After all, creativity in developing curriculum and responsibility for decisions and content selection are new aspects of teacher obligation. The teacher's goal may become fixed on carrying out her idea and on having the children support her in this. She may derive intense gratification from this support. Indeed it is important for teachers to develop a rich curriculum, but even more important is the response from children, which is the touchstone of validity for these curricular developments. The teacher may have internalized the importance of one without the other or may not have even begun to internalize that even more important than the children's response to the *teacher's* program is the teacher's obligation to respond to the children's connections and "wonderful ideas" (Duckworth, 1972). Annoyance is inevitable if the children's response to the teacher's interest and provision is inadequate, i.e., if six respond but several do not. Although the material, the brilliant idea, is not present in whole-class fashion, whole-class involvement (at some level) is expected, and the teacher has not provided for the contingency of *no* response. Seldom does the teacher question the adequacy of provision in the event of nonuse.

Difference and Development

We are at the beginning of developing sophistication in the search for a positive connotation of differences and for the positive developmental thrust in each child, implicit in our assumption of educability. For example, in some of our classrooms the teacher may actually be following the prescribed curriculum that spells out, admittedly with some flexibility, the defined math program. If the child is not using or cannot use the material in a way that fits within the teacher's recognition of expected development, the child is "allowed" to play with the material. Play is in itself a good thing, supportive of the child's development. However, what may be missing is a serious response to the child's interaction with the materials — a response that acknowledges the child's activity as having interest, purpose, and meaning and that may lead to further interaction and activity that is consistent with the child's own structure. Without such response, transition to and connection with the further possibilities in use of the material may be delayed. Without such response, *allowing* may be reminiscent of the *tuning out* and *ignoring* that used to accompany the statement "I've referred him."

Even in the context of these beginning and imperfect efforts, our heterogeneously grouped classrooms quickly achieved some reputation for successfully coping with difficult children. Principals brought them down saying, "They'd probably be better off with you." This happened so often that our groupings began to be, in a way we had certainly not planned, heavily weighted with "difficult" children. It was interesting that over and over again, although the teacher complained about ten or twelve "problem" children in her room at the beginning of the year, the number was often reduced to two or three at the end of the year. In fact, it did seem to be easier for children to live in our type of classroom, and quite frequently, with or without the teacher's help, the child was able to restabilize himself. In open classrooms, where this did not happen, the child who was creating trouble less often interrupted the whole class because the teacher was not trying to have a pinpoint focus and was able to make special arrangements for at least some of these children some of the time.

Perhaps the overwhelming difficulty that teachers face is their inability to provide for the time a child might need to "put it together." The realization of how long it takes to grow, the conceptualization of time in development, is a slow-growing one. Teachers tend to see children in a nine-month span of development and conceptualize their development over this period. Having made enormous effort to produce growth within that time span, they have an investment in growth that can be observed in this period and their judgments about failure and success may sometimes have a quality of rigidity about possible change. Parents whose children have grown up in the Open Corridor have made contributions that we have come to see as essential to our ability to understand time and continuity in the process of development. It is true that in mixed-age groupings of the Open Corridor the pressure of speed in performance is eased. Children need not repeat a prescribed grade curriculum and need not be stopped in their continuous progression even when it does not match with grade progression, yet the "space" and "time" given to these groupings in the Open Corridor are still only partial. The fact that children have different time sequences of development is still far from being accepted.

STUMBLING BLOCKS TO IMPLEMENTATION — THE INSTITUTIONAL FRAME

Even when teachers make efforts to develop settings and procedures that are more responsive to children's learning and are backed with a maximal level of understanding and commitment, they face difficulties. Teachers work within an existing institutional frame, and their ability to make changes is more often than not inhibited by the prescriptions laid down by the overall school system. It is true that the weight of these prescriptions varies within schools, and the climate for change set by a school administration may be in varying degrees more supportive than constricting.

Nevertheless, school arrangements are only beginning to be humanized. Lunch and toilet facilities and arrangements for arrival and departure have hardly been examined. Although their importance for a child's orientation to and understanding of the world, for relief of physical tension, and for use as stabilizers is well known, provision for sand, water, clay, wood, movement, and dramatic play is still sparse in most situations. Further, nowhere is the teacher able in more than a very limited way to provide for the time a child may need to consolidate and stabilize himself. This inability to provide the time necessary for development is certainly more a result of the continuing pressure of grade-level arrangements than a result of the teachers' limited understanding of the developmental process. Even with heterogeneous and mixed-level groupings grades are still the norm of organization. Test results are reported in grade-level terms.[4] Present promotion and retention practices relate to

---

[4]For a critique of grade-level reporting, see the *New York Times* Education Supplement, May 1, 1977.

these grade-level test reports, and the prospect of increased stringency in retention regulations or of regulations more closely based on grade-level test reports is imminent. Naturally, in this context it is difficult if not impossible for parents to be calm about their child's development over time. They fear, with or without reason, that their child may be found to be functioning below grade level, and they fear that retention will be an immediate consequence.

The pressure on the teacher, reflecting pressures on the parents and pressures parents bring to bear on the school system, is to follow mandated prescribed remedies. The pressure on the teacher is to try to "beat" the tests, to "teach to the test," to "play it safe," and to drill the children in whatever seems to be needed for this purpose. Teachers are offered programs that purport to *guarantee* better performance on tests. Surrounded with such offers it is difficult for them to remember that such drill and rote programs were used for years with *no* obvious impact on the tests. Even the new, more structured programs, said to be effective, although not in all situations, report success only in narrow segments of the tests and do not seem to relate to the comprehension demanded of older grades. Of course in many, perhaps most situations, decision on these matters is not left up to the teacher. The teacher is required to use the programs that are mandated either by the district, by the school, or by a particular program within the school.

Reading

It was in the context of the teacher's growing understanding of a child's active search for meaning and of a child as an active learner that teachers gradually began to support a child's entrance into reading in ways that went beyond basal readers and rote drill. Even in early open classrooms, reading had begun to spread into all areas, rather than being confined to a specific period and defined in specific skills. As open education developed, teachers showed evidence of a growing understanding of the different ways in which children were becoming readers. All classrooms continued to be subject to the standardized reading tests, but since there is no evidence that the performance of children in the Open Corridors on reading tests is affected negatively by their membership in these classes, many teachers over the 10-year-period of development of Open Corridors developed a professionalism that included studying, for its relevance to their work, the burgeoning literature in psycholinguistics.[5] Teachers made de-

---

[5]Important work on reading is being done by Frank Smith (1971) and others. Bussis, Chittenden, and Amarel (1976) of Educational Testing Service have also been conducting a collaborative research project with teachers on reading. In addition, the National Consortium on Testing, a group consisting of more than 40 organizations, has been meeting for several years to discuss the issues of standardized testing.

cisions to adapt their plans for reading in response to what they understood about a child as they observed him in the classroom. However, in the context of the new intensity of fear about the impact of grade-level test reporting, it is becoming extremely difficult for the teacher to continue to maintain his commitment to support a child's search for meaning or her commitment to provide a context that will assist a child in this search.

How then shall we react? Our commitment both to teacher and child and our belief in intelligence as characteristic of humans gives us no choice. Even when the teacher is surrounded by mandates that restrict her function and decision-making with "teacher-proof" material, understanding can give her the space to reject the stance of taking the blame for test results. Understanding can also help her find whatever space can be retrieved to maintain a child's connection with meaning and context.

Testing

We continue to criticize the narrow definition of the reading process that is used in the formation of reading tests. The critique of testing and the research seeking an understanding of the reading process has burgeoned in the past ten years (see Footnote 5). One could almost characterize as schizophrenia what is going on in classrooms pushed by test-result pressures to adopt structured programs that see reading as segmented skills and the development of psycholinguistic and reading research. The differences are suggested in a critique by Rudolf Arnheim (1969) that is not generally known. For example, Arnheim proposes alternative interpretations of responses to a subsection of the Wechsler-Bellevue adult intelligence test:

> A person, asked in what way wood and alcohol are alike, is given a zero score if he answers: 'Both knock you out.' No doubt, this answer testifies to a bright intellect. It comes from a person capable of finding at the spur of the moment a striking common feature in two things not obviously alike. In life, we would reward him with an appreciative smile. If nevertheless his cleverness makes him fail the test, it is because the examiner prefers logical categories of scientific classification. He is justified in doing so if he wishes to find out whether the testee's mind is geared to the kind of logical operation practiced in academic settings. But if the purpose is to reveal productive intelligence, the zero score is misleading. [Arnheim, 1969, p. 200]

Discussing the failure of brain-injured patients given a section of the Goldstein-Scheerer test of ability to classify abstractly, Arnheim says:

> Clearly, the patient 'fails' not because he cannot abstract but because his procedure of abstraction differs from the one taken for granted by the experimenter. By no means can one conclude that he did not see the relation among all the hues present to him. [Arnheim, 1969, p. 199]

Arnheim goes further in discussing the copying of model figures in the Goldstein-Scheerer test:

> ...the patients do have trouble in copying model figures.... They may use the right colors but change the shapes and the arrangements.... Quite often, the faulty solution, as it does in this case, amounts to rendering a relatively complex model by a structurally simpler organized pattern — an adaptation to the level of visual comprehension accessible to the person. This sort of simplification, so well known from the drawings of children, does not necessarily prove that the person was unable to grasp the pattern of the model. It rather represents a perceptual abstraction, indicating an elementary level of conceptualization, but no cognitive defect.
>
> One of the reasons for 'incorrect' reproduction is that unless a person has received specific instruction in mechanically correct copying he tends to look for the overall structure of the model rather than imitating it painstakingly, piece by piece. [Arnheim, 1969, pp. 197–8]

These last two quotations from Arnheim criticize test conclusions that he considers to be an inadequate analysis of the factors inherent in visualization. Although they are taken from material relating to the brain-injured, they give one pause because of the similarity to test conclusions on the normal population.

Finally, at the end of this critique, Arnheim comments:

> Our educational system, including our intelligence tests, is known to discriminate not only against the underprivileged and the handicapped but equally against the most gifted. Among those capable of becoming most productive in the arts and sciences are many who will have particular trouble with the formalistic thought operations on which so much of our schooling is based, and will struggle against them most strenuously. To what extent do our schools and universities serve to weed out and retard the most imaginative minds? Intelligence test scores and creativity correlate poorly, and the mentally more lively children tend to be a nuisance to their teachers and peers and a liability in class work. These are ominous symptoms. [Arnheim, 1969, p. 207]

NEW LABELS FOR OLD

The current context presents additional problems not only as a result of budgetary crises but because Federal monies are being used in a way that in a very real sense narrows the definition of the norm. The obstacles to the development of classrooms for *all* the children mount. New funding for treatment of learning disability and for special education creates new pressures for additional classification and for special groupings in which a child can get prescribed and specific help with focus on separate problems, on separate deficits, or on specific behavior or activity. In these groups, it is argued that such help, usually considered fixed, constant, and inflexible, will better "fit" the child to the school context.

The experience with regroupings within New York City schools in 1975-77, the period of mass firings in response to budget crisis, is instructive. As teachers were fired because of budget cuts and as class size mounted, teachers feared it might be impossible or very difficult to pay separate attention to any single individual. In circular argument some teachers thought that at least a partial return to whole-class methods would ease their difficulties, but what they really wanted was a chance to reduce class size. Thus, when many teachers were asked to point out which of their children were "troubled" or achieving "below grade level," they were quick to respond to the invitation to nominate children for possible new groupings.

Further, teachers who had already been fired welcomed the new groupings because of the prospect held out to them that they might be rehired to staff these groups, either as class teachers or as specialists, i.e., experts offering periods of remedial experiences to these children. Regardless of who was hired as the learning disability teacher — by virtue of the terms of that hiring and of being defined as a "disability" teacher — the tendency was to segregate the child in terms of his deficit and thus narrow the child's connectedness and the resources from which he could draw to contend with his deficit. Few teachers criticized this paradoxical response to the budget crisis — firings that increased class size to unmanageable levels and then rehirings to remedy that situation. It was too easily accepted that these new learning disability groupings, formed because of the pressures of mounting class size, represented a process of exclusion from the previously existent continuum of the norm.

It was no wonder that such was the case. It became easier to turn to such solutions because the groupings seemed to be temporary ones that promised the child's eventual return to the mainstream, rather than the fixed kind that were so frequent in the older homogeneous grouping of children. The whole issue of heterogeneity was confused by this discussion of grouping in terms that sounded different from a simple return to old homogeneous methods. Who would refuse help to those who are learning-disabled, and who would not welcome the new funds that were becoming available for such help? However, in the search for funding, the descriptions became vague and the figures on how many required help seemed to grow. The need for special expertise was argued but very little was written about the instances and circumstances where special help could be given *within* the already existing classroom.

Individualization or Segregation?

Even where the child remained in the classroom and was only removed from the classroom for periods of help in some curriculum area, the practice has been segregative. Whereas whole-class teaching had been arranged in supposed homogeneous ways, now a "fine" individualization of children has been sought through more and more refined screening processes separating out more and more detail about perceptual or motor process. In fact, this form of individualization has been a categorizing kind of individualization whereby a class of children with a certain defect has been taught in a certain highly prescribed way. The class has been smaller, but the relationship of the teacher has still been to a whole class, not responsive to the individual. In this kind of arrangement, the very children who needed support that comes from context and meaning, who needed the stimulation to develop interests that emerge from a rich environment, and who might in a mixed classroom be carried into new experiences through interaction with others were often separated from the content and continuities and relationships that could support their connections and continuities.

The arguments for prescribed and specific help seemed to avoid the fixed and global racial categorizations attached to IQ in Jensen's work (1969). They seemed quite different than statements about irreversibility. From Jensen's data and from arguments for irreversibility, recommendations had been developed for more permanent specific educational methods emphasizing rote and bypassing efforts to engage with the child, as active learner. Under the new label of learning disability — supposedly different from IQ labels — and in the midst of supposedly integrated and inclusive situations new segregations threatened. It was still the reading tests that were uppermost in the labeling and in the segregation. It was the theory of reading process underlying the tests, in which a child's perception, motor skill, and sensory reaction were viewed as separate and specific, that focused diagnosis and treatment of learning disability on aspects of perception viewed in an isolated, segmented fashion. The emerging theoretical discussion about the reading process as an active process of making-sense, a process related to other integrative processes in the child, was bypassed.

The narrow confines of reading test discussion became even more evident when these test scores were used to define the gifted — another diversion from responsibility to the "ordinary" classroom that is now emerging. In too many instances, instead of depth and richness of curriculum, what is offered is only *more* of the same — an intensification of pace and of quantity of work, speeded-up and stretched. Instead of the rich stimulation of the corridor of inclusive classrooms and of mixed-age groupings, the gifted child is offered *concentration*. Little credence is given either to changing interests or to the need for mulling over and speculation on the part of those who are gifted. There is a devaluing of what is gained from a context of diversity and of helping each other.

There is an assumption that only a focus on the task will "get the child ahead." It is understandable that parents — depressed by the aura surrounding the mainstream of public education, both in funding commitments and in opinions on effectiveness — who think their child has a chance to be considered for a gifted class, work for this opportunity. While many parents have put such value on the Open Corridor community that they have fought against the IGC (Intellectual Gifted Children) classes, others begin to feel it is an opportunity not to be missed. What is unfortunate is that remediation and special grouping may well divert some teachers from their search for direct and indirect ways within their classroom to assist a child's further progress by supporting his multifaceted developmental potential. Teachers may well be diverted from their search for ways in which they can influence the conditions that surround a child's learning. Moreover, they may even be prevented — by school acceptance of funding for special groupings — from implementing their commitment to the potential of each child.

Mainstreaming

No discussion of labeling can avoid the issue of mainstreaming. I have said that our focus was not on those already sorted out from what I have called the broad continuum of the norm, but those already categorized and labeled as within the purview of special education. Mainstreaming is the talk of the day and as *inclusionists* we have welcomed and encouraged interaction and inclusion wherever this has been possible, but in truth little has been attempted. The efforts at inclusion are few. Mainstreaming, seemingly directed against segregative practices, seems to be an inclusion within the public school building of separated and segregated classrooms, as in the already familiar CRMD classes (which are still not integrated), or in classes for the orthopedically-impaired, emotionally disturbed, etc. So far, mainstreaming seems to take place on the minimal level of joining assembly programs and lunch periods. In some of our Open Corridors a little more has developed. For example, children in Open Corridor classrooms may join children in special classrooms to help them in some way. Sometimes there is common effort on art programs, but all of this is a long way from mainstreaming. One can only hope that the rubric of mainstreaming does not cover up budgetary devices that deprive children with special needs of truly needed services.

ONCE AGAIN, THE ISSUE

Thus, classification is still an important issue. The present drive toward classification, promoted by the atmosphere of accountability and fear for jobs, is also bolstered by the new rationale that reiterates a one-dimensional view of human capacity, in which difference is deficit and is judged by external demands to which adjustments must be made within a grade progression and a strictly limited time space. Such a view of human organization separates behavior from understanding, and cognition from affect. It is derived in large measure from discussions on IQ, as related to race, on learning disability, and on behavior modification. What is paralyzing about some of this material is the weight of what looks like "fact."

We cannot accept such "fact." We are obliged to study these arguments so that we can knowledgeably defend our own commitment to a view of complex and fluid potentiality and a view of difference that is seen as a positive aspect of humanness. This perspective contributes to our ability as individuals and as a species to perceive and adapt in new ways.

Fortunately we can also turn to literature that can directly support our position. (For example, see Mercer, 1974, and Hobbs, 1975.) This literature offers evidence of widespread misclassification that in effect rouses us to renewed efforts to redefine compulsory education. In particular, the preponderance of misclassification among children of social and ethnic minorities rouses us to moral indignation.

EXPERIENCES WITH INCLUSION

Even in the midst of crisis, teachers who are past the initial hurdles of classroom organization and the early floundering about the arrangements for open teaching have discovered that, if they manage to create boundaries that can support the survival of themselves, the class, and the individual child, they can get past that first feeling of helplessness with the difficult child. They can face their responsibilities to what is now a larger class, and they can accept the universe of their classroom, avoiding the exclusion that at an earlier time seemed to be the only solution. Some teachers have found that in many instances the problem posed by the difficult child in their classroom has eased over time.

Now in our tenth year of Open Corridor classrooms, several classes of children have completed six years of primary school in open classrooms. As we re-examine and analyze the history of these classes, we have found many instances where children were maintained within the classroom (although with difficulty the first year, with perhaps less difficulty the second year) so that by the third year they were hardly identified as the same difficult children. We have found that an amazing number of the children for whom the issue had been possible exclusion in their first year had found self-stabilizing forces within themselves and had found the ability both to cope and to contribute by the fourth, fifth, and sixth years.

We point to this because the actual structures within the schools — the overcrowded classes, the testing, the expectation of progress within a certain period, and the fixed time period for development — contradict and impede response to the complexity of human development. It is amazing that within these unchanged structures, where our limited effort was to help things bend and to find flexibility within these structures, we are able to report on child after child where this eased pattern of development over time has been utilized. Certainly in the old set-up it was difficult to report such instances. The "difficult" child was categorized so that the teacher's experience of the child's resiliency as it developed over time could not occur.

Teachers who have lived through such adjustments, who have been able to find ways of supporting the child's growth, and who have spaces and time for the child's development and for his latching onto resources within himself, have been particularly pleased that under conditions of crisis they have still been able to find these ways. In their reports on how they coped with crisis, overwhelmingly, this question of their success with the inclusion of children is in the forefront of their thoughts.[6] Excerpts from some of these taped reports illustrate this process:

> At the beginning of the year I wanted the child C out of my room. He was 'too destructive, too nasty to everybody,' I'd say to myself. The children kept writing to me about how C was bothering them, getting in their way. He had one foot in my class and one foot in the guidance class. But luckily — because it turned out to be very helpful to me in my own growth — he stayed in my class. His mother started working in the classroom every Wednesday, a day when the student teacher wasn't there. And to my amazement, this mother with a messed-up kid was fantastic in the classroom. She did a great reading job with the reading group. She moved easily from one place to another. She was not put off if I corrected her. And C really did change. He didn't turn into a little angel, but he learned to respect the other person.
>
> Not too long ago C took charge of a kindergarten child who had come into our room at 11:20 to wait for his mother to take him home at noon. At our class meeting I noticed that C was sitting with his arm around this little 6-year-old. It was a beautiful thing. It's very important, I think, for children to have some reflection of what is happening to them over a period of time. It's valuable for them to see how their strengths and our experience with them strikes us, when we're not involved with them outside school. So I said to C later, 'Do you know, I remember your brother and how really nice he was with my daughter when she came in and she was little. You were nice like that to the little boy.' And C smiled.

> Children have a tremendous tolerance for other children. I know this from my own daughter's years in elementary school. She would be in classes with some child whom we might call disruptive and that child would be her best

---

friend or at least someone she would relate to very well. It always strikes me that the children manage well with each other as long as they don't feel they're being victimized. They have alternate ways of dealing with the other children.

Often when a child is disruptive I'll tell another child: 'You have got to help so-and-so.' It is not up to me alone to maintain the class, it is also up to every child in that class to help the ones who are having trouble. A part of them can enjoy a lot of the acting-out and provocative behavior, things they might not be ready to do themselves. On the other hand there are things that really disturb them and my feeling is, they just better learn to do something about it. They've got to learn to move away, to avoid certain things, or to face them in a way that's going to be helpful. And then the class will work. This is part of taking the long view of the year. When you've had a lot of experience you realize that the class is going to work, but it's going to take time.

Now I have much more of a sense of the year as a whole block of time. I know that what happens in September and October is not necessarily what's going to happen in November and December. If things are messy in October or September, it doesn't mean that they're going to be messy later on in the year. I know there is a kind of time needed for things to jell, which means that some things are more disorganized at the beginning of the year. So I'm not as worried and scared as I was when I first joined the Open Corridor. At that time I thought 'This is it' and 'Where am I going?' I wanted to know 'Is it always going to be this way?' But after being in it a few years, you do see the time it takes for children to really get a feel of what they should do when they finish something, and where they should go, and how they should get involved with someone else, and whether they can help somebody, or do something by themselves. It does take time to set up a room so that it will be responsive to what is happening with the individuals coming into that room.

These same teachers, experienced in open education, came together at the Workshop Center in 1976–77 to study Lois Barclay Murphy's work, *Vulnerability, Coping and Growth* (1976). They were seeking a deeper understanding of their role as teachers, and of their responsibility for "the universe of all the children" who were given over to their care (see Haskins, 1976). They were seeking a broader frame for their understanding of vulnerability, not only for a learning-disabled child but for the human condition — a condition we all face, although differently. Equally they were seeking an understanding of the resiliency that helps us survive. Fortunately, most children do find the resilience within which to survive, given the time and an environment that is not so narrowly spelled out that only children's deficits achieve prominence.

As we work toward understanding the difficulties teachers face in attempting to relate to all the children for whom they have accepted responsibility, it is interesting to find that many teachers who identify themselves as special education teachers come to us attempting to find more supportive, more responsive, and more flexible ways for their own work and for the relationships that they are attempting to build with each child in their classrooms. They are finding too many limitations in a prescribed approach that is centered on perceptual deficit. Teachers search to find continuities of development and to provide a context rich enough to support potentialities previously unobserved in children. Gene Binder (1976) has described this attempt to build an open classroom with his special needs children. Peter Knoblock (1973) and others working with handicapped children have reported on their experiences with these children in flexible environments.

This turning to us for ways of supporting children's strengths is comparable to rediscovering the wheel. It is a phenomenon that I find among early childhood teachers, who ask me, "Can one have an open classroom with young children?" It is as though the early childhood and special education people recognize something in our work that applies to them but, sadly, do not know it is their own tradition from which we drew at the beginning of our work. I used to pass by CRMD classrooms when we were first getting started and see the children "playing," see the teacher's effort to form an attachment to the child, and I would ask myself, "Does one have to be a CRMD child to have an interesting environment that supports the child's learning?" Where special education is trying to be open education, it is following the earlier creative therapeutic model of Lilli Peller (1946, 1948, 1956) and others, who sought to mesh with the individual child, to find within the child the humanness that could be expanded and brought to bear on weaknesses. The departure from this framework is what is amazing.

EDUCATION FOR *ALL* THE CHILDREN

The difficulties of the teachers committed to inclusion have been so great that there has always been a temptation to romanticize the ease of homogeneous grouping, to reach for easy solutions, and even to call for exclusion. It is our conviction that if the teacher's intent is to find ways in which she can support each child's developmental thrust, then she can be helped to look at the impediments that stem from her own arrangements or from the inadequacy of school provision.

Teachers who possess the intent and commitment to try, muster the energy for the task and make the necessary arrangements, with a great deal of ingenuity, compassion, and humanity. With such considerations set before them, teachers can be helped to try to adapt arrangements so that the child can manage. Thus, they continue to move toward the incompletely realized goal of a setting responsive to the needs and the active impulses of each child, a setting where each child can use his positive strength.

Our Open Corridor teachers help each other toward this goal, sometimes simply by offering a change of setting for the restless child or by providing a respite, a breather, from an abrasive or overly intense situation. Teachers have seen that a child's restlessness may change with time of day, in different contexts, and in different relationships, but they offer each other a deeper support, the mutuality of commitment to educability, to maintaining connectedness and wholeness in learning. Teachers share their problems and solutions and through such interaction refine their understanding and implementations. The Open Corridor communities are not exclusive; only voluntarism, intent and commitment are required for membership. Therefore, they too are heterogeneous in composition, based on respect for person, belief in educability (of teachers), and the possibility of positive contribution from each member.

These relationships mirror what must exist in heterogeneously grouped classrooms — a mutuality of respect and interests and an expectation of positive contributions and helpful participation. Helpfulness is maximized in the mixed-age grouping of the corridor community, connecting with the intergenerational family and neighborhood relationships already familiar to the child. Not only is the older child relating to a younger child, but each child may have something to offer in which he is more expert than another child. For many, sharing further clarifies and consolidates a newly gained power.

I speak of cognitive clarification — the experience of every teacher in teaching — but I see no need to avoid speaking of moral development. We want to establish an atmosphere of respect, of helpfulness, of empathy, and of mutuality. We want to support, with interaction, response, and interest in all areas, the child's growth toward empathy, and reciprocity. A child may be deprived in many ways, but a child who has had *no* experience of giving and of sharing is truly deprived.

Our changes are incomplete; we are still beset with difficulties, and it is more than obvious that it is difficult to effect change. A battle on several fronts seems to be necessary. Our primary, continuous focus is inevitably on our own efforts, but it cannot remain so narrowly set. What we do takes place in a setting and that setting is, to some extent, defined by the force of law and administrative ruling. Testing decisions, mandated remediation prescriptions external to the teacher's responsive adaptations, and the like all stem from the institutional bureaucracy.

Our ability to make decisions about heterogeneous grouping, about class size, and about exclusion of children is limited by the public framework. Although the institutional frame by itself will make neither a good nor a bad teacher, it does render some teachers' efforts more or less impossible. Of course not only direct constraints affect the teacher's efforts. Fear of accountability or of loss of job creates its own constraints, self-limitations, and rationalizations for retreat from change.

The teacher is an adult, functioning not only in a classroom with children but as a citizen within the institution with an obligation to comment on and contribute to its function. It is in this context that the teacher seeks to give meaning to compulsory education through a commitment to educability, potentiality, heterogeneous grouping, and the positive connotations of difference.

REFERENCES

Arnheim, R. 1969. Visual Thinking. University of California Press, Berkeley.
Binder, G. 1976. Open and special. Notes from Workshop Center for Open Education. 5:17-20.
Bussis, A. M., Chittenden, E. A., and Amarel, M. 1976. Beyond Surface Curriculum. Westview Press, Boulder, Col.
Carini, P. F. 1975. Observation and Description: An Alternative Methodology for the Investigation of Human Phenomena. North Dakota Study Group on Evaluation, Grand Forks, N. D..
Cicirelli, V. G. et al. 1969. The Impact of Headstart. Ohio University: The Westinghouse Learning Corporation, Athens, Ohio.
Duckworth, E. 1972. The having of wonderful ideas. Harvard Educ. Rev. 42:217-231.
Haskins, K. 1976. Morgan Community School. Notes from Workshop Center for Open Education, 5:7-10.
Hobbs, N. (ed.) 1975. Issues in the Classification of Children, 2 volumes. Jossey-Bass, San Francisco.
Jensen, A. 1969. How much can we boost I.Q. and scholastic achievement? Harvard Educ. Rev. 39:1-123.
Knoblock, P. 1973. Open education for emotionally disturbed children. Except. Child. 39:358-365.
Mercer, J. 1974. A policy statement on assessment procedures and the rights of children. Harvard Educ. Rev. 44:125-142.
Murphy, L. B., and Moriarty, A. 1976. Vulnerability, Coping, and Growth. Yale University Press, New Haven.
Peller, L. E. 1946. Incentives to Development and Means of Early Education. Psychoanalytic Study of the Child, Vol. II. Yale University Press, New Haven.
Peller, L. E. 1948. Character development in the nursery school. Mental Hygiene 32.
Peller, L. E. 1956. School's Role in the Promotion of Sublimation. Psychoanalytic Study of the Child, Vol. XII. Yale University Press, New Haven.
Smith, F. 1971. Understanding Reading. Holt, Rinehart & Winston, Inc., New York.

Designing Developmentally Optimal Classrooms for Children with Special Needs

Anita R. Olds

THE ENVIRONMENT IS THE CURRICULUM

Schools and other institutions designed for the care of children in our society (hospitals, day care centers, special treatment facilities), can best be characterized as being environmentally barren, cold, and sterile. These settings reflect an incongruous response to the needs of young, developing children, who require not reduced but enriched physical facilities to support the fundamental interactive experiences necessary for growth.

Development is a process of adaptation whereby children, in order to grow, effect changes in their environment and, in turn, adapt to the demands that the environment places upon them. Development is their active engagement with people and objects, it is their movements as they perform activities. It is achieved when children invent anew, for themselves, the knowledge being sought, by observing the consequences of their personal operations upon materials and events outside of them (Piaget, 1963, 1973).

The motivation to interact with the environment exists in all children as an intrinsic property of life, but the quality of the interactions is dependent upon the possibilities for engagement that the environment provides. Hence, in all its manifestations, the environment is the curriculum and the physical parameters of classrooms, as much as books, toys, and work sheets, must be manipulated by teachers as essential aspects of the educational process.

Children with special needs develop more slowly or in ways that differ from established norms. The necessity to interact with the environment in order to traverse an invariant sequence of developmental stages is

91

characteristic of all children. Except for the physically handicapped, it cannot be claimed that particular disabilities require special and differing environmental supports. Rather, schools will be both educationally and therapeutically improved if they can meet at least three needs of all children, which the design of most classrooms has not yet adequately addressed: the need to move, the need to feel comfortable, and the need to feel competent in the educational setting.

The Need for Movement

The first design requirement of any preschool classroom should be to allow children the greatest possible bodily movement. To operate upon external forces children must be active and in motion. Few creatures alive are busier or more energetic than the preschool-age child, who engages in shouting, singing, doing, manipulating, climbing, running, crawling, hopping, and spinning on, under, around, and inside everything (see Isaacs, 1967).

However, to adults nothing is quite so aggravating and enervating as the incessant, unpredictable activity of many little bodies, each moving to its own separate drummer. To orchestrate such cacophony and reduce it to tolerable proportions, teachers typically intervene with rules, admonitions, or the withdrawal of materials and facilities in order to *stop* children's movement. They eliminate gross motor equipment in the classroom to constrain running and jumping indoors, in ways they would not limit it on a playground, because the indoor context does not seem to support the adult's capacity to keep the behavior within manageable limits. Similarly, teachers try to restrain movement by restricting the territory available for action, by requiring children to sit in chairs, or by engaging in activities generated by materials whose accessibility is totally controlled by the teacher.

To deny activity is to halt development at its source. Insofar as the interaction between a child and his environment is an intrinsic property of life, it is doomed to failure. A child's needs to perform and to move must express themselves, despite constraints, prohibitions, and inadequate environmental supports for activity. Thus, children fidget in their seats when they cannot get out of them, they incessantly try to gain access to prohibited materials behind the teacher's back, and they continue to chase one another around a room even if it means knocking over furniture and other classmates.

Such unchanneled and undirected needs for movement usually emerge as disruptive rather than constructive behaviors. They can quickly become repetitive or lead individual children to fail consistently to behave in accordance with established rules of conduct. Then teachers may begin to locate the causes for misbehavior *within the child* and suspect personal deficiences, such as poor motivation, lack of intelligence, emotional disturbance, hyperactivity, etc., as the root of the difficulty.

The common response to such behaviors, "How can I motivate the children in my class?" is a mis-statement of the problem. A more accurate statement of the problem is, "How can I get particular children in particular contexts to achieve those child-environment interactions that lead them toward ends deemed desirable in their culture?" In other words, the problem is less the source of the behaviors and more the match between the child and the classroom's social and physical context.

In some cases, assessments of deviancy are correct, but it is certainly not the case that all disruptive behaviors in classrooms are due to the shortcomings of individuals. It is equally likely that restrictions placed upon learning environments that limit opportunities for movement and active engagement contribute substantially to, if not actually cause, many so called behavioral and learning difficulties.

Environmental Supports   Instead of placing arbitrary and uniform limitations upon movement without regard for the developmental needs of children, thought must be given to the environmental supports needed to allow activities their fullest reign within an overall physical plan that makes such movement tolerable for all. Through environmental design, the tension between the child's developmental need for movement, and everyone's need — especially the teacher's — for organizing the movement, can be resolved. Over such external forces, rather than over internal psychic ones, teachers can exercise control.

In cases in which a child possesses physical or perceptual deficits, provisions for movement must be given great priority, because primary faculties often weaken or atrophy without proper exercise. Some disabilities do cause excessive bodily movements that require training in inhibition and restraint, but most disabilities tend to restrict rather than increase a child's capacity for full interaction with his environment. Therefore it should be the function of the educational/therapeutic setting to set the balance aright by promoting, wherever possible, the fullest exercise and use of all the abilities, however minimal, that the child possesses.

Furthermore, this exercise must be performed by the individual child and not consist simply of the passive reception of information and experience, characteristic of many programs for children with handicaps. Research has demonstrated (Held and Bossom, 1961; Held and Hein, 1963) that adequate development depends upon experiences that are self-induced by learners and afford them feedback about the consequences of *their* operations upon materials and *their own movements* through space. Wheelchairs, braces, crutches, and caregivers can support a body as it grows, but they cannot provide sustenance for the eyes, ears, hands, brains, and muscles that become limp, useless, and restless with passivity and disuse. Only by daring, risking, doing, failing, redoing, and succeeding will each child grow properly. Over-protective caregivers, parents, and educators who, in the presumed interests of health and safety or in avoidance of legal culpability, prevent the special needs child from experiencing the activity and risk-taking essential for normal development, simply retard and prejudice a disabled child's chances for a positive developmental outcome.

The Need to Feel Comfortable

Teachers often complain that preschool-age children in general, and special needs children in particular, have short attention spans and are unable to attend to activities long enough to get beyond superficial levels of involvement with materials. In contrast, it is maintained that sustained inquiry and experimentation are necessary for mastery and learning.

Yet young children will not engage in genuine exploratory and discovery behaviors unless they first feel comfortable and secure in their physical surroundings. In-depth inquiry requires an ambience in which children can "lose" themselves, not in the sense of being confused and disoriented, but in the sense of feeling safe from attack, intrusion, and exposure, which makes them self-conscious about their performance. Comfortable surroundings foster playful attitudes toward events and materials that help lower anxiety, promote understanding, and enable children to be more open in divulging their personal responses to events, thus giving teachers a more knowledgeable basis upon which to individualize learning. While stress and deprivation may motivate learners to initiate tasks, they are not effective strategies for generating intensive involvement over hours or even days. To support the development of attentional processes, memory, and mastery, it is quite important that classrooms be inviting, comfortable places that entice learners to pause, play, and stay for awhile.

Physical settings that provide moderate, rather than over- or under-arousing, levels of sensory stimulation are usually perceived as comfortable. Most institutional spaces are uncomfortable places in which to spend time because they tend to be either over- or under-arousing.

Some over-arousing aspects of schools are the vastness of the building and its rooms in relation to the size of the children, the unfamiliarity of spaces and materials, and the ambiguity of groups of people behaving in accordance with mysterious social norms. The impersonal, public nature of the school setting also makes preschool-age children vulnerable, often for the first time in their lives, to exposure, censure, competition, and ridicule. For any child with difficulties, such experiences can be particularly stressful.

In contrast, the barrenness and homogeneity of the physical parameters of classrooms can deaden arousal and interfere with children's capacities to stay alert and attentive. Cold, shiny, tile floors, multiple chairs and tables of identical design and hard finish, dull-colored walls lacking recesses or changes in texture, ceilings of uniform height, which dwarf the size of the room's occupants, and fluorescent lights, which spread a constant, high-powered glare over all activities indiscriminantly, all contribute to feelings of boredom, listlessness, and dislike for the settings in which learning takes place.

Variety and Richness   To counteract these negative institutional messages, and hence to use the environment in the service of learning, teachers should introduce variety and richness into classrooms and make them warm, welcoming, and interesting. Indeed, the old adage, "Variety is the spice of life," is the best guideline for creating comfortable and functional spaces. This variety should be considered on two levels: 1) variety in the sensory quality and physical parameters of facilities, and 2) variety in the types of spaces and activities provided.

Elements used in personalizing homes (pillows, plants, soft furniture) are valuable "softening" devices that provide sensory richness, as is the intentional variation of parameters, such as *scale* (small spaces and furniture for children, larger ones for adults, areas for privacy, semi-privacy, and whole group participation, materials at child eye level and at adult height), *floor height* (raised and lowered levels, platforms, lofts, pits, climbing structures), *ceiling height* (mobiles, canopies, eaves, skylights), *boundary height* (walls, half-height dividers, low bookcases), *lighting* (natural, fluorescent, incandescent, local, indirect), *visual interest* (wall murals, classical art, children's paintings, views to trees and sky), *auditory interest* (the hum of voices, mechanical gadgets, music, gerbils scratching, children laughing), *olfactory interest* (cookies baking, fresh flowers in a vase, plants in warm earth, animal fur and habitats), *textural interest* (wood, fabric, fur, carpet, plastic, formica, glass), and *kinesthetic interest* (things to touch with different body parts, things to crawl in, under, and upon, opportunities to see the environment from different spatial vantage points).

Such variation of a classroom's sensory and physical qualities can transform it from a stark, stressful ambience into a comfortable and pleasant place to be. This sensory variety can be put to its best advantage when used to create many spaces within a room, which are perceived as unique and separate "places" for engaging in particular enterprises. Just as homes have kitchens, living rooms, and bedrooms to support different functions, moods, body postures, and levels of interaction, so too should classrooms present spatial options for activity and a change of scene. In fact, the success of many preschool programs, particularly if they provide all-day care, is often proportional to the number and variety of types of places that can be created within the four walls of the setting. Thus, there should be places that are warm, cozy, and comforting, others that are hard, sterile, and isolated, some that are dark, others that are light, some that are large, some that are small, some that are noisy, some that are quiet, etc. Varied mini-spaces prevent boredom, disinterest, and discomfort by enabling children to seek out activities and levels of stimulation appropriate to their own moods, needs, and levels of arousal at different points in the school day.

Notions of introducing moderately varied levels of sensory and spatial stimulation into classrooms may have relevance for hyperactive children. Usually, it is argued that hyperactive children suffer from overactive nervous systems that need to be quieted and calmed by reducing environmental stimulation. However, it has been shown clinically that amphetamines, which energize the average adult or child, tend to slow down hyperactive children. In consequence, some research (Zaporozhets, 1957; Gellner, 1959; Satterfield et al. 1971, 1972, 1973) tentatively suggests an alternative interpretation of the hyperactive syndrome: The nervous systems of such children may, in some sense, be asleep or under-active, and such children move excessively in an attempt to provide for themselves the sensory stimulation necessary to keep them alert and able to function at levels characteristic of their classmates. Amphetamines make the hyperactive child appear more outwardly calm because, in operating in a fashion consistent with their effects upon normally active and distractible individuals, the drugs heighten arousal levels and function for hyperactive children as do their own bodily movements.

Although speculative, according to this interpretation, the prescription to strip environments bare for hyperactive children only serves to exacerbate their problems. It reduces environmentally derived sources of stimulation and forces them to rely almost exclusively upon their own activity for the basic stimulation that their nervous systems require. If the physical environment of the classroom is made rich and varied, hyperactive children may be able to find requisite sources of stimulation outside themselves, which free them to settle into activities for more sustained periods of time.

While every child stands to benefit from a comfortable learning environment, it is important to realize that limitations in the behavioral repertoires of children with special needs may give them low tolerance for and reduced ability to deal with the extreme arousal properties of the typical educational setting. Many sensory, emotional, and physical deficits cause discomfort and pain with which the special needs child must live constantly. In addition, if the classroom is poorly designed or impoverished, it renders the child doubly disabled, first by personal and then by external conditions. Rather than aggravating existing levels of distress, pleasant and appealing surroundings may help compensate for a child's disadvantaged position and optimize his abilities to perform competently. At the very least, a comfortable, relaxed atmosphere makes handicaps appear less formidable and minimizes the magnitude of those aggravated by tension.

The Need to Feel Competent

In addition to needs for movement and comfort, every child wants to feel successful or competent at his endeavors, not stymied by his immaturity and incapacity to do most things well. White (1959) has argued that the motivation to perform competently is intrinsic to growth and is manifested by the child's unceasing efforts to interact with and operate upon his environment. Obviously, one of the roles of schooling is to help children become competent at those things that teachers and the culture deem significant for the child's future.

However, environmentally induced sources of strain often interrupt children's attempts at mastery. Some primary sources of environmentally induced incompetence are: physical facilities poorly scaled or in poor working order, confusing layouts, disorganized arrangements, inadequate material, and spatial provisions for desired activities.

There is perhaps no more visible evidence of one's ineptitude than to be hindered in activity by physical facilities (doors, stairs, sidewalks) that do not operate according to one's expectations or strength. A doorknob that fails to turn, or falls off when manipulated hardly increases anyone's feelings of competence about his abilities to open doors. Similarly, children's immaturity and small size in relation to many physical elements of the environment constantly force them to confront intimidating and embarrassing experiences, such as light switches too high to reach, faucets too tight to turn, clay too hard to pound, or spaces and surfaces hidden from view. Montessori (1964) claimed that the primary task of preschool education was to help children achieve control over *the instrument,* by which she meant their own bodies and physical coordination. Thus, she designed light, movable tables and chairs, special cupboards and mats, and listening and movement exercises to aid in the development of mastery.

Classrooms should be designed to maximize the abilities of children to interact easily with their surroundings by adjusting the scale, height, and weight of physical elements to the dimensions and abilities of the child or by providing props that act as extensions of the child's limited capabilities (child-sized furniture, step stools, hooks, strings, etc.). Facilities designed so that children can fulfill basic personal needs (hanging up coats, toileting, putting on smocks, getting a drink of water) or so that they can be helpful to themselves and others without adult assistance are important sources of independent behavior and proof of children's capacities to care for and do things by themselves. Equally important are provisions that respect a child's ability to understand and contribute to prevention, treatment, and control of therapeutic concerns, such as being able to take braces off or put them on, listening for a timer, which signals when to take medicine or go to the bathroom (if the child is incontinent), learning how to adjust the volume on a hearing aid, or asking to go to the time-out room before a tantrum erupts.

In addition, the competent execution of most tasks, whether for self-help or mastery, depends upon the availability of proper tools, in good working order. Sharp saws, oiled scissors, flowing glue, and paint that is rich in texture and color prevent the termination of impulse and enthusiasm by easing the transition from idea to finished product.

Confusing or disorienting physical layouts may prevent execution of the simplest human activity — getting where one wants to go. In contrast, an understandable physical plan, designed from the child's eye level and reinforced by good orientational devices (clear pathways, visible boundaries, qualitative differences in the spaces, markers signaling dangerous or varying levels), enables children to see where they can go and know something about what is happening around them.

Organizational Aspects of Facilities   Classrooms certainly exacerbate feelings of incompetence when they allow the organizational aspects of facilities to get in the way of a child's goals for completion and positive execution of tasks. Take the case of the ubiquitous, "never where you want it when you want it" roll of tape. Billy wishes to tape pictures onto a large sheet of paper to create a collage or fanciful design. He carefully lays out the pictures, turns for the roll of tape, and not finding it nearby, walks around the room in search of it. Some time and many inquiries later, he returns with tape in hand only to find his pictures disarrayed and scattered. In the face of so much frustration, he decides the idea of making a collage is not worth the effort and abandons the task. Billy's ultimate feelings of incompetence are especially unfortunate when it is realized that the roll of tape was only an instrument for his activity, not his goal per se. Had the tape been in a centrally located position to which all children returned it habitually, half the battle would have been won.

Thus, well-organized storage and display of materials, which enables children to see what is available, where it belongs, and where to use it, is critical to the success of most activities, as are tools in good repair and in good working condition. Basic order is especially necessary when children have difficulty focusing attention or retaining information about spaces and events over time, since order helps clarify ideas and the possibilities for their execution once they have been initiated. Materials and tools always grouped together in consistent locations can be found easily when needed to extend a developing concept, while those that are predictably available allow activities to be carried over from one day to the next and be given time to evolve apart from their making. Protected, well displayed works-in-progress, such as paintings and sculptures still growing and changing, a scientific experiment in process, and a wood structure not yet complete, all provide evidence of children making, thinking, and learning, which reinforces a spirit of inquiry and "success through doing" in the room.

However, physical and organizational supports are of limited value in promoting feelings of efficacy unless they are buttressed by the availability of interesting things to do, an attitude of trust and encouragement for independent inquiry, and a range of options. Crayons kept locked in a closet except when the teacher gets them out are not, from the child's standpoint, "something to do," nor are a few materials placed haphazardly around a room. Usually, for lack of diversity and appropriate storage and display, materials end up being abused and ignored in short order.

Instead, classrooms must provide materials that are visibly and attractively displayed and accessible for active manipulation. These materials should be located in physically identifiable, protected play areas, with work surfaces that invite use by a child alone, groups of children, or adults and children together. Such spaces and materials legitimate children's rights to occupy themselves with things they, as well as the teacher, find interesting. The mutual support systems that grow out of collaborative enterprise help attenuate the loneliness, frustration, and embarrassment that can accompany incompetence and disability.

It is characteristic of most children, particularly those with special needs, to fear exposing their weaknesses and to try to undertake things with which they feel most competent. Therefore, in addition to being accessible and interesting, the materials and spaces in a classroom should represent a broad range of activities and choices. This will ensure that each child finds at least one thing with which he can be successful and through which he will reveal himself by allowing the consequences of his actions to become manifest. As a result, the teacher can begin to know something about the child's interests, abilities, level of understanding, and the environmental circumstances that inspire his activity. Eventually, because of the options available, shortcomings will be revealed, which the teacher can help the child overcome through the use of facilities at which the child feels less adept. For example, the irresistable attraction of wood-working may enable some children to work on under-developed fine-motor skills in ways that differ from the manipulation of puzzles. Private spaces may help shy children express abilities and feelings that are kept secret under public surveillance. An aggressive child may learn to constructively redirect his anger away from other youngsters onto a piece of clay, a punching bag, or a foam tumbling mat.

Ultimately, the ability of children to work competently and productively is affected by: 1) the number and variety of things there are to do, 2) the number and variety of places there are in which to do them, and 3) the organization and accessibility of those things and places within the classroom space.

The industriousness of school-age children is predicated upon experiences in infancy and early childhood that give them the opportunity to trust their environment, to behave autonomously without shame or doubt, and to exercise initiative without feeling guilty. (Erikson, 1950). Unfortunately, by age three or four, many special needs children are already burdened with feelings of mistrust about their world, doubt about their abilities to affect that world, and shame and guilt about their behavior in the eyes of others. More than physical handicaps, emotional disturbance, delayed maturation, and learning disabilities, these feelings of inadequacy are the issues that mainstreaming programs must affect by supporting each handicapped child's need for autonomy, initiative, and trust in self and others.

To ensure lasting changes in development, children must themselves effect changes in their own lives and have direct proof of their own capacities for improving themselves and their world. Out of the freedom to explore, to experiment, to make mistakes, and to master new skills comes the self-confidence of knowing they can do it, which is the best guarantee that they will be able to do it in years ahead.

DESIGNING A CLASSROOM

Despite differences in the sizes and shapes of rooms, the sizes and ages of groups, or programmatic and educational requirements, the following pages present general strategies for planning and designing most classroom spaces so they will meet each child's need for movement, comfort, and competence.

Functional Requirements

Architects who design schools are hired to provide adequate exits and entries, square footage, light, heat, and ventilation for classrooms, but they are rarely asked to attend to the day-to-day movements and events that will transpire in each room. In contrast, teachers must base the design of their rooms upon what they know best: the functions and activities of the room's occupants, such as sitting, eating, lying, reading, pretending, drawing, etc., and the needs for movement, comfort, and competence discussed above.

To begin, each teacher should list the activities, materials, and projects that he most wishes to utilize in promoting personal educational goals. Such a list might contain traditional subject headings, such as reading, art, science, and dramatic play, but it can be extended to include mud streams, foam punching areas, and bean bag alleys. Typical preschool functions include reading, math, science, animals, plants, painting, collage, clay, water, sand, woodworking, large blocks, small blocks, gross motor play, fine motor play and manipulatives, doll and kitchen play, fantasy play, store fronts, puppets, wheeled toys, large construction toys, listening, viewing, rhythms and movement, musical instruments, a group meeting space, private and time-out spaces, one-to-one spaces, dressing, undressing, coat storage, personal storage of classroom work, snack and/or lunch, cooking, toileting, napping, and cot storage.

The terms used in describing the activities matter little provided that all activities that the teacher deems valuable appear on the list, in some form, and are not excluded simply because there seems to be no way to make them happen. For example, water play should not be deleted because the closest water source is far down the hall. Activities rejected at this stage may be buried forever. Similarly, the list should not be limited to those items and materials already in the room, such as two electrical appliances for one outlet or table-top activities, because there are only 6 tables and 30 chairs. The purpose of the list is to expose fully all activities and materials of educational merit so attempts can be made to provide for each requirement and enrich the classroom's educational potential, rather than foreclose possibilities at the outset. Teachers should expect the nature and number of functions to change over the year as experience tests the merit of each and reveals new areas for consideration.

There is no magic or ideal number of functional requirements; each list will vary from teacher to teacher, reflecting the variety he or she feels most comfortable in handling. Highly developed preschool classrooms may support as many as 15–20 different activities simultaneously. However, in meeting the wide range of preschool and open classroom interests, and the special circumstances of a classroom that enrolls handicapped children, at least six different categories of play experience seem necessary:

1. Quiet, Calm Activities
   (listening, viewing, meeting, reading)
2. Structured Materials / Activities
   (puzzles, construction toys, blocks, manipulatives, group games, and instruction)
3. Craft and Discovery Activities
   (paint, clay, collage, pens, crayons, blackboards, woodworking, science, plants, and animals)
4. Dramatic Play Activities
   (puppets, store, fantasy, masks and dress-ups, kitchen and doll play, miniatures)
5. Large Motor Activities
   (climbing, sliding, crawling, hanging, tumbling, swinging, rocking, balls, Velcro and magnetic darts, ring toss, nerf basketball, large blocks, punching bags, and bo-bo punching clowns)
6. Therapeutic and Therapeutically Educational Activities
   (inflatable and foam equipment — water bed, air mattress, etc. — with therapeutic value for sensorily and physically disabled children. Casts, braces, X-rays, and models of organs, to educate special needs and normal children about disabilities and development).

Once a list of functional requirements has been completed, the design will attempt to provide a separate, fully equipped activity area for most, if not all, requirements. By creating a variety of spaces within a room, each supporting a different function, it becomes possible to keep apart noisy and quiet, messy and clean, and expansive and contained activities, and to provide a wide range of choices for movement and activity within a single space. Areas encourage dispersion throughout a room, enabling the use of all available facilities for most of the day, and preventing the congestion and tension that arise when everyone tries to use the same materials in the same space at once. When many activity areas are used simultaneously, the teacher's ability to be present in all places at all times is limited. Children must be trusted to be more independent and work things out for themselves. However, well-organized activity areas regulate behavior and the use of materials by giving everything a place and by providing places where, within clear physical limits, things can be found, explored, and put away. Teachers are then freed to help children settle into activities for extended periods, so they may be enticed beyond the superficial aspects of materials to the point where true inquiry and experimentation transpire. A teacher's increased ability to supervise and participate in each child's explorations allows meaningful questions to be asked and necessary skills to be worked upon.

The Concept of an Activity Area

Contrary to common practice, a table and chairs arranged in a space or corner do not suffice to make an activity *area,* but only to make a work surface and seats. An activity area has five defining attributes: a physical *location,* with visible *boundaries,* indicating where it begins and ends, within which are placed *work and sitting surfaces,* and the *storage and display of materials* to be used on the surfaces in performing the activities for which the area is intended. Ideally, an area, similar to a room, should have a *mood* or personality all its own, which distinguishes it from contiguous spaces. Activity areas, particularly for preschool-age and special needs children who do not read or who require clarity and lack of ambiguity, must visually entice children to explore and use the materials. The two variables most often neglected in achieving this goal are physically visible boundaries and materials displayed for use. Each of the five variables is considered in turn.

Location   To establish a location for each of the activity areas, one should empty the room psychologically, if not physically, of all movable elements, so only the fixed features remain (doors, windows, lights, outlets, heaters, sinks, etc.). Fixed features speak strongly to all users of a space about its basic functional parameters and are powerful orientational devices that frequently take precedence over other perceptually salient characteristics of a room. Instead of ignoring them, the room's design must proceed from them. First, a single path through the room, from entry to exit, should be created to maximize the territory available for activity areas and minimize the amount of unprotected, exposed space. If transit zones are multiple or confused, the elimination of some doorways and/or relocation of ones of primary use should be attempted; most fire laws do not require more than two exits.

Second, the fixed features determine the two prime factors to consider in placing areas within a classroom: the position of major transit zones and the location of protected areas outside those zones. Activities requiring tables or the motion of children on their feet can be contiguous with transit pathways, and are appropriate in open and busy spaces, whereas activities that can use the floor or low platforms as sitting and work surfaces require a great deal of protection and seclusion. Children's use of materials may proceed with a minimum of interference and with the least necessity for solid barriers around these areas that might cut off visibility and communication throughout the room.

Locating activities in protected zones, in order to use the floor as a sitting and work surface, is a critical means of controlling children's movement and effecting a successful classroom plan. The virtues of the floor are many. Most importantly, when children are down low, their energy of involvement is reduced to levels appropriate to a busy but subdued classroom. On the floor, they may still be moving, but they are not traversing classroom space, therefore their distracting actions are less perceptible. Since it takes more energy to go from the floor to standing on one's feet than it does to go from a chair to standing, once children are down low, they tend to stay there. Use of the floor reduces occlusion of an area by furniture, especially chairs (although a few small, low tables might be retained), and makes a space more flexible for varied uses. When working in groups or socializing, children can then contract space at will so they need not shout across physical barriers to communicate with one another. Use of the floor as a work surface allows the child to adjust his viewing height, by sitting or kneeling, so as to modify his field of vision. Since young children do not spontaneously scan arrays, a wider field of vision enables them to take in more at a glance, and hence overcome a developmental handicap.

Using the floor helps create a more tranquil and productive classroom, provided that the floor surfaces are protected by physical boundaries that structure the area limits and prevent transit across it (i.e., there is a need to locate such areas in geographically protected zones). Activities requiring the greatest protection and seclusion are small unit blocks, small construction toys, and manipulative materials. Other activities, such as reading and listening, require physically protected areas but can tolerate more exposure if necessary. Too frequently, small unit blocks are located near a doorway, instead of in a corner, because the teacher recognizes that entry areas provide free space in which to build. However, rarely are blocks that are located in such a way used, since no child wants to work at something that will be trampled upon. The only transit that should occur in areas where children use small construction toys is that of children going to and from the storage and display units.

More exposed areas of the room are appropriate locations for activities involving work at a table, such as art, science, or water, where the child's focus is on the table and his back acts as a barrier to the movement behind him. Art areas, where children love to stand, involve much movement to and fro for supplies, clean up, etc., and thus are appropriate near transit zones as are store fronts, puppet theatres, and some dramatic play activities.

Besides protection and exposure, there are additional factors to consider in locating areas. Messy activities should be contiguous and separate from neat activities. Messy areas should be located near a sink, if possible. The quiet activities are better separated from the noisy, and the expansive activities are better separated from the contained. The presence of windows often suggests locating reading, art, or writing areas nearby for the natural light that windows provide. Wherever possible, areas requiring electrical appliances (fish tank, cooking) should be located near outlets, but if this forces inappropriate compromises in layout, extension cords should be used instead. Lastly, contemporary spaces too often lack the special structural touches that give older buildings their character and charm. Therefore, unique architectural features of a space, such as a beautiful view, a niche, a fireplace, or a change in ceiling height, should be capitalized upon by making them functional parts of activity areas; thus, structural variations become salient and integral to the classroom design.

After applying these general strategies, if there are still spaces and activities unaccounted for, the task is somewhat comparable to that of fitting the remaining pieces into a jigsaw puzzle. Experiment and experience, as well as consideration of the other four variables for area definition, should achieve a workable, effective layout. Several classroom floorplans, based on the above stated principles, are shown in Figure 1.

No teacher should feel that once a comfortable layout is achieved, it is unalterable. As the functional requirements of a classroom change, so too must its design. On the other hand, it is extremely time-consuming for teachers and unsettling for children to have the room rearranged frequently, and young children, particularly those with special needs, often require a sense of place and predictability about their world. It is the case that some small and/or architecturally poor classroom spaces may admit only one layout that will accommodate a broad range of functional needs appropriately. Therefore, although the overall layout of a room may remain fairly stable, the design and development of activity areas should always be subject to change, in terms of its work surfaces, boundaries, mood, materials, and storage and display, as time and curriculum progress. The areas themselves, rather than the overall layout, are really the locus of the room's educational program.

Boundaries   Once activity areas, based upon functional requirements, have been mapped in the room, the areas must be defined, bounded, and developed. A boundary can be as solid as four walls, as fluid as taped lines on the floor, or somewhere in between. Regardless of its permanence or fluidity, each area must have a boundary that signals where the area physically begins and ends. Boundaries help to distinguish and limit activities and reduce disruptive behaviors that occur as a result of activity congestion or the inadequate and improper physical separation of tasks.

Typically, boundaries are created by encircling a space with bookcases, storage units, or other furniture. However, if this were done to all

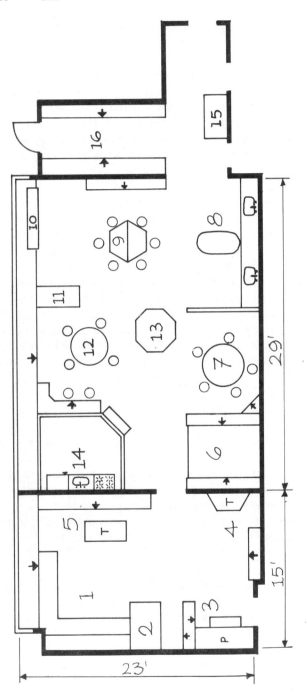

A

Figure 1A.   Floorplans showing the location of well-defined activity areas in several open, mainstreamed classrooms. 1, reading and group meeting area — risers and book display; 2, quiet loft; 3, musical instrument display and piano; 4, math area — table and storage; 5, writing area — table and display; 6, small unit block area — 5″ high platform and storage; 7, cooking and snack area; 8, water play area; 9, art area — tables and storage; 10, wall easel; 11, low clay table; 12, science area — table, storage, and display; 13, sand table; 14, play house area — 4″ high platform with ramp entry; 15, woodworking area; 16, coat cubbies.

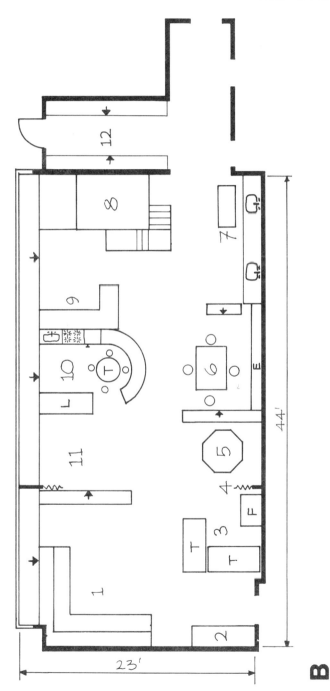

Figure 1B.   1, reading and group meeting area — risers and book display; 2, two-story quiet loft; 3, science area — tables, display, and fish tank; 4, collapsible wall; 5, sand table; 6, art area — storage, wall easel and table; 7, water play area; 8, dramatic play platform and stairs with grab bars; 9, woodworking area; 10, playhouse area and small loft; 11, small unit block area; 12, coat cubbies.

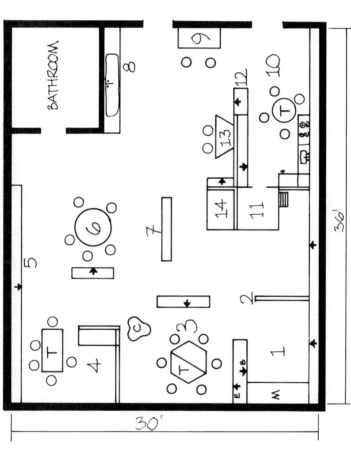

Figure 1C.   1, group meeting and reading area — mattress and book display; 2, blackboard; 3, art area — easel, tables, low clay table, and storage; 4, woodworking area — workbench, tool display, and glue table; 5, coat cubbies; 6, game area — table and storage; 7, sand table/planter; 8, sinks and water play area; 9, cooking area; 10, playhouse area — kitchen play, table, and lower level of loft structure; 11, two-story, fully enclosed loft with access to lower portion from playhouse area, and to upper portion via ladder cut into loft wall; 12, play store/puppet theatre; 13, science area — table and storage; 14, platform — 1 foot high; 15, manipulative play area and storage.

areas in a room, the effect would be to make users feel somewhat like rats in a maze, following defined pathways into enclosed, discrete boxes. Such procedures make a room appear cluttered, fail to visually entice children into activities, block visibility across areas, and inappropriately confine activities requiring freedom of movement. While protected areas of the room and activities using the floor will require fairly solid boundaries, alternatives are needed for areas demanding greater fluidity.

An effective way to create a fluid boundary is to change the floor level of an area by raising it onto a platform four or more inches high, so that the perimeter of the platform delineates where the area ends. Another alternative, not available to most, would be to lower the level of the floor. This effect can be achieved by using an L, U, or rectangular arrangement of low carpeted risers to enclose a space, so that the internal floor level appears lower than its perimeter. (See Figure 2.)

In addition to creating fluid but perceptible boundaries, changes in level may be intentionally introduced into classrooms for their educational and therapeutic value. Most young children enjoy perching up high as much as they enjoy working on the floor. In fact, their cognitive maps of the room are shaped by experiences that allow them to look at spaces from different perspectives. Piaget (Piaget and Inhelder, 1956) described the egocentricity of the pre-concrete operational child's topography. There is also indication (Ayres, 1973) that children cannot adequately distinguish the orientational variances of symbols on a page (the difference between b and d depends upon which side of the line the circle is on) until they are able to discriminate orientational variances spatially. Thus, opportunities to go under, over, above, across, below, inside, and upon different surfaces and to perceive the world kinesthetically, as well as visually, from a variety of spatial vantage points, may be a critical means of preparing preschool-age children for reading and other symbolic enterprises.

Bounding effects comparable to a change in floor level can also be obtained by changing the level of the ceiling, via eaves, canopies, trellises, streamers, and mobiles or by changing the lighting, so that the space under a spotlight or subdued lamp appears and feels distinct from surrounding zones.

In addition to all these possibilities, the most powerful way of demonstrating boundaries is through the use of color. Color is an excellent visual organizer and busy classrooms are visually chaotic places at best. Using color does not mean painting the door and window frames one hue, the walls another, and the ceiling a third. This effect is colorful but draws the eye to inconsequential features of the environment. Instead, color should be placed on the work surfaces, display units, and

Figure 2.   Low, carpeted risers form an enclosed play "pit."

dividers to areas, at levels where children work, so that areas begin and end where particular hues begin and end. The specific hue matters little, since there is no conclusive proof of the psychological effect of soft versus vibrant colors on behavior. A child standing in the room should be able to see a yellow space, a blue space, a green space, etc., and should be able to know that where the colors stop, the areas and the activities delimited by the colors also terminate. To achieve this effect, it is sometimes necessary to apply color or paint to new furnishings, since a classroom composed entirely of lightwood bookcases, tables, and chairs unfortunately appears as homogeneous and undifferentiated as one built entirely of formica.

In designing boundaries for areas, height, mass, and permeability should be considered. A necessary ingredient of an active open classroom is the contagion, or cross-area, effect that activities initiated and sustained by some children can have upon others. When given the chance to watch others at play, children can be relieved of their boredom, solitude, or confusion about what to do next. Easy visibility across areas aids children in transitions from one task to the next, especially when these tasks involve going from independent to whole-group endeavors (clean up, meeting) or vice versa. In addition, teachers certainly need to be observant of all events that transpire, although they may not want to participate directly in each activity. Thus, for stimulation, communication, and supervision of children, boundaries should be kept low, in scale with the size of the children, and/or varied in height and permeability. High or cluttered boundaries (paper bags and boxes stored on top of shelves, etc.) are distracting and overpowering. Those that vary in fluidity, scale, and color introduce variety into a space and enable a room to appear spacious and less congested.

The Size of Activity Areas   Rarely are so many people placed together for such long periods of time, in such confined space, with so few options for withdrawal, as are children in schools. While the developmental consequences of this practice are unknown, it does suggest that the sizes of areas in the room should be varied to provide options for privacy, for small groups, for a whole-group meeting, and for one-to-one interactions between a child and an adult.

Most areas should be scaled to accommodate about four children comfortably. Physically limiting the number of occupants in an area allows for quiet, cooperative interaction and discourages the potentially distracting, leader-dominated quality of a large group. It also ensures that children will be dispersed throughout the room, making maximal use of all facilities available, under conditions of minimal congestion. Thus, tensions are minimized and positive participation is enhanced. Many handicapped children lead relatively isolated lives while at home. The intimacy of classroom activity areas can increase their opportunities to interact with peers and to form friends whom they may invite home or visit, a dramatic addition to their social experience.

Private spaces in a room provide shy children with opportunities to explore feelings, moods, and inner turmoils that are not easily exposed to public surveillance, and allow those who may occasionally not feel like working with peers to retreat and behave according to their mood. A fiberboard barrel, obtainable without charge from chemical companies and hospitals, makes an easily transported private bubble, for reading, resting, or getting away from it all. The barrel may be cut with varied openings, decorated, and lined with foam, mylar, or fake fur to give it interesting textural qualities. (See Figure 3.) Distressed, bored, or disengaged children may spend as long as an hour in one of these barrels, seemingly unengaged. However, such children tend to monitor and assess on-going activities and emerge from the barrel when calm or energized, better prepared to join something.

Working and Sitting Surfaces   Most classrooms are cluttered with tables and chairs that are the child's typical work and sitting surfaces. Since standard tables and chairs have four legs each, and the average child has two, the total number of legs per child in the room can sometimes be as many as ten. Aside from the difficulties such protrusions cause the perceptually and physically handicapped, at child eye level the environment

Figure 3.   A fiberboard barrel makes a comfortable private bubble.

appears more populated with legs than other features. To introduce variety, increase spatial versatility and make room for different work surfaces, the number of tables in classrooms should be minimized and those

Figure 4.   A low table at which children kneel, or sit on the floor, is extremely functional and versatile.

retained should be kept small in scale, i.e., for four to six persons. Rather than crowd a room all day with tables used by the whole group for twenty or thirty minutes at lunch or snack time, alternative eating surfaces should be considered, such as tables that stack and flip up or down, counters, or platforms that double as work and eating areas. Covers placed over water and sand troughs can transform them into tables, or the cover can be used alone, on the floor, perhaps supported by a few cinder blocks, as another work and eating surface.

Given the freedom to choose their own work spaces, children frequently employ odd surfaces, such as floors, storage unit tops, and chair seats, instead of tables. Much has yet to be learned about the child's perception of appropriate surfaces for the execution of tasks. Lacking this information, a variety of table shapes, heights, and sizes should maximize the teacher's chances of providing surfaces that are functional, appealing, and useful to different ages and physical conditions.

A table only ten inches high, at which children kneel or sit on the floor, is much preferred by preschool age children to normal table height. This level, similar to the floor, allows children greater visual command, and the freedom to put the full force of their body into their work. Low tables are especially good for working with clay and construction materials. (See Figure 4.)

Casual conversation occurs most readily when people are oriented at right angles to one another and can easily engage or disengage eye contact. Thus, round tables will promote verbal interaction (provided the diameter is not too great), whereas rectangular tables, if large, tend to pull people apart, especially those seated in the middle. Despite manufacturer's claims, most tables are too large and too high to be used effectively in preschool classrooms. Tables of this type bring too many children together at once, place great stress on a leader to keep the group intact, and raise noise levels by forcing people to fight the table surface in order to make contact. Strategies that decrease the physical separation of interlocutors (use of the floor, small, low tables, etc.) help lower the overall noise level of a room and support conversational intimacy.

For activities, such as art and science, where children are on their feet and moving about, child counter-height surfaces are often preferred to sit down tables. Also attractive is a draftsman's table, where a child may sit on a high stool, looking very important, with his work spread out on an inclined surface. In fact, the availability of at least one surface with variable angles of inclination might be worth experimenting with for children with special needs who, for reasons of visual or intellectual impairment, may perceive symbols better when the symbols are not presented exclusively in a horizontal or vertical plane.

Typically, straight-backed wooden or plastic chairs are provided as sitting surfaces for classrooms. However, stools are often preferable to chairs because when children work at tables they tend to lean forward and inward over their work, and rarely recline or use a back support. Stools slip easily under work surfaces when not in use and, if they are made from fiberboard tubes with round bases,[1] cause less problems with tripping and unbalancing than four-legged chairs. The tubes can also be used to make chairs with backs, cut in fanciful designs, or according to the support needs of children with physical handicaps. (See Figure 5.) Retaining-straps or belts can be added if needed. Stacking tables conserve floor space and help keep table size small over all.

Sitting surfaces that vary in the presence and height of backs, arms, cushions, and angle of inclination should be considered, including air-filled and bean bag chairs, arm chairs, couches, risers, pillows and cushions. Modular foam units that open partially or fully to form semireclining and lying surfaces are especially useful for physically handicapped children. Rocking chairs are invaluable for promoting physical contact between an adult and a child, for comforting tired, weak, or ill children, or for giving energetic children constructive opportunities for movement.

---

[1]Twelve-inch diameter tubes are available in most cities, free of charge, from the International Paper Company.

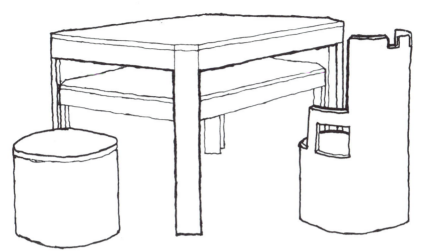

Figure 5   Stacking tables conserve floorspace and help keep table sizes small overall, while stools and chairs made from fiberboard tubes are attractive and do not tip.

The Orientation of Working and Sitting Surfaces   Perhaps because we do not have eyes in the backs of our heads and thus cannot protect ourselves from attack from the rear, people feel most secure having something solid at their backs with the opportunity to monitor visually and aurally what approaches them head-on. Thus, the arrangement of sitting and work surfaces in an area should orient the children's backs toward or perpendicular to a wall, not toward the room and its activities.

Physical security also depends upon being able to have some contact with and make resonable predictions about events beyond one's immediate spatial sphere. In fact, too little information or too much environmental protection can be as harmful, distracting, and unsettling as too much immediate physical or visual input, for the child feels cut off from things around him and is unable to know what might occur to interfere with his own activity and position. By properly orienting work surfaces and by varying boundary heights and permeability, a child seated in an area should be able to have visibility outward on at least one side. Such visibility provides moderate levels of visual stimulation that are calming, whereas total enclosure and protection are arousal-inducing and appropriate only on occasion. As long as sufficient space exists between the working child and the potentially distracting events, the external events will not impinge upon him against his will, and the option to visually scan all areas of the room will be comforting because of the "monitoring" information it provides.

Teachers who fail to acknowledge these two orientational needs often experience difficulty with group meetings. Instinctively, they may place their own backs against a wall and spread the children out on the floor before them. Invariably, the children at the rear, furthest from the teacher, start to squirm and lose interest first, since, psychologically, they feel the most vulnerable because their backs are exposed to the room. In contrast, an L-shaped seating arrangement, especially two tiers of risers, which places the children in the corner and leaves the teacher's back exposed, may help to make meeting times go more smoothly. Children then have a solid wall at their backs, and the occasional opportunity to scan the entire room, which keeps them awake, attentive, and free from having to watch one another's squirming backs. A right-angle orientation allows all children to make eye contact with one another, puts them equidistant from the teacher (if she sits at floor level in the middle of the L), promotes group intimacy and cohesion by reducing the territory the group occupies, and eliminates the "Teacher, I can't see," syndrome by placing some children at a level higher than others. When built 15–18 inches deep, the risers can double as work and reclining surfaces.

Storage and Display of Materials   The first priority of most teachers redesigning classrooms is for more storage space. Yet, large locked cabinets that are convenient for storing bulk supplies put the teacher in the role of being a purveyor of materials, if items have to be transported from the storage units to the child. Instead, storage space is best gained by placing materials directly in the classroom, immediately accessible to children's work and sitting surfaces, so that children know what is available, where it is to be used, and where it belongs. In fact, a child's invitation to play is communicated only by the visual presence of play materials, and not by furniture, play platforms, and work surfaces. For example, cushions on the floor next to an empty bookcase do not make a reading area, whereas the presence of books on the shelves clearly indicates that the cushions are to be sat upon while reading.

It is impossible to over-emphasize the importance of clear, visible storage and display for the effective operation of a special needs classroom and for children whose handicaps complicate their lives and make them dependent upon unambiguous physical surroundings for orientation and limit setting. Similar to a storekeeper who arranges his merchandise aesthetically, the teacher can, by the placement and attractiveness of the materials displayed, capture a child's attention and curiosity and entice him to an area and the things in it. Once there, the child should be able to find and easily replace the materials he needs for his activity. Each visible material in a room is an opportunity for exploration and discovery. A broad range of options allows each child to feel competent at something and abets the chances that the unique interests of individuals will be met and that varying levels of complexity will be available to challenge children at different stages in their development. The message conveyed by

Figure 6. A storage unit for manipulative play area shows good display and clear organization of materials.

locked cabinets and empty shelves is: "Hands off. These materials are too precious to be put out for your use. You can have only what I choose." Whereas the message of well-stocked shelves at child height is: "Look, children, at my beautiful wares. Come touch them, come use them, come learn from them."

The quantity of materials displayed affects their perceptibility, accessibility, and use. Too few materials make a place seem drab and uninteresting, as if there is nothing to do; too many materials make it appear chaotic, so it is impossible to know where to begin. Appropriate quantities to be displayed vary over time and situation. Periodic rotation of the supply of materials available for use and relocation of those on continuous display can often awaken or renew interest in materials.

Similarly, the arrangement of individual items within the total physical context affects how each is perceived. (See Figure 6.) A puzzle can be irresistible when invitingly placed on a wide counter, but it generates little interest stacked in a puzzle rack or haphazardly piled on a shelf, pieces disarrayed and missing. Massing, color, height, and quantity are all display tactics that teachers, as display artists, need to practice and employ continually for the ultimate effective functioning of their classrooms.

Many disruptive and dependent behaviors in classrooms occur because of insufficient and poorly organized material supports for tasks. Once the desire to do something is initiated, children have little tolerance waiting for the activity to be "set up" or sustaining interest across periods of interruption while someone searches for the necessary tools. The full, constructive execution of an activity requires that all the props necessary for performing it are near at hand, in sufficient supply when needed, and that there is a balanced stock of items. Therefore, prior to the child's entrance, teachers must take the time to organize and set up the classroom for child use. While this must transpire during after-school time, it frees the teacher during class hours to be an educator and facilitator of learning, rather than a custodian, and supports a child's basic needs for self-sufficiency and independence.

Two additional forms of storage/display to consider for most areas are spaces and surfaces for works-in-progress, so unfinished projects can be continued over time securely protected, and vertical tack surfaces for graphic and informational displays, which enrich communication and stimulate an interest in symbols. It is often useful to provide paper and writing implements in every activity area, so children are encouraged to draw and write about all their activities. The visible display of children's work and of written and graphic materials throughout the room encourages a general attitude of talking about and sharing what one is doing, which helps strengthen vocabulary and communication skills and generates feelings of mutual pride and respect for work well done.

The easiest way to encourage proper care and respect for materials, as well as a cooperative spirit of cleaning up, is to have the attractiveness of the classroom itself convey such respect. If storage shelves and bins are clearly labeled, fit the items they should hold, display them attractively and distinctly, and if the containers hold all the pieces at once, are light enough to carry yet small enough not to usurp all the work surface, then children will be encouraged to care for and put things away because there are cues by which to do so. Transport, loss, and extraneous movements through the room are further minimized when storage units are placed adjacent to the work surfaces on which the stored materials are to be used. Participation in clean-up allows children to learn basic self-help skills, to practice primary motor skills, while sweeping, sponging, mopping, washing, and storing things away, and to be useful contributors to the sustenance of their room.

A child's willingness to risk personal treasures from home on the neutral territory of the school is confirming evidence of a classroom's successful, supportive design. Instead of viewing such items as an annoying source of clutter, they too should be given proper display and applauded as children's spontaneous desires to personalize their room, to affirm their presence in it, and to reveal themselves in the environment by having a stake in its composition.

Mood   The mood of a space is created by the same decorative techniques used to personalize homes and make them sensorily rich and varied: plants, pillows, colors, textures, fabric, knick-knacks, and furniture design. A tablecloth and flowers on the table at luncheon and subdued lighting or candles in jars at snack time are all part of the good life which children are entitled to share. As areas vary in size, function, and layout, so too should they vary in mood, so that children go from place to place within the four walls of the room and experience spaces that are soft and hard, dark and light, cold and warm, colorful and bland. The appropriate mood for a particular function can be gauged by the level of activity, movement, and physical energy that children expend in performing it. Low, tranquil activities tend to go with warm, soft, textured spaces, while wide, expansive activities go with spaces that are cooler, harder, more vibrant in tone.

As the largest organ of the body, the skin is probably a vital source of stimulation for the arousal system (Montagu, 1971). Ayres (1973) suggests that increased tactile and somatosensory stimulation may improve the form and space perception of children with learning disorders. Thus, decorative elements that introduce texture into the room seem particularly important for creating a mood, softening institutional blandness, and therapeutically aiding children. Similarly, objects that move, grow, or change shape (mobiles, wind chimes, mirrors, interactives, plants, fish, animals) add visual interest, pattern, and excitement to the environment, encouraging both passive and social interaction.

Once a comfortable, well-functioning classroom layout has been achieved, care must be taken to maintain it. This usually requires providing the custodians with clearly labeled floorplans and explanations for the diversified arrangement, so their support may be enlisted not to, by force of habit, push all the furniture back against the walls.

SPECIAL CONSIDERATIONS FOR PARTICULAR AREAS

Possibilities for designing and implementing the above strategies are limited only by imagination and resources. Unfortunately, versatile facilities for classrooms, especially those for special needs children, are rare and available only on a limited commercial basis. The following pages highlight a few considerations, which can enhance the development of particular activity areas, and present some ideas using recycled, remade, and custom-designed facilities developed by the author to stimulate new

Figure 7.   A reading area formed by cushions on the floor. Diagonal supports placed inside the shelves of a standard bookcase permit viewing of book covers.

approaches to the creation of exciting, functional classroom environments.

Reading Areas

Books for young children are best displayed with their covers outward so that the jacket design, as well as the title, informs the child of the book's theme. A comfortable sitting area, next to the book display, should provide adequate back support if readers are to be encouraged to linger for awhile. A mattress is often too deep for this purpose, but old couch cushions function effectively. Horizontal book displays can be achieved with wall-mounted shelves (as in Figure 2) or by wedging a board or piece of triwall, i.e., triple-strength, cardboard at an angle, inside regular shelves (See Figure 7). A strip of half-dowelling across the front of the shelf will prevent the books from slipping.

An A-frame structure built of plywood (measuring about 40 inches high by 6 feet long) can double as a book rack and room divider. Both sides of the frame can be designed to hold books or one side can be surfaced with homosote, an inexpensive fiberboard sold by lumber companies, to provide an easel. The easel accommodates various sizes of paper, allows communication between children working side by side, and is washable when covered with two coats of polyurethane over two coats of semi-gloss paint. Therapeutically, it enables children to paint from as far down to as far up as they can reach and to use their upper bodies ex-

Figure 8. *Left:* An A-frame book rack and room divider. *Right:* A 6-foot long easel formed by attaching a sheet of homosote to the backside of the book rack.

pansively. Homosote panels may be mounted floor to ceiling to create a "painting wall," or cut to fit backs of bookcases and cabinets, providing an excellent bulletin board surface for individual areas. (See Figure 8.) Large sheets of newsprint are most efficiently stored vertically in a tube or in a wastebasket.

Block Areas

It is advisable to place large and small unit blocks in two separate areas. Large blocks require children to be on their feet moving about, whereas small blocks are best used when children are sitting or kneeling on the floor. The former can go in open areas, but the latter need considerable enclosure and protection. If combined, children tend to use the small blocks to fill in the holes in constructions made of the large blocks, therefore failing to appreciate the mathematical properties inherent in the smaller units. Small blocks should always be displayed with their longer dimensions visible and are enhanced by the presence of miniature cars, animals, and people. Outlines of the blocks painted or pasted on the shelves assist in clean-up and help children learn to match a three-dimensional object to its two-dimensional representation. (See Figure 9.)

Water Play Areas

Messy play with water and sand is an excellent activity for young children since it encourages individual expression, is calm, and is slow paced. An inexpensive water trough can be created with a galvanized double wash-

Figure 9.   Small unit blocks in a secluded location are well displayed with their long dimensions visible and their shapes outlined on the wall and shelves. Small toys add possibilities for play.

tub or a small animal feeding trough, raised on a platform to a height of 24 inches. A narrow board (6–8 inches wide), with cleats on the underside to enable it to slide across the top of the trough, will provide a surface for vessels and containers used in play. (See Figure 10.)

Much custodial work can be eliminated if the trough is mounted onto an existing faucet and drain or if it is custom-designed out of plywood, lined with fiberglass resin to make it waterproof, as a built-in feature of the room. Troughs can also be built to accommodate a child in a wheelchair. Covers for the troughs provide additional work surfaces. Water faucets can have temperature controls and lockable turn-offs if desired. (See Figure 11.)

Gross Motor Play

Most preschools suffer from insufficient *indoor* provisions for large muscle play (climbing, tumbling, hanging, sliding, swinging, crawling, rocking, jumping). Wherever possible, a designated, well-provisioned interior space for jumping and climbing is much preferred by children to the exploitation of couches and tables for the same purposes. The climbing structure in Figure 12 is only 4 feet by 6 feet and, despite appearances, is free-standing, not attached to the wall. It has graduated spacing between the rungs, two platforms, which children can relocate, and a detachable slide that can be mounted on the platform to the right (not visible). A

Figure 10.   Water play in a small animal feeding trough. Filling and emptying is aided by hook-up to an existing faucet and drain.

beam with a hook on it allows suspension and interchangeability of many props over the course of a long winter, such as the "bird cage," a tire swing, a rope to shimmy up, a punching bag, a monkey swing, etc. Without the structure, versatility can be achieved by mounting a swivel hook in a ceiling. Additional gross motor facilities to consider are an air mattress, foam- and air-filled wedges, bolsters, mats for rolling and tumbling, balance beams, portable climbers, rocky boats, "tunnels of fun," etc.

The Playframe

A custom-designed unit called a Playframe is an extraordinarily versatile work surface, especially for dramatic play and games of skill, providing as many as twenty different activities in as little as a 4-foot square space (easel, puppet theatre, busy board, play house, play kitchen, dart games,

Figure 11.   Built-in water play troughs, including one to accommodate a child in a wheel-chair, form part of a messy play area that includes a table and open storage for crafts activities. Water troughs have covers and lockable faucet turn-offs.

nerf basketball, mirror and sketch board, miniature doll house, etc.).[2] Play panels supporting the different activities may be interchangeably suspended on any of the four sides and placed at varying heights to accommodate children seated, standing, or in wheelchairs. Panels and other items can be stored in the upper portion of the frame. Where space is extremely limited, wall-mounted supports for the panels, rather than the entire frame, can enable comparable versatility. (See Figure 13.)

Dramatic Play Areas

To be truly effective in stimulating dramatic play, house equipment should never be simply lined up against a wall, but it must be arranged to form a small, fully enclosed space designed to simulate the four walls of a room, within which children can retreat from adult presence to fantasize. Kitchen furniture, whether purchased or homemade, must be supplemented by manipulable items, such as small but real pots and pans, dishes, silverware, and recycled cereal boxes, juice and milk containers, tin cans, soda bottles, etc. The latter items are the "stuff" from which

[2]Plans for constructing the Playframe can be obtained from the author.

Figure 12. A free-standing climbing structure, with graduated spacing between the rungs and two movable platforms. The swivel hook on the protruding beam enables suspension of this "bird cage" climber and other equipment, such as a tire swing, a rope, a punching bag, etc.

"meals" are prepared and can be replaced periodically by supplies children bring from home. Enclosures, which enable a child to rest, hide, or put a doll to sleep, add to the "homelike" setting of the playhouse area. (Note foam mattress on floor of structure at right rear in Figure 14, left. Lower portion of loft in Figure 14, right, can be a crawl-in resting space or a place to display dress-up clothes.)

In addition to traditional playhouse areas, preschool-age children have many role-playing themes they frequently need to act out (batman, spacemen, farmers, doctors, etc.). These themes are often expressed by children who, lacking a specific place for play, usurp transit areas, stairwells, and open space around tables and chairs as the territory for running wildly about "shooting" targets or competing for power and speed.

4'x 4' interchangeable panels

Figure 13.   *Left:* The Playframe, a free-standing unit from which interchangeable panels can be hung at varying heights, provides a wide variety of activities in a small area. Panels are stored in upper portion of unit. *Right:* Wall-mounted uprights can support the play panels when space is too limited for a free-standing unit.

Rather than being stifled, such children are far less disruptive and more creative when given a *place* in which to act out their fantasies. The dramatic play area can be at floor level, often incorporated with large blocks, or on a suspended or free-standing loft 3–5 feet above ground. Three such lofts are shown in Figure 15: one with a woodworking area, one with a small block area, and one with storage space for 30 cots underneath; a fourth loft is visible to the left of the climbing structure in Figure 12. The unfinished house struts on the loft in Figure 15, right, encourage children to build on and embellish the structure.

Use of the dramatic play platform by both sexes occurs when teachers help children enact themes of a bisexual or asexual nature (restaurant, camera shop, puppet theatre, etc.). Movement up and down the ladder expends energy, while the height and enclosure tend to keep children in one place and make their movement less disruptive to on-going classroom activities. No platform should exceed 6 feet by 7 feet, so that it does not become comparable to a second floor level, encouraging much movement and expansive behavior. Partial enclosure is required to pre-

Figure 14.   *Left*: An enticing doll corner is enclosed on four sides and well-supplied with utensils and containers. The loft at right rear provides a small hideaway for putting dolls to sleep or for resting. *Right*: This loft adds two crawl-in, resting spaces to a house corner, or the lower portion can be used to display dress-up clothes.

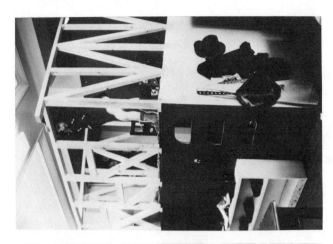

Figure 15.   *Left:* A dramatic play platform suspended from the ceiling with a woodworking area underneath. *Center:* A free-standing dramatic play platform is being transformed into a gas station with a small unit block area below. *Right:* Two stacks of fifteen cots each fit under this loft that has a dramatic play area above. The unfinished house frame encourages fantasy play and embellishment of the structure.

vent falling, but total enclosure is extremely unsafe as it provides a false sense of security, restricts a child's knowledge of his whereabouts, and may challenge a child to scale the barrier. Vertical ladders or ladders formed by making cut-outs in the wall of the structure are safer than staircases and diagonally braced rungs that can be tripped over. A vertical ladder requires the child to take note of where he places his hands and feet and increases his awareness of his transition from the floor to a higher level. The addition of a ramp with cleats or rope enables physically handicapped children to pull themselves up to such a level.

Areas for Quiet Work and Reclining

Two tiers of carpeted risers built into a corner create an effective group meeting space. This can also become a reading and manipulative play area when buttressed by contiguous storage and displays of books and construction toys. (The shape on the wall in Figure 16 is a giant felt board cut in a fanciful, graphic design.)

Smaller platforms and lofts for reading, quiet play, or the retreat of one or two children can be created in many ways and are especially appealing when carpeted or cushioned. The platform in the foreground of Figure 17, left, is approximately 4 feet by 3 feet by 1 foot high and easily moved to any location. Low walls on two sides, while permitting visiability to most areas of the room, provide back support and enclosure for several children working with puzzles, games, or books. The structure in Figure 17, right, designed to conform to the 4 by 8 foot dimensions of plywood, has an internal level 4 feet above the floor, and measures 4 feet by 4 feet by 8 feet high at the peak. The roof was intentionally provided to create privacy and sloped to reduce the structure's bulk. It has one cut-out through which a child can poke his head in order to experience a bird's-eye view of the room.

In Figure 18, a 4 foot by 5 foot by 1 foot high platform enclosed on three sides and softened with throw pillows and bolsters provides a nook for storytelling or sharing a few relaxed moments with friends.

A two-story loft, more open than that in Figure 17, right, is shown in Figure 19. The ceiling of the lower portion is intentionally raised to accommodate a seated adult, for one-to-one exchanges with a child, or for reading and resting. The upper portion has a low roof to prevent children from standing and to provide a place that children perceive as uniquely their own.

Woodworking Areas

Woodworking activities, as in the case with sand, water, and clay, are invaluable for their unstructured properties and for the energy they allow

Figure 16.   *Left:* A group sharing a story, while seated on two tiers of carpeted risers built into a corner. *Right:* The same group meeting / quiet area uninhabited. The shape on the wall is a giant felt board cut in a fanciful, graphic design.

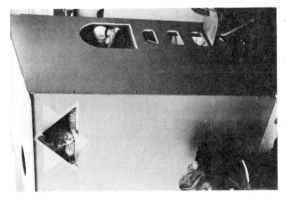

Figure 17. *Left:* Two quiet platforms provide functional and spatial variety. The platform in the foreground sits almost in the room's center but receives constant use for work with puzzles, games, and books because of its raised height and low walls on two sides that provide back support and outward visibility. *Right:* This structure, designed for privacy and quiet play, has an internal level 4 feet above the floor. Children sitting there can enjoy a bird's eye view of the room by peeking through cut-outs in the walls or roof.

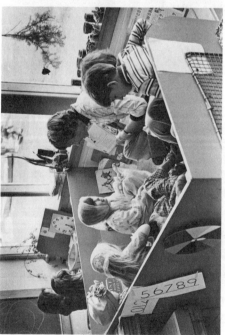

Figure 18.   *Left:* A low platform enclosed on three sides makes a cozy nook for story-telling. *Right:* With pillows, it is a nice place to rest and share a few quiet moments with friends.

Figure 19.   A two-story open loft designed for encounters between an adult and child below or for two children alone above.

children to release. No more than two children should be allowed to work at the bench at one time. Since children work fairly close to their bodies, the workbench need not be wide and should provide a trough or sectioned-off portion that keeps nails, screws, and scraps of wood from falling off its surface. Noise is reduced primarily by making the *surface* of the bench as thick as possible. For children needing experience with hammering, a tree stump of *soft* wood takes many nails, almost noiselessly. In large, acoustically poor rooms it may be necessary to cover the bench surface with carpet or rubber matting to control sound, although this destroys the aesthetic of working with wood on wood. Adult-sized tools, and bins for wood of different sizes, should be well displayed. Since children often become frustrated by their poor carpentry skills and prefer to glue their structures together, a separate, washable table for gluing should be provided nearby, to keep the workbench clean.

Figure 20.   A well-designed woodworking area for two children, complete with storage bins for wood, a glue table, a tree stump, and wall display of tools (not visible). The workbench has a central recess to keep nails, screws, and wood scraps securely on its surface.

Modifications for Physically Handicapped Children

As indicated above, the group of children requiring specialized design facilities are those with physical handicaps that limit mobility or sensorial receptivity. Adaptive equipment for such children is of limited commercial availability and must usually be custom-designed to fit the individual case. National and local parent or self-help groups organized for particular disabilities (spina bifida, multiple sclerosis, cerebral palsy) often informally distribute useful designs and adaptations of standard equipment that members have created.[3] A few considerations and recommendations are offered to guide teachers in this challenging design area.

[3]See also N. R. Finnie's book, *Handling the Young Cerebral Palsied Child at Home,* (Second Edition, 1975, E. P. Dutton, New York) for many useful, adaptive suggestions.

Mobility and Transport   The greatest environmental barrier for the physically handicapped is lack of *access* to desired spaces and facilities. Classrooms that serve children wearing crutches or braces or in wheelchairs should provide extra-wide, clear transit pathways for easy passage through the room and wide entrances to areas with firm boundaries. Sufficient space in each area is required for the child to put his crutches on the floor. Expandable metal grips can be fastened to the sides of chairs and tables or onto walls to hold the crutches upright and out of the way.

Raised levels should not be eliminated in deference to such children, as changes in height frequently challenge the exercise of limbs and faculties that can profit from use. However, the height and design of the raised levels should be modified to support access by the physically disabled. Platforms less than 1 foot high may need a gradually sloping ramp at the entry (see Figure 1A), with or without steps for the nonhandicapped. Lofts and structures 2 or more feet high require a ramp of more rapid slope supplemented by cleats, rope, or grab bars on the ramp surface or sides by which the child can pull himself up to the higher level. As a ramp increases vertically, it must project at least an equal amount (usually twice as much) horizontally out into the room, potentially usurping floor space and getting in the way of children's movement. Therefore, the structure's height must be weighed against the projected length of the ramp, enabling a reasonable balance between the two to be achieved. In the case of high structures, the ramp can double back on itself to conserve space (see Figure 1B).

A child who must remove his braces in order to climb a ramp should be provided with a proper seat and storage space for the braces near the ramp's entry that will not interfere with any child's movement around the structure. A transport substitute for braces and wheelchairs is a board on casters, which the child lies across on his abdomen and propels with his arms. Where it is difficult for children in braces to make frequent transitions from sitting to standing, a straight-backed chair that allows their legs to hang straight down can be moved about easily if mounted on casters.

Sitting Surfaces   Contrary to their advantages for most children, the floor, stools, and risers without backs are uncomfortable sitting surfaces for physically disabled children, who require considerable back support and ability to have their legs in line with their bodies (standing or lying) or hanging straight down from the knees. A fiberboard tube cut to form a chair (see Figure 5) can provide a reassuring support and an alternative to ladderback chairs. Facilities for lying down and stretching out (platforms, water bed) relieve muscle tension and encourage relaxation. In areas where floor level activities cannot be conducted from a prone or supine position, a table and several chairs (for friends), kept small in size and placed near storage units in such a way as not to dominate or negate the floor level quality of the area, enable a physically handicapped child to participate in the area's offerings. Since most table surfaces limit play with small unit blocks, attractive alternatives for table top use are minia-ture block sets and geoblocks. Seats with backs, in self-help areas (coat cubbies, toilets), maximize the handicapped child's independent activity.

Work Surfaces   Tables with cut-outs clearly extend the work sur-face available to a child in a wheelchair or with restricted torso mobility. However, to be useful, these tables need to be higher than the standard chair and quite large. They can quickly overpower a space. Teachers should be aware that major manufacturers do produce trays for wheel-chairs, in a variety of sizes, shapes, and designs. Despite appearances, these do not usually isolate the child from peers any more than large tables with cut-outs and they conserve space.

Tables at which physically disabled children stand to work, such as a sand table, may require a semicircular support to brace the body and may need to be higher than tables for nonhandicapped children. In contrast, a water table may need to be lower, to both support the body and free the child's arms to reach over and into the water trough. Spilled water under-foot is dangerous; therefore, bath mats and throw rugs should always be provided to absorb water. Workbench activities tend to throw the dis-abled child's body backwards and make him lose his balance. Additional bracing, by means of sturdy chairs, body straps, or placement of the workbench parallel to a wall, may be helpful.

In most cases, it is not necessary or advisable to change the height of storage and display units for the child confined to a wheelchair since this can interfere with accessibility, visibility, and the design of boundaries for the other children. However, the tops of storage units, especially if widen-ed, can become good work and display levels for children in wheelchairs.

Modifications for Deaf Children   For a deaf child, good visibility into and out of areas increases his contact with on-going events and the ability of others to make contact with him from a distance. Materials and surfaces that transmit vibrations, especially wooden platforms and lofts, are useful facilities for increasing the child's cognizance of ambient move-ments and sounds.

Modifications for Blind Children   The use of ramps to raised areas and the elimination of facilities with protruding, irregular boundaries are as important for blind children as for physically disabled children. Divid-ers and bounding elements should be free from clutter so children can use these as tactual orientational guides. Textural changes (wood, carpet, for-mica, brick, etc.) in floors, boundaries, and levels should be capitalized upon as significant clues for orientation and mobility. There is also indication (Bower, 1977) that blind children may utilize echoes in detecting environmental features, if not all surfaces in the room are sound absorbing. Even legally blind children frequently have some minimal vision and light sensitivity. Good lighting, but not glare, can support such minimal capacities if there are options, such as floor and table lamps, that children can adjust to their own needs.

Most blind children are fearful of moving through space, are light on their feet, and are tense in their upper bodies. Comfortable, soft furnishings encourage muscle relaxation, while gross motor equipment, which holds a child securely but encourages him to propel his body multi-directionally in space (swings, tumblers, rockers, trampolines), is an invaluable therapeutic and mobility aid.

ACKNOWLEDGMENTS

Photographs by Anita R. Olds and Henry F. Olds. Figures 2, 6, 11 and 13 are reprinted by permission of Grune & Stratton, New York, from A. R. Olds, "Psychological considerations in humanizing the physical environment of pediatric outpatient and hospital settings," in: E. Gellert (ed.), *Psychosocial Aspects of Pediatric Care,* 1978.

REFERENCES

Ayres, A. J. 1973. Form and space perception. Sensory Integration and Learning Disorders. pp. 190–206. Western Psychological Services, Los Angeles.

Bower, T. G. R. 1977. A Primer of Infant Development. W. H. Freeman & Company, San Francisco.

Erikson, E. H. 1950. Childhood and Society. W. W. Norton & Company, New York.

Gellner, L. A. 1959. A Neurophysiological Concept of Mental Retardation and Its Educational Implications. J. Levinson Research Foundation, Chicago.

Held, R., and Bossom, J. 1961. Neonatal deprivation and adult rearrangement: Complementary techniques for analyzing plastic sensory-motor coordinations. J. Comp. Physiol. Psychol. (54)1:33–37.

Held, R., and Hein, A. 1963. Movement-produced stimulation in the development of visually guided behavior. J. Comp. Physiol. Psychol. (56)5:872–876.

Isaacs, S. 1967. The Children We Teach. 2nd Ed. University of London Press, London. Reprinted in C. E. Silberman (ed.), 1973. The Open Classroom Reader. pp. 181–182. Vintage, New York.

Montagu, A. 1971. Touching. The Human Significance of the Skin. The mind of the skin, pp. 1–42. Harper & Row Publishers, New York.

Montessori, M. 1964. The Montessori Method. Schocken Books, New York.

Piaget, J. 1963. The Origins of Intelligence in Children. W. W. Norton & Company, Inc., New York.

Piaget, J. 1964. Quoted by Eleanor Duckworth in "Piaget Rediscovered," The ESS Reader. Education Development Center, Newton, Mass.

138   Olds

Piaget, J. 1973. To Understand Is to Invent. Grossman, New York.
Piaget, J., and Inhelder, B. 1956. The Child's Conception of Space. Routledge and Kegan Paul, London.
Satterfield, J. H., Cantwell, D. P., Saul, R. E., Lesser, L. I., and Podosin, R. L. 1973. Response to stimulant drug treatment in hyperactive children, prediction from EEG and neurological findings. J. Autism Child Schizo. 3:36–48.
Satterfield, J. H., Cantwell, D. P., Lesser, L. I., and Podosin, R. L. 1972. Physiological studies of the hyperactive child I. Am. J. Psychiatry 128:1418–1424.
Satterfield, J. H., and Dawson, M. E. 1971. Electrodermal correlates of hyperactivity in children. Psychophysiology 8:191–197.
White, R. W. 1959. Motivation reconsidered: The concept of competence. Psychol. Rev. 66:297–333.
Zaporozhets, A. V. 1957. The development of voluntary movements. In: B. Simon (ed.), Psychology in the Soviet Union, pp. 108–114. Stanford University Press, Stanford, Cal.

Informal Assessment and Individualized Educational Planning

Lane W. Gunnoe

IDENTIFYING INFORMAL ASSESSMENT

Educational assessment focuses on identifying children's strengths and weaknesses and assisting teachers in utilizing classroom activities and options to enhance children's growth and development. A fundamental objective of early childhood assessment is to increase the number of children who are capable of participating in the mainstream of the social and educational childhood experience. An essential step in this process is the recognition of specific factors about the child that may require that the educational mainstream be modified. An ideal progression for specifying and identifying these critical factors would include the following activities: childfind, screening, evaluation, and individual program planning. Figure 1 lists the activities involved in this progression and places them in a context of increasing complexity and specificity.

This chapter discusses in depth one assessment procedure — informal assessment — and demonstrates its role in the planning of individualized educational programs for handicapped and nonhandicapped children. This chapter shows that the key to productive use of informal assessment is the teacher's ability to observe and evaluate children's activity within the natural classroom setting, to interpret these observations in terms of a developmental perspective, and to relate this information to the multiple learning functions inherent in classroom materials and activities.

Preparation of this chapter was supported in part by Grant GOO-75-00230 from the United States Office of Education, Bureau of Education for the Handicapped.

Figure 1. The relationship between early childhood identification, evaluation, and intervention procedures (from Meisels, 1978b).

	CHILDFIND	SCREENING	EVALUATION	INDIVIDUAL PROGRAM PLANNING
PURPOSE	Initial contact and awareness	To identify children who may need further evaluation	To determine existence of disability and to propose possible remediation strategies	To determine individual educational plan, program placement and curriculum activities
PERSONNEL	State Personnel, School Staff, Volunteers, Community Members, Pediatricians	Teachers, Other Professionals and Paraprofessionals, Parents	Educators, Psychologists, Parents, Clinicians, Physicians, Social Workers	Teachers, Parents, Evaluation Team Personnel, Other Professionals
ACTIVITIES	Census taking, newspaper and media publicity, posters, leaflets	Administration of screening instruments, medical examinations, hearing and vision testing, and parent questionnaire	Formal evaluations, parent conferencing, evaluation team meetings	Informal evaluation, development of instructional objectives

Childfind

In certain important respects informal assessment includes each of the activities included in Figure 1. For example, the entire assessment procedure may be initiated because of informal observations of disturbing behaviors, because of a potential lag in the child's development, or because of a previously diagnosed problem that is seen as a possible obstacle to the child's future educational development. Parents, pediatricians, and other health workers or early childhood education personnel who have observed the child over a period of time may decide that they want an additional perspective in which to place their informal observations. For children without obvious handicapping conditions, but who seem to be educationally at risk, participation in developmental screening would seem to be appropriate.

Screening

Although screening procedures vary from community to community, the selection of a screening instrument that focuses on the child's development in a number of areas (e.g., language, gross and fine motor, cognition) is probably more useful at this point than is a procedure that focuses solely on the child's readiness to undertake a preconceived and absolute program of instruction. There are two reasons why such "readiness" testing is inappropriate: first, the child is participating in screening in part because a modification of the mainstream is anticipated for him; second, children vary enormously in their rate of development. Nowhere is this more evident than in the ages 2 through 6. Readiness tests do not reflect this variability. However, a developmental screening test enables the trained examiner to describe a child's skills within a range of abilities, rather than treating those skills in a limited pass/fail modality. Thus, at their best, formal developmental screening instruments reliably and validly can be used to place a child's abilities within a general profile or developmental continuum. Initial informal observations, which may have preceded screening, can then be compared to the child's performance.

Evaluation

Following screening, the next step in the assessment process is diagnostic evaluation. Unlike screening, evaluation is principally a formal procedure designed to determine whether or not a child has a disability that will interfere with his ability to learn. At the evaluation stage the information that is collected should be used to determine how the child's regular classroom program should be modified or what type of program the child may require. Ideally, such determinations are made by a cross-disciplinary team, which reflects medical, educational, and parental expertise and concerns for the child.

The next step in the identification and evaluation process is to translate the information that has been accrued into a cohesive individualized educational plan that reflects the child's strengths, remediation needs, and general developmental abilities. Although individual program planning can be conceived as a collaborative effort (see Figure 1), such planning is typically the primary responsibility of the classroom teacher, and it makes substantial utilization of informal assessment techniques.

Informal Assessment

Informal assessment may be defined generically as the process by which an individual who is knowledgeable concerning early childhood development utilizes that knowledge to evaluate a child's level of functioning and ability in a number of key areas of performance and learning. The "testing situation" for informal assessment may be a day care classroom, a pediatrician's office, a regular or special education classroom, the child's home, or any other site that provides an opportunity to observe the child utilize language, gross motor skills, fine motor skills, reasoning abilities, and abilities to interact with adults and children. Utilizing this definition, informal assessment can serve as the first step in the process of early recognition and intervention. Clearly, this is not always the case. With some handicapping conditions the child's impairment can be determined at, or soon after, birth. In other instances, trauma or accident may determine the need for intervention. However, in general, informal assessment may be considered to be a form of continuous screening because it implies that the professional serves as a "sifter," attempting to identify those children who display one or more skill areas in the questionable range of a developmental continuum.

Fortunately, the orderly progression of identification, evaluation, and intervention, which is described in Figure 1, is becoming more the norm than the exception. Local special education mandates, as well as federal legislation (P.L. 94–142), are having a significant impact on systematizing childfind, evaluation, and remediation procedures. However, it is still frequently the case that a child is not identified as educationally at risk prior to his entry into the regular classroom. Occasionally, problems are simply not identified, or sometimes a "wait and see" attitude is adopted by those who have concerns about the child. Thus, the preschool or kindergarten teacher may be the first person to review, assess, and initiate systematic remediation for a particular child. The teacher must be prepared to utilize his knowledge of development and of the materials and possibilities of the classroom to assess the child's functioning and the child's educational needs.

Informal assessment plays its most prominent role in the classroom. Techniques of informal assessment can be used by the teacher to assist in the development of individualized programs for children whose handicaps have already been diagnosed, as well as for children who do not have specific disabilities. In the classroom the teacher can utilize regular materials to monitor the progress of individual children. Thus, classroom informal assessment becomes individualized assessment in which the child's skills and abilities serve as the criteria for success. For example, at the beginning of the school year, the teacher who observes a 4-year-old who uses two hands on a pair of scissors to snip paper, who cannot stack table blocks consistently, and who spreads glue or paste indiscriminately across paper and the gluing table may hypothesize that the child has poorly developed fine motor abilities. The teacher would then focus some of the child's activities on this area. If, within four to five weeks, the child is able to use one hand on the scissors for random snipping into the edge of the paper, can stack up to five blocks consistently, and spreads paste only on the object or paper to be pasted, the teacher can consider that the child has demonstrated significant success. In other words, the teacher has used the child's own activity within a developmental progression to assess the child's progress.

Informal classroom assessment should be individualized and process-oriented. That is, the teacher attends to variables that accompany the child's learning, such as the style with which the child learns, situations in which he learns best, and the length of time needed to acquire a skill. In addition, the teacher is concerned with actually reaching the goals of cutting with scissors, block-stacking, etc., as vehicles for assisting the child in fine motor development. All of this takes skill and ability: the ability to identify and carry out individualized objectives within the classroom routine and the skill to develop a curriculum capable of reflecting multiple objectives for a variety of children. Classroom teachers engaged in informal assessment and individualized programming should have at their disposal knowledge about the parameters of normal development in areas such as language, gross and fine motor skills, reasoning skills, and personal/social development. Moreover, a teacher should be able to:

a. Identify behavioral objectives,
b. Develop activities to meet objectives,
c. Utilize a variety of record-keeping procedures to monitor change,
d. Evaluate progress through the use of informal and formal assessment procedures, and

e. Plan and implement additional short-term goals that extend and unify previous objectives.

Thus, the classroom teacher should be able to assess abilities, as well as regulate the learning environment, in order to encourage development and mastery in particular curriculum areas. Utilizing the child's activity in the classroom for informal assessment allows a skilled professional, the teacher, both to undertake the development of an educational plan for a child and to select or create prescriptions that meet the plan.

Efficient utilization of classroom informal assessment, as an ongoing and integral part of teaching, requires careful characterization of elements in the informal assessment process. Elements of observation, goal-setting, describing behavioral objectives, developing activities to meet those goals, and monitoring progress are essential. In addition, a description of the teacher's function, the child's learning features, and characteristics of the curriculum must be clearly understood in order to systematically design the elements of the classroom for the purpose of effecting planned change in the child.

This chapter introduces and discusses the elements of teacher function, child learning features, and curriculum characteristics. The primary focus is on classrooms and teachers that serve children 3 to 6 years of age. However, many aspects of early childhood informal assessment are also germane to classrooms that serve older children. Although the open classroom structure may lend itself more readily to the development of multiple instructional objectives that are essential to classroom informal assessment, even the most traditionally structured classroom can be modified to make use of informal assessment techniques. The elements generally in need of modification in traditional classrooms are: attitudes about the function of the teacher, the relative importance of child learning features in curriculum planning, and the use of curriculum activities that are able to serve multiple needs of different children.

FUNCTIONS OF THE TEACHER AND INFORMAL ASSESSMENT

Frequently, when requested to outline and explain the daily schedule used in their classrooms, teachers find themselves referring to a variety of outside activities (art, music, gym) or imposed expectations (workbooks, curriculum kits, reading groups) that act as interlopers in the planning of a defined and responsive daily schedule. One of the problems highlighted by this kind of response is a weakness in conceiving the teacher's role. A major function of the teacher is to understand and develop the relationship between the needs of each child and the role of classroom curriculum in meeting those needs. The teacher who principally reacts to demands that emanate from outside the classroom as he plans curriculum undoubtedly has difficulty developing a cohesive educational program that utilizes activities inside and outside the classroom as part of a framework designed to meet individual and collective goals set for the children. Systematic program development occurs with more regularity when the teacher has an overview of the function and purpose of elements in the curriculum, rather than when she simply moves along as part of a plan not well understood. The teacher is the architect or designer of the classroom, not simply the implementor of other's ideas and priorities.

The Teacher as Architect/Designer

When the teacher is viewed as architect of the classroom, her role is more easily seen as one of developing expectations and procedures for children in the classroom. Within this framework the teacher must understand the learning process and must have the ability to relate this process to the general developmental range of 3- to 6-year-old children, as well as to the particular abilities of individual children in the classroom. Using this knowledge, the teacher focuses on curriculum as the vehicle for relating activities to the needs of children and the goals set for those children. The teacher is then in a position to think of a particular child simultaneously as one of a group of children who may be pursuing a given art activity and as one who needs to improve eye-hand coordination, using art activities as a vehicle toward achieving this goal. The teacher develops a curriculum capable of being individualized to meet multiple instructional objectives, that is, a curriculum with activities that can be utilized to meet the various needs of a number of different children. The ability to individualize is critically important for the teacher/architect in providing a flexible curriculum and in developing informal classroom assessment techniques to support the goals of the curriculum and to evaluate the effectiveness of those activities.

The Teacher as Observer

The role of the classroom teacher can be conceived as architect/designer, but it must also include the role of observer. As an observer, the teacher may have at least four distinct purposes. *First,* the teacher uses knowledge of the parameters of child development to assess the abilities of the children in the classroom: Do the fine motor skills of this child roughly approximate those to be expected for children of this age, at this time of year, with this kind of experience? If this inquiry results in questions or concerns about individual children, the teacher uses observation for a *second* purpose: the testing of hypotheses and the clarification of initial observations about particular children. Pursuing this second purpose in observation requires clarity on the teacher's part about the underlying components of curriculum activities. The teacher must be capable of providing the child with a variety of experiences that call upon the abilities under scrutiny. In other words, the teacher tests hypotheses by using classroom activities as vehicles for examining the child's abilities in a particular area.

The results of the second set of observations may yield information that leads the teacher to set behavioral objectives within the identified skill area. The teacher will individualize curriculum for the child in order to assist him in the acquisition of certain skills. In an effort to determine how to best individualize, the teacher observes with a *third* purpose in mind: What are the child's strengths? What does he enjoy doing? What can be used as a vehicle for individualization? It may prove useful to keep a record that focuses on activities and materials that the child selects spontaneously, situations he avoids, children he prefers to be with, his ability to function in small and large groups, etc.

The *fourth* purpose served by teacher observation generally takes place after individualization, for the child has been implemented for a specific period of time. At this point the teacher must find out the effects of the individualized program: Were the goals realistic? Were the activities appropriate? Was the child interested and involved? Have the child's skills and abilities changed? Observing the child's manipulations of the same activities or materials used in the second series of observations may be useful, or the teacher may draw from a different area of the curriculum that she knows taps the abilities in question. The purpose of this fourth observation, then, is test-retest. Having established the need for assistance in a given area and having provided additional experience in that area, the teacher now expects to see increased ability.

The Teacher as Evaluator

As architect, the teacher has developed an overall plan for the classroom. As observer, the teacher has detailed and implemented strategies to individualize that plan to meet the needs of particular children. The third function of the teacher is that of evaluator. The role of the teacher as evaluator is varied and on-going. At the outset, the teacher evaluates the appropriateness of classroom curriculum to the developmental level of the children with whom she will be working. Next, the teacher evaluates children who may have special needs for the purpose of curriculum modification. These needs may or may not have been identified prior to the child's entrance into the classroom. The teacher follows these evaluations by examining the child's pattern of strengths and weaknesses and decides on the most useful way to individualize curriculum for the child. Evaluation of the progress made through individualized programming occurs next. At this point the teacher evaluates the elements discussed earlier: Were realistic goals set? Were elements in the child's pattern of strengths and weaknesses overlooked? Were the activities selected appropriate to the behavioral objective? Evaluation continues as the teacher determines the next step to be taken in the child's individualized program: Will new activities be introduced? Should the focus be shifted?

The classroom teacher functions as architect, observer, and evaluator. She uses space, materials, and activities of the classroom to represent the physical manifestations of her concept of individual and group needs. Workbooks and gym classes are then used as a part of the process, but no single element determines the process.

CHILDREN'S LEARNING FEATURES AND INFORMAL ASSESSMENT

Throughout this chapter reference is made to the variability of skill levels in young children. One 3-year-old child may cut with scissors easily and be able to hop on one foot, once or twice. Another child may be completely unable to manipulate scissors and be incapable of hopping. However, both children display fine and gross motor skills that fall within the normal range for children their age. The classroom teacher should provide activities and materials appropriate to the range of skill of a general developmental level. However, the teacher must also focus on individual developmental levels, or variability, within the expected range. Materials and activities should be examined to assure the teacher that the items can be used by children at differing skill levels.

As children progress through a developmental continuum, they display a "readiness" to learn and to be challenged. In order to determine a child's readiness in this developmental and generic sense, the teacher must focus on the framework of development, as well as on the immediate activity of the child. Thus, the teacher can use the general parameters of development and experience as a guideline (Gesell, 1940; Werner, 1948; Piaget, 1951; Erikson, 1963), but the teacher must also find out if a particular child is interested in exploring certain materials or certain experiences. In other words, the teacher must determine if the cognitive, motor, and/or personal/social systems of the child are poised to begin exploration in a given area. In the developmental sense, achieving "readiness" for the next experience is an ongoing part of the *child's role* in the classroom informal assessment process. For a new experience or notion to have meaning for a child, he must have some predilection to make sense of the new material, to come to terms with the new phenomenon in the light of previous experiences, and to bring the entirety into harmony

(Piaget, 1952). In other words, once the child's interest has been aroused, he will generally explore and integrate until mastery has occurred (see White, 1959). Once mastered, that skill or knowledge becomes the "readiness" factor for a new encounter or new experience.

Classroom teachers observe this process repeatedly throughout the year. For example, a child enters the housekeeping corner. He explores clothes, tries on a shoe, opens cabinets, handles pans, and looks over the doll in the high chair. Later the child may try on the clothes, hold the doll and then observe himself in the mirror. Eventually he may participate with other children in cooperative role-taking and dramatic play. Integration of the experiences and materials of the housekeeping corner with issues or skills already a part of the child's repertoire may be reflected in these role-playing activities, in classification skills (organizing the kitchen tools by use), or in other skill areas. In other words, the child has encountered the new materials, explored them, and utilized them to expand his own developing system of competence and effectiveness.

Informal assessment of the child's learning features can be determined by observing the quality of the child's interactions with carefully developed classroom activities. The teacher develops activities to enable the child to approach materials, to explore them, and in time, to master them. Materials should also be organized to permit the exercise of previously developed skills and abilities. In this way the child is afforded the opportunity to develop new skills, while remaining in touch with experiences in which he already has expertise. For example, a 6-year-old who has been reading for a year may select a book to read that he mastered when he first learned to read. His return to the less difficult material serves to remind him concretely of his general competence in reading, as well as the particular achievement that was his when he originally mastered the book.

The teacher should permit this type of "regression" to occur, and it should form a part of the teacher's informal assessment information: How often and under what circumstances does the child return to an experience already mastered? What role does frustration with new skills play in this behavior? Is the child reminding himself of skills already acquired? Is the child unwilling to face a new challenge?

In examining child learning features the teacher must consider the relationship of readiness, exploration, practice, and mastery to the child's interaction with materials. The teacher uses informal assessment procedures of observation, planning (goal-setting), and activity selection related to individual program goals and record-keeping in order to monitor progress and change.

By carefully structuring classroom activities, the teacher can help individual children use already developed skills in order to explore and master new ones. As many classroom activities as possible should draw from a variety of skill areas and levels of difficulty. In this way several children can participate in the "same" activity, each taking from the experience what he is capable of and each having his particular learning features validated.

CURRICULUM AND INFORMAL ASSESSMENT

Materials, activities, teaching strategies, and goals comprise the elements that a teacher uses in constructing a curriculum. The purpose of the curriculum is to serve as a vehicle for the growth and development of skills in children and to provide experiences that expand the children's language, personal/social, reasoning, and motor skills. The broader the curriculum, the more opportunities the teacher has to provide options for individual children within the more general framework of group needs. *Breadth* of curriculum refers to the number of skill or interest areas in which activities can be developed. For example, most preschool or kindergarten classrooms contain the following activities: language arts, number skills, cooking, science, gross motor movement, music, creative dramatics, arts and crafts, carpentry, sand, and water. This series of activity areas enables the teacher to provide individual children with a wide spectrum of experiences.

Within each of the above areas specific activities can be developed. The number and kinds of skills that the teacher draws upon in these activities reflects the *depth* of the curriculum. Using a simple activity focus, such as growing a pot of chives, the teacher can organize activities that focus on language skills, fine motor skills, reasoning, and number skills, as well as elements of personal/social development. Flexibility in curriculum, which is essential for individualization, evolves from this type of potential for multiple activities.

Figure 2 illustrates the use of the chives growing activity with considerable depth across a wide number of curriculum areas. In pursuing this focus, the teacher might choose to extend the theme of growing things throughout the classroom for the period of time it takes the plant to go from seed to harvest. In the initial phases, building a planter, planting the seed, discussing germination, drawing pictures of the seed underground, and having children move their bodies as if they were newly opening seeds are potential activities. Several weeks later, after the first harvest of chives is made, a cooking activity might be included. In the interim, many of the

CURRICULUM AREA	ACTIVITIES
LANGUAGE SKILLS	Discuss jobs in caring for the plant; record growth and change in the plant; follow directions and steps in building the planter, planting the seed, watering, etc.; discuss other growing projects at home.
NUMBER SKILLS	Measure ingredients to make potting soil; count the number of seeds per pot; record the plant's growth.
COOKING	Collect recipes that include chives; talk about how chives are used in cooking; cook something using the chives grown.
SCIENCE	Discuss seeds, varying kinds, where they come from; bring seeds from home and display them, cut them open and talk about their parts; discuss germination, and the role of water, soil and light in growing; what is required for children to grow?
PERSONAL/SOCIAL	Share jobs; cooperate; be a leader and sometimes a follower; talk about how plants grow and change and the analogy to children.
GROSS MOTOR/ MOVEMENT	Be a seed germinating, a plant desiring water, a plant in the warm sun, a big bushy plant waving in the wind, and a tiny baby plant just coming up.
MUSIC	Make instruments using seeds for noise makers inside small boxes; choose differing rhythms to reflect the movement you have selected: robust for the bushy plant, quiet for the small plants, etc.
DRAMATICS	Create a play about seeds who are friends and who make a journey from inside a seed packet all the way to full-grown plants; let children make costumes and determine how plants should

CURRICULUM AREA	ACTIVITIES
DRAMATICS — *continued*	appear at various stages of change and growth.
ARTS/CRAFTS	Chart plant growth; build seeds and plants of clay; draw pictures of how the plant feels in the sun; make a book that tells the story of the play in pictures; draw pictures of all the things you eat that are made with chives.
CARPENTRY	Build a small box for seeds and larger boxes for plants.
SAND/WATER	Make the potting mixture;water the plants.

Figure 2. Growing chives. An example of curriculum depth.

other activities could be used with individual children or groups of children.

The chives activity stretches across a number of curriculum areas. It also presents multiple opportunities to individualize for different children. For example, in one classroom, a child who was involved in the initial activity of building a planter was also asked to be in charge of drawing a mural depicting the construction of the box, and the gathering of nails, hammer, seeds, and other necessary materials. This child, who enjoyed carpentry projects, had a speech impairment that made it difficult for other children to understand his expressive language. Nonetheless, his excitement at being a leader for a group project motivated him to make an extra effort to be understood. The other children involved in building the planter and drawing the mural shared his pleasure in the project and made a special effort to understand his directions. The group activity reinforced a behavioral objective for the speech-impaired child, namely, to practice articulation while working in small groups.

To be used effectively in informal assessment, an early childhood curriculum must present a broad range of activities and potential experiences that can be pursued at different levels, depending on the needs and abilities of individual children. The broader the curriculum, the more options the teacher can provide. The deeper the curriculum, the greater the number of abilities that can be focused on in a given curriculum area. However, teachers do not always have to devise special themes or activities in order to achieve curriculum breadth and depth. Regular classroom activities and materials can be used for informal assessment and individualized programming. Figure 3 lists a number of classroom materials and identifies some of the ways in which they may be used in informal assessment. As the teacher observes the child working with these materials and eventually making progress with them, the classroom becomes an ideal "observation booth."

Informal assessment in the classroom utilizes the planning, activities, behavioral objectives, and evaluations collected by the teacher. In short, informal assessment relies on the classroom curriculum. The more a teacher is able to develop a curriculum with breadth and depth, the more he will be able to use that curriculum to obtain baseline descriptive data, plan activities, and individualize within the regular classroom.

A MODEL FOR CLASSROOM INFORMAL ASSESSMENT

Classroom informal assessment has been defined as an ongoing process used to identify and address individual and group characteristics. Informal assessment has been shown to be facilitated by the teacher's view of herself as architect, observer, and evaluator of this process. In this chapter, this information is integrated into a cohesive model for classroom informal assessment. Of course, the model that is illustrated is not definitive, but, by its nature, informal assessment varies according to several classroom and teacher characteristics that are listed below. The usefulness of the model lies in its organization of the elements of informal assessment into a structure that allows the teacher to identify, plan, implement, and evaluate the educational needs of individual children.

A number of variables influence the use of this model by the classroom teacher:

1. *Child/Teacher Ratio*   A preschool or kindergarten classroom that has more than twenty children and only one teacher with no aides or assistants presents particular challenges and issues. It is possible for the teacher to utilize curriculum with multiple instructional objectives. However, a classroom with a child-teacher ratio of twenty or more to one may restrict the amount and complexity of individualized programming that can take place. Classroom informal assessment, with its emphasis on the needs of the individual within the group, should therefore be modified. In such a situation the teacher is advised to review the possibility of obtaining classroom assistance from sources such as parents, high school home economics students, senior citizens, college interns, and student teachers.

2. *Child-Directed Activities versus Teacher-Directed Activities*   A number of educational approaches are predicated on organizing the cur-

riculum to support the child as the initiator of activities. One example of such an approach is the open classroom. This chapter presents a view that is consistent with an approach that supports the child in his own selection and exploration of materials (Bussis and Chittenden, 1970). Nevertheless, the classroom teacher's conception of the way children learn and his comfort with child-directed activities bears heavily on the frequency and success of such activities. Other issues to consider include the ratio of children to teachers and the characteristics of a particular group of children. The more opportunities that exist for child-directed activities in a classroom, the better the fit of that classroom with the informal assessment model that is presented here.

3. *Organization of Classroom Space*   The manner in which a teacher chooses to organize the classroom is determined by a number of factors, including the age of the children and the number of children in the class, as well as the relationship perceived by the teacher between the organization of space and teaching. The manner in which the teacher organizes classroom space will influence the number of activities that can be self-initiated, the number of small group activities that can occur simultaneously, and the breadth of curriculum. The organization of space is a critical feature in informal assessment to the extent that these variables influence the quality and quantity of planning for individual and group goals.

4. *Group or Individual Focus*   Throughout this chapter the parameters of informal assessment are described as involving a dual focus: the group and the individual. As previously stated, a teacher working alone with 22 children will find a greater challenge in meeting their individual needs than a teacher who is aided by several assistants or working alone with only ten children. However, more than sheer numbers is at issue when one considers group versus individual needs. Teachers need not make a choice between "total" individualization or teaching to the mean, that is, teaching to the average abilities of the group. Rather, a compromise between these two extremes entails that the teacher views children as both uniquely different learners and members of a group. To the extent that the teacher keeps in mind developmental, cultural, and social continuities, as well as children's individual approaches to these continuities, the classroom focus will be balanced and appropriate.

5. *Class Population*   The model to be presented is appropriate for homogeneous or heterogeneous groupings of children — whether these groupings are based on age or educational need. Several of the variables discussed above should be considered with greater care in heterogeneous groupings simply because diversity poses different teaching challenges than homogeneity. A multitude of strategies are available to assist the teacher in an integrated or mainstreamed setting (see Gunnoe and

Figure 3. Examples of the use of regular classroom materials and activities for informal assessment.

Area of assessment	Materials/Activities	Observation features
Fine Motor Skills		
adaptive skills	cooking	How does child: -pour? -spread peanut butter? -mix batter?
	clay painting	-use and build? -grasp brush, combine elements?
hand preference	crayons scissors using tape getting dressed	-grasp -effectiveness -control -zippers -buttons
perceptual-motor	magic markers copy forms cubes color cubes	-control and representation -copy and trace forms -build and follow patterns -control; towers
motor planning	music games	-clap rhythms and imitate -body awareness in space

Area of assessment	Materials/Activities	Observation features
Gross Motor Skills		
movement	music stairs	-identifying body parts -using feet going up and down
self in space	big blocks	-climbing over and on -following instructions
body control	ball	-catching and throwing
Cognitive		
seriation	manipulatives, blocks	-order
classification	attribute blocks	-groupings
numbers	manipulatives	-counting groups of objects regardless of configuration
matching	classroom objects, lotto	-identifying shapes, sizes
sequencing	macaroni beads, color cubes	-following a pattern
initial consonant sounds	picture cards	-give sound before getting to hold card
rhythm and beat	music	-clap to music and get beat
ability to follow directions	clean-up	-follow two- and three-part instructions

Meisels, 1978). However, the use of informal assessment procedures is important whether the group is labeled homogeneous or heterogeneous, for each child varies developmentally from another.

The model of classroom informal assessment that is detailed here includes seven elements, all of which assist in the development of individual child programs:

1. Behavioral objectives (goals)
2. Baseline descriptive data (assessment)
3. Outcome objectives
4. Activities
5. Record-keeping procedures
6 Evaluation
7. Next steps

These elements serve two purposes. First, they help the teacher organize information necessary to the informal assessment process. Second, each element addresses a particular content area within the assessment process.

Goals and behavioral objectives are established by the teacher at the outset of the informal assessment process. Initially, goals may be stated in summary terms, such as personal/social, cognitive, or motor. Specificity is obtained when the goal set by the teacher is described in behavioral terms. Several objectives that were utilized in a mainstreamed early childhood program are outlined below (see Meisels, 1978a). In order to establish behavioral objectives such as these, the teacher must carefully identify the skill area within which there is concern, as well as the specific aspect of the skill area that is at issue for a particular child. For example, it is useful to be able to say that a particular child must improve his personal/social skills, but the classroom teacher will only be able to plan activities if a goal is specified and is related directly to classroom behaviors. Such a specific goal would be to help a child "express anger verbally and not hit children." The outline of behavioral objectives provides an illustration of the logical progression of objectives, from global to general to more specific. Although it only contains a limited selection of potential objectives, it gives a clear indication of the range of objectives that are possible to establish with a group of young children.

Examples of behavioral objectives.

I.   *Personal/Social*
    A.   To accomplish successful separation.
        1.   To separate from parent and become involved in classroom activities.
        2.   To separate from parent and express appropriate feelings.

3. To separate from parent and become able to play with other children.
4. To help a child transfer physical dependency on parent to attachment to teacher.
5. To help a child feel confidence when separated from parent.

B. To establish positive relationships with adults.
1. To encourage a child to say "hello" upon entering classroom at beginning of the day.
2. To encourage a child to speak to adults during classtime.

C. To increase positive interactions with peers.
1. To help a child acquire a friend by playing with other children in the classroom.
2. To help a child feel comfortable in a group setting.
3. To assist a child in developing role flexibility in relationships.
4. To help a child learn to talk directly to another child, without using an adult or nonhuman (doll) intermediary.
5. To teach a child to display appropriate affect with peers.
6. To enable a child to share people with whom he has relationships.
7. To help a child with speech limitations make a friend.

D. To acquire skills for appropriate resolution of peer conflicts.
1. To help a child listen to another child's concerns without resorting to tantrum behavior.
2. To enable a child to use words, rather than tears, to resolve conflicts.

E. To develop the ability to express one's feelings.
1. To learn to express anger verbally, eliminating inappropriate affect.
2. To encourage an impassive child to express verbally appropriate anger.
3. To encourage the verbal expression of feelings and concerns about sharing.
4. To enable a child to express feelings spontaneously.
5. To improve a child's vocabulary and repertoire of feeling-oriented experiences.
6. To encourage the use of specific materials as creative media, rather than as objects of aggression.

F. To improve ability to make transitions and follow classroom routines.
1. To help a child accomplish successful classroom transitions.

       2.   To help a child accept and utilize outdoor time.

       3.   To help a child anticipate and accept end-of-school departure without tears and fighting.

  G. To cope with crises outside of school.

       1.   To help a child deal with the birth of a sibling.

       2.   To help a child cope with death.

  H. To increase impulse control and the ability to accept limits.

       1.   To help a child inhibit his impulses to flee physically from adult when in the midst of conflict.

II. *Cognitive*

  A. To increase exploration and mastery of a broad repertoire of curriculum experiénces.

       1.   To help a child utilize fantasy play in order to deal with family/social interactions.

       2.   To engage a child in active scientific investigation.

       3.   To involve a child in sand activities for simple exploration and purposeful play.

       4.   To involve a child in "messy" curriculum experience.

       5.   To involve a child with areas and materials that he usually avoids.

  B. To improve prereading and early reading skills.

       1.   To acquire identity of "a reader."

       2.   To improve overall auditory discrimination.

       3.   To improve a child's understanding and use of story sequence.

  C. To improve visual memory and visual discrimination.

       1.   To learn to discriminate and label, as "big" or "small," objects of different size.

       2.   To learn to discriminate among colors.

  D. To increase the ability to attend.

       1.   To have a child remain at an activity for 3–5 minutes.

       2.   To help a child stay and participate at a large group activity for several minutes, maintaining eye contact with teacher.

III. *Motor*

  A. To stimulate gross motor development.

       1.   To foster mastery of gross motor skills by decreasing timidity and increasing involvement.

       2.   To teach a child to jump from a low step, remaining upright on both feet.

  B. To improve fine motor abilities.

       1.   To help a child feel competence and comfort with fine motor tasks.

2. To teach a child to hold and use scissors.
3. To teach a child who cannot stand unsupported how to use a hammer.
4. To help a child successfully trace over letters in name.

Behavioral objectives are most accurately and appropriately formulated when the teacher carefully monitors the child's behavior for a period of time and then organizes these observations into baseline descriptive data about the child. This information, such as the case study of Vickie, assist the teacher in her planning.

CASE STUDY: VICKIE

> *Assessment*   Vickie, small for her age (5-years-old, developmental delay), seldom climbs ladders or stairs. She stands passively watching the other children act out the song, "Jump to M'Lou." Although general motor activity (walking, stair climbing) is smooth, she still single steps when climbing up and down stairs, unsure of her body management. She does not experiment with her body and is generally constricted in her movements.

The teacher kept a log over several weeks to acquire this information. Such an anecdotal record includes behaviors under scrutiny (gross motor), as well as other behaviors considered important (e.g., activity on playground, possible vision problems, fine motor problems, etc.).

After noting the baseline descriptive data or assessment about the child, the teacher is then prepared to set outcome objectives for the child's individualized program. Outcome objectives are specific behavioral statements that state the specific goals of individualization. In Vickie's case, the teacher translated her assessment of Vickie's gross motor development into concise objectives:

> *Outcome Objectives*
> 1. Vickie will increase her gross motor attempts and general gross motor involvement: jumping up and down, falling down, turning around, and balancing.
> 2. She will learn to alternate feet while climbing stairs.
> 3. She will learn to climb ladders.

The teacher's next step is the integration of these outcome objectives into a series of activities that are either a part of the daily classroom repertoire or are specially designed to meet Vickie's needs. In the activities listed below, Vickie's teacher has combined teacher-directed activities (1) and activities especially designed for Vickie (2), as well as activities that involve Vickie with materials her other classmates will be using (2, 4, 5):

Activities
1. Present "railroad track" equipment on both horizontal and vertical levels. Also use large boards and blocks as walking boards and bridges — a "train" or "bus"
2. Start song "Jump down, turn around" during music time to encourage jumping off step and turning around.
3. Suggest many body movements: e.g., "Hop to M'Lou."
4. Place alluring dramatic play equipment, such as magnets at end of fishing lines, baskets on ropes for hauling objects up and down, etc., on both high climbing structures in the room.
5. When outdoors, encourage running in ballgames, climbing on fire engine, or swinging on tire swing with special friend.

The plan developed for a child should be implemented within a specific time span. During the period of individualization the teacher should record progress and change. Vickie's teacher developed an anecdotal record-keeping system to which aides, teachers, and others who worked with Vickie contributed. Such a system presents a quick and useful way to collect information essential in monitoring the progress of a child, such as Vickie.

A summary of the anecdotal report follows:

Record Keeping
Record actual amount of time spent in gross motor activity. Briefly describe its nature. (See Figure 4.)

Evaluation of the progress made in an individualized program of activities may rely on the record keeping throughout the period that selected activities are implemented. On the other hand, a test-retest situation may be used to enable the teacher to judge change. Additional information indirectly related to the behavioral objectives, but considered important reflections of change, may be included in the evaluation. Such information is demonstrated in Vickie's case as follows:

Evaluation
1. Vickie seems to be showing signs of becoming more experimental — more relaxed around music time.
2. She has shown an interest in using large boards and blocks.
3. Quantity and quality of gross motor involvement seem to be increasing as weeks progressed — 40–65 minutes.
4. Does not alternate feet on climbing. Still frequently awkward and stiff— needs continued encouragement and teacher support.
5. Has not attempted ladder climbing.
6. Has ignored railroad structure in favor of build-it-herself project with friend.

Based on the evaluation, the teacher should begin to develop the next steps to be taken in planning for a given child. Perhaps the goals that were

Figure 4. Record of Vickie's gross motor activities.

Day		Type of Gross Motor Activity	Duration	Success/failure — brief qualitative description
Mon	1.	Climbing on large equipment-stairs.	10 min.	Ascent and descent became smoother.
	2.	Rearranging large blocks and boards, climbing.	20 min.	V. negotiated the complex board and block structure — she and friend constructed a "bus" with only one fall and a few stumbles. Passive — little body motion.
Wed	1.	Play on large blocks and boards.	25 min.	Good control of large materials — no falls, two stumbles.
	2.	Music movement.	10 min.	Practiced jumping, falling down, turned around awkwardly.
	3.	Played ball-roll outdoors.	5 min.	Movements jerky and uncertain-almost toddler-like, fingers straight out.
	4.	Climbs on fire engine.	20 min.	Hampered by dramatic play equipment — purse, hat falling off.
Fri.	1.	Large blocks.	25 min.	No stumbling.
	2.	Large equipment "fishing."	10 min.	Does not alternate feet, but smoother.
	3.	Fire engine.	20 min.	Puts handbag down and negotiates well.
	4.	Tire swing.	10 min.	Slightly more body motion?

set were not realistic, or only a portion of the plan has been realized and other issues now need to be addressed. Next steps for Vickie include:

1. Use large board and block building in planning and as objectives.
2. Have adult dramatic play equipment available while Vickie is climbing or involved in gross motor activities so her hands and feet are unencumbered by handbag and dress.

The use of classroom materials and activities as tools in various stages of the informal assessment process is well-illustrated in the following case. In addition to the elements already introduced, other features to note include the teacher's use of multiple record-keeping methods and the extension of the individualized plan through several phases. The child in this case, Lou, is a 6-year-old boy with aphasia who has been mainstreamed into an open classroom setting containing 4- and 5-year olds.

CASE STUDY: LOU

Phase I

Goal   Cognitive

Behavioral Objective   To acquire skills of group participation.

Assessment   Lou always leaves a large group activity and wanders around the room. In particular, he:

1. Hides outside when it is time to join a large group activity
2. Extends eating snack to avoid going to a large group activity
3. Hides in the room
4. Does not watch the teacher when at the large group
5. Touches other children
6. Does not participate in any of the group activity
7. Pulls out accessible materials and plays with them
8. Leaves the group
9. Goes to the bathroom to avoid being at group
10. Gives no eye contact to adults while at large group activity

Outcome objectives:
1. Lou will stay at a large group activity for two minutes.
2. He will actively participate in the group for that two minutes.
3. He will have eye contact with the teacher who is leading the large group activity.

Approximate time period   Three weeks. Re-evaluate progress at end of this period and if successful go on to Phase II.

Activities
1. Warn Lou that a large group activity is about to happen, e.g., "Look, Lou, see the children coming to story," or direct his eyes in that direction and indicate this to him.
2. Have the same adult warn Lou and take him to the large group.
3. Have the adult set up a routine of actually getting to the group, e.g., "Let's jump to story," and hold his hand and demonstrate jumping.
4. Have him sit in the lap of the special adult.
5. Have a child who he likes sit next to him.
6. Have a theme song to start the large group activity, or have the same record on every time the large group meets.
7. Have Lou leave after two minutes to have a story by himself with an adult. Make sure all the children are told where he is going, e.g., "Lou has a hard time listening to story so he is going to have a little story with Joe."
8. Have Lou's tutor demonstrate how to follow a story, e.g., she sits in a chair and demonstrates how a book is held and how the pages are turned. She also demonstrates how to follow a story, e.g., have Lou watch two children doing it.
9. Have other children actively involved in getting him over to the group, e.g., "Let's go and jump with Lou to story." "Let's help Lou come to story by singing his favorite song."
10. Reinforce the two-minute stay with lavish praise, e.g., with smiles and words, "Lou you did stay well!"

Record-Keeping Procedures
1. Team meeting to evaluate the two-minute stay; how it went and how it could be improved.
2. Anecdotal records, e.g., a record of the day Lou stood up and directed the singing of "Going to the zoo, zoo."
3. Meet with his tutor and coordinate activities and keep both sides up to date with progress.
4. Have a neutral observer watch the two-minute stay over the three weeks to see if there is marked progress or not.
5. Have a checklist to evaluate the three-week period.

day	time stayed	comments
Wednesday	1½ minutes	not held in lap so left

Evaluation
1. At the end of three weeks Lou stayed at a large group activity for two minutes.
2. He wanted to stay longer at the activity and started to object when he was taken to story by himself.
3. He came more willingly when it was fun to get there or when some children jumped along with him.
4. The theme song acted as a stimulus and he started to come over automatically.

5. He learned the words of the song. (Unfortunately, he perseverated in this and sang this song through any other song that the rest of the class sang.)
6. The other children actively sought him out to make sure he came.
7. No eye contact with teacher yet.

Next steps
1. Make sure that the tempo is swinging so he has no chance to wander from the activity.
2. Start a new plan aimed at having him at story or large group time for four minutes.

Phase II

Behavioral objective   To acquire the skills of group participation.

Assessment: Lou can stay at a large group activity for two minutes, but he leaves the group after that time and is unable to stay longer. In particular:
1. See the list of observable behaviors recorded in Phase I.
2. He now leaves the group to have a story with an adult after two minutes.

Outcome objectives
1. Lou will stay at the large group activity for five minutes.
2. He will actively participate in the activity.
3. He will have eye contact with the teacher leading the group.
4. He will want to stay longer.

Approximate time period   Three weeks. Re-assess after three weeks and adjust if necessary.

Activities
1. Repeat the activities of Phase I.
2. Add a second theme song so that there is a lengthened time of familiarity with the activity, e.g., "Itsy bitsy spider" so Lou can also involve his body.
3. Have Lou perform the actions so he is partially released from the adult's lap and he experiences a limited amount of freedom.
4. Have the storybook or musical instrument right in front of his nose so he knows what is coming next.
5. Start the activity by purposely attracting his attention, e.g., clap hands or blow a whistle as a cue that the activity is about to begin.
6. Have Lou "play" at watching a book read or an instrument being played. Have him do this by himself so there are no distractions.
7. Toward the end of the three weeks, introduce new variations to the two theme songs so it can introduce a gradual variety into the routine, e.g.:
   a) show pictures of zoo animals as you sing
   b) bring a spider to the activity
   c) make spiders and use them as "itsy bitsy" props
   d) puppets
   e) change the words to "itsy bitsy crocodile went up the water spout"
   (A tribute has to be made to the other children who sang the two songs for six weeks nonstop with a minimum of complaint!)

Record-Keeping Procedures   Record-keeping procedures are the same as in Phase I.

Evaluation
1. Lou stayed for five minutes provided that the activity was well-planned and moved along quickly.
2. He became used to the cue that a new activity was about to begin.
3. He learned the words of the second song.
4. He started to use his body and watch what the teacher was doing so that he could copy.
5. Sometimes he wanted to stay longer, sometimes he did not.
6. The introduction of new ways of doing the two songs led to a problem of Lou refusing to sing unless we sang about kangaroos.

Next steps
1. Evaluate progress.
2. Introduce more new materials until the theme songs are not needed.
3. Have Lou leave adult and sit by himself, e.g., on his own cushion.

This example illustrates each of the elements that have been noted in this chapter as critical to successful informal assessment and educational planning. In the generic sense, screening occurs as the classroom teacher observes and records behaviors of concern to her. In setting an outcome objective and developing classroom strategies for achieving that objective, the teacher has attempted to design a classroom experience that conforms to both her expectations and the child's learning style. The teacher has designed the child's program to encourage him to initiate appropriate behaviors with minimal teacher direction (e.g., upon hearing the meeting time "theme song" the child will bring himself to the circle), and the teacher has also included a number of teacher-directed strategies to assist the child in becoming more self-directed (e.g., demonstrate how to follow a story, limit initial time with group, etc.). Throughout her individual planning the teacher uses a variety of record-keeping procedures to monitor and evaluate the child's progress. Thus, by carefully planning the child's program, the teacher functions as architect of the classroom experience, rather than as a respondent to unanticipated events. Time spent in planning has not only benefited the child and the classroom as a whole, but it has been fundamental to the implementation of an adaptive, individualized educational plan.

SUMMARY

Informal classroom assessment is a critical element in the development of a child's individualized educational plan and is often a beginning point in the comprehensive evaluation of children with special needs. It is a process that is influenced by the way the teacher defines his role in the classroom, by the degree to which the child's learning features are understood, and by characteristics of the classroom curriculum.

The teacher who views herself as the architect of a curriculum, with sufficient breadth and depth to meet individual and group needs and whose classroom relies heavily on child-initiated activities, will find informal assessment, as described in this chapter, a systemization of much that already occurs in that class. This approach requires time from the teacher and close attention to detail. However, the majority of the time that is required is planning time — time to sift through observed behaviors and relate them to displayed strengths and weaknesses, time to correlate those strengths and weaknesses with classroom curriculum, and time to develop strategies for evaluating progress. The model that is illustrated utilizes a documentation format that facilitates this planning process and has the potential for enhancing the quality of each child's educational experience.

ACKNOWLEDGMENTS

The teachers at the Eliot-Pearson Children's School, especially Ann Handman, Martha Keller, and Florence Longhorn, provided me with valuable examples of classroom activities. I am grateful for their assistance. Figure 3 and the outline of examples of behavioral objectives were derived from material developed by Project LINC (Learning in Integrated Classrooms), Eliot-Pearson Children's School, Tufts University.

REFERENCES

Bussis, A. M. and Chittenden, E. A. 1970. Analysis of an Approach to Open Education. Educational Testing Service, Princeton, N.J.

Erikson, E. 1963. Childhood and Society. W. W. Norton & Company, Inc., New York.

Gesell, A., et al. 1940. The First Five Years of Life. Harper & Row Publishers, New York.

Gunnoe, L. W., and Meisels, S. J. 1978. Mainstream Challenges: A Manual for Early Childhood Educators. Project LINC Outreach, Tufts University, Medford, Mass.

Meisels, S. J. 1978a. Open education and the integration of children with special needs. In: M. J. Guralnick (ed.), Early Intervention and the Integration of Handicapped and Nonhandicapped Children. University Park Press, Baltimore.

Meisels, S. J. 1978b. Developmental Screening in Early Childhood: A Guide. National Association for the Education of Young Children, Washington, D.C.

Piaget, J. 1951. Play, Dreams, and Imitation in Childhood. W. W. Norton & Company, Inc., New York.

Piaget, J. 1952. The Origins of Intelligence in Children. International Universities Press, New York.

Werner, H. 1948. Comparative Psychology of Mental Development. Follett Publishing Company, Chicago.

White, R. W. 1959. Motivation reconsidered: The concept of competence. Psychol. Rev. 66:297–333.

Developmentally Oriented Classrooms

Some Observations on the Integration of Handicapped Children in British Primary Schools

Murray Levine

In the United States, a combination of legislation, litigation, and professional rethinking of the value of special and segregated programs versus normalized programs for the handicapped has renewed interest in the problems of maintaining children with special needs in regular classes (Blatt, 1976; Pitt, 1976). Analogous considerations faced local educational authorities in Great Britain after Parliament passed *The Education (Handicapped Children) Act* in 1970, making the education of handicapped children the responsibility of local education authorities. In at least one local education authority in England, Oxfordshire, policy was established to maintain all children with special needs (the retarded, the emotionally disturbed, and children with other handicapping conditions) in regular classrooms, as much as possible. Financial considerations may have been involved in that decision, but Oxfordshire was also very proud of its primary school system. The Plowden report (Central Advisory Council for Education, 1967) called world-wide attention to the child-centered philosophy and open education practices of many of England's post World War II primary schools. The Plowden report suggested that since normal children seemed to be thriving in open education programs, such school programs should be adaptable for the handicapped.

In anticipation of problems of implementation subsequent to the 1970 Education Act, a committee was established in Oxfordshire to consider methods for implementation. The committee originally proposed a special class program, using child-centered methods, and implemented that proposal on a trial basis in one school. The experiment failed

This report was prepared while the author held an NIMH Special Post-Doctoral Fellowship (1F22 MH 00111-01) during the academic year 1974–1975.

miserably, but in order to salvage the children, the suffering teacher, and the experimental program, the headmaster of the pilot school distributed the special children to his regular classrooms, at first on a part-time basis and then full-time. This initial experiment worked out very well. Many of the children's problems disappeared as they were normalized, according to folklore that came across the Atlantic. The school district adopted mainstreaming, although not by that name, as its strategy for educating handicapped children.

I had been conducting research, in collaboration with my colleague Richard Salzer and a group of students, on problems of emotional disturbance in traditional and open classrooms in the Buffalo area. I had seen a number of excellent programs in our area, and our research was producing intriguing findings. Coming from a background in community psychology (Sarason et al., 1966) I was interested in the potential of differences in classroom practice and in social atmosphere for either producing or preventing problem behavior. To put it simply, my theory is that a problem child is a problem because there are inadequate solutions for that child's difference within the normative structure of a given classroom. If the range of permissible behaviors were enlarged, then the child's difference, within broad limits, would present less of a problem to the teacher, to other children, and to himself.

About this time, I had the good fortune to meet Mr. John Coe, then head advisor in the Oxfordshire system, and Mr. Francis Backhouse, Headmaster of the Longfields School, where the original experiment had taken place. Both men impressed me greatly because of the feelings for children that each projected and because of the exciting educational programs that they described. When I had the opportunity for a sabbatical leave, I decided to spend the 1974–1975 school year in Oxfordshire, studying the adjustment of children in the Oxfordshire primary schools.

This chapter describes some characteristics of classroom organization that support the integration of children with special needs within the normal classroom setting. Emphasis is on observations in the classrooms that follow the modern British primary approach, variously called open education, child-centered philosophy, or the integrated day. There are probably as many variants of the approach as there are teachers (Bennett and Jordan, 1975), but most have several features in common, whether the classes take place in large open areas or in smaller, self-contained classrooms.

THE BRITISH PRIMARY SCHOOL

The British primary school has been so well described that it would be superfluous to attempt to repeat it here. In general, in the classrooms that

I observed, the rooms were usually richly endowed with a variety of materials, and often the display of children's work was beautiful and visually exciting. The classrooms typically allowed a large measure of freedom of choice for the children. Usually, there were multiple activities taking place. Sometimes the activities were widely varied, and sometimes it was variation on a common theme (e.g., different kinds of work in mathematics, or choice in a project topic and how the topic was to be developed). In many of the classrooms, children were allowed to speak to each other most of the time. Similarly, children were free to move about as they wished. Although the crowded physical arrangements of desks limited free movement in some of the rooms, children did not have to sit at their desks all day. Many of the schools incorporated two or more grade levels within the same classroom. In one school, children from ages four to eleven were integrated into the same group under the same team of teachers, and in another school, the group ranged from ages seven to eleven.

I emphasize these particular features of the classroom because these are the elements that make it possible to integrate children who have a wide variety of educational and personal needs into the same classroom. The variety of ages and activities, the possibilities for movement and choice, and the materials necessary to support a wide variety of activities help to create a situation in which varied ways of being are normatively acceptable in the same classroom. In this chapter I describe how these characteristics of classroom organization, along with the attitudes fostered by the classroom teacher, support the special child in the normal classroom.

METHOD

These observations were made in 70 classrooms in 14 schools. I spent one to three days in each school. All were normal classrooms. The schools ranged from a large suburban institution with more than 600 children to a one-room, village school with two teachers and about 60 children. A few of the schools served areas with a fair proportion of working-class children who lived in nearby public housing. I did not visit any urban schools or schools with any sizable number of children of nonwhite immigrants. I visited the classrooms of teachers who voluntarily accepted me. Not all teachers let me visit. I had a research protocol, which I followed from the beginning. This protocol required me to make specific observations in order to classify the classroom. I spent additional time observing children who were either emotionally disturbed and under treatment or who were retarded. In a few instances, I observed children who were physically handicapped as well. I took extensive notes for periods as long as forty minutes, trying to describe the special child's behavior in as much detail as possible. In addition to my observations (which I shall report here in the first person to emphasize their subjective nature), Ms. Susan Stalbow, an Oxford undergraduate, undertook systematic observations in one school of 14 children who had been identified as having special educational needs. She compared their behavior with 14 normal children matched for age and sex in the same classrooms. Pertinent observations and findings from her study are reported here.

THE INDIVIDUALIZATION OF INSTRUCTION

If there is any feature that makes it difficult to integrate children with special needs into the ordinary classroom, it is the tendency to teach to the average children, losing the slow children and boring the brighter ones. In contrast, modern British methods of primary education emphasize a form of classroom organization in which individual instruction is not only possible, but is an integral part of the program. Many classrooms have more than one age level within them. A few, designated as vertically grouped classes, have children ranging over the full span of the primary years, from infants, children who are 4 years old, to upper juniors, who are 11 years old. The varied age ranges make it necessary for a teacher to program for different developmental levels and for individual differences in aptitudes and personality.

VARIED TASKS AND MATERIALS

Even when all the children in a classroom are directed to work on their math, there are often three or four groups working in different levels of workbooks. Because most classrooms emphasize an individual pace of work, the children work on different pages in the workbook. Moreover, the math program in use is varied in its approaches. In any single math period, it is possible for children to work at an abstract symbolic level or to shift to more concrete tasks, using games and puzzles to illustrate fractions, to use counting objects (pine cones, coins, spools of thread, etc.), to measure aspects of the environment (walls, playground dimensions) with string, hands, bricks, rules, or trundle wheels, or to use scales to weigh various objects. The math program calls for such activity, and most classrooms seem well supplied with the necessary materials. It is possible for the teacher to find or to allow the children to find a math activity in which they can be successful, and hopefully learn and progress. Since children of different ages and different sizes are in the same room, and since they are constantly moving about or regrouping, a larger, older child working on easier work is not conspicuous. There is a place for such a child and there is work for the older child to do, which is normal for that classroom.

Individual Standards of Accomplishment

Individualization can be observed in many other aspects of the program as well. Even if all children are doing the same kind of work (e.g., listening to a BBC broadcast and then writing a story or poem about it), the products may vary in length, complexity, felicity of expression, and neatness of handwriting. My impression is that teachers have individual norms for children. They tend to respond to the effort, rather than to the product. That does not mean teachers accept any work at all. On the contrary, I observed numerous instances in which teachers required children to repeat an assignment or to improve it in some aspect. On occasion I observed a teacher harshly criticizing a child's work and calling it "rubbish," but that was said to a bright child who was capable of doing much more.

Individualization took many forms. For example, I observed one child copying material directly from a book for a project. When I asked the teacher about it, he said that he was satisfied that the child was working at all and that the child would have a project book comparable to the others. The teacher said that he would not accept copying from another child of greater ability. Another teacher told me that she would deliberately demand more of a brighter child in order that the child understand that effort was necessary for accomplishment. Still another teacher, who described the same practice, said that he wanted his brighter children to understand that things could be difficult, therefore the brighter child would have a way of empathizing with the duller child. If it becomes noticeable that one child is less able than another in some sphere of activity, several teachers told me that they will deliberately point out to the class that each person is different, that some are more able in some tasks than others, and that's the way it is. The teacher conveys by manner, by action, and by word that different levels of production are acceptable and that the lesser performance is not to be treated with contempt.

Lack of Competitiveness

Classroom organization is such that children do not readily become aware of each other's failures. In many classrooms, the children bring their work to the teacher to show they have completed it or to ask for assistance if they are unable to do the work. The vast bulk of contacts between teacher and child are brief and individual. Few papers receive a formal letter or number grade. The teacher generally makes a tic mark next to a workbook item to show right or wrong. In general, the children do not recite publicly. I observed very few whole-class lessons. Fifty percent of the teachers told me that they spent less than ten percent of class time in whole-class teaching. Evaluation then is limited. It tends to be task oriented, and almost always private, rather than public. Although praise was not lavish, it far exceeded negative comments.

As an American observer, I was struck by the apparent lack of overt competitiveness among the children. On numerous occasions, I was surprised to see children point to a child and say that he is the best artist in the class or to hear a child state that he was the best in math without having other children criticize or dispute the statement or reveal any sign of jealousy. I asked children who were working side by side at different levels in the same math series, or in some other identifiable series, why they were working in different books. Invariably the children would tell me that one series was more advanced than the other, but, with one exception, I never heard a child tell another that it meant that one was smarter or dumber than the other. It was always a statement of fact, rather than a competitive comparison with an implication of superior and inferior.

By and large teachers agreed with these observations when I called them to their attention. When I asked what they did to produce a noncompetitive atmosphere, most had to stop and think. The response to the unexpected question was that they seemed to do it naturally. It evidently represents not only an educational practice, but it may also represent a cultural characteristic that differentiates British and Americans to some degree. Perhaps the competitiveness is more muted. However, teachers, nearly uniformly, told me that other children were very kind to those who were less capable, and rarely were the less capable teased on that score. An obese child who could not tumble during the physical education period, and whose difficulty became obvious, would be more likely to be the butt of derisive laughter than an intellectually slow child. It is my belief that the noncompetitive atmosphere is a critical factor in allowing teachers to cater to individual differences, making it possible to have special children tolerated, if not totally accepted, in the normal environment.

Curricular Freedom

I have already mentioned that the age-grading system contributes to the acceptance of individual standards of performance. For historical reasons (Levine, 1976) year by year achievement tests have never been as important in British schools, as they are in American schools. The curriculum is also extremely varied, school by school. The curriculum is the responsibility of the headmaster. It is often established by consultation with the teachers and the headmaster, but each teacher is given considerable leeway in implementing the curriculum. In general, teachers have age-norms in mind, and have general expectations for children at given age levels, but there does not seem to be any expectation that all children will necessarily master some predesignated level in math or reading. Teachers want as many children as possible to accomplish as much as possible, but I never received the impression that a teacher would judge his own work by the number of children who attained grade-level performance, nor did I receive the impression that teachers were so judged by headmasters.

It seemed to me that the absence of an externally defined standard for each age-grade level allowed the teacher to think in terms of individualized standards. I never encountered the universalistic-particularistic argument: if I let Johnny do that, everyone would want to do it. Individualized standards seem to be very much a part of the thinking of teachers. Whenever I asked how the teacher thought about such matters, the reply came quickly and frequently in the same words — "the child's own best standard" was what the teacher aimed for.

Summary

The emphasis in education on variability in methods of instruction, the cultural muting of overt competitiveness, the emphasis on the individual's own best standard, and the blurring of age-grade lines in the junior and infant schools, all seem to contribute importantly to the possibilities of maintaining special children in the normal classroom situation. There are a great many structural supports for individualizing instruction, even to the level of children with special educational needs. I think it is because of that background that I heard few intensive complaints about slower children in the normal classroom. I never heard any teacher refer to slower children as burdens to the normal classroom. The variations in ability provided a more complex task for the teacher, but it was never expressed as unfair or impossible, at least not to me. Teachers with very large classes said it was difficult for them to work with special children, who required time and attention, but their complaints were focused on class size and were not directed against the idea of individualizing instruction. The attitudes toward individualization described above must be kept in mind when thinking about the possibilities of adapting a program from one cultural context to another.

THE INTEGRATION OF SPECIAL CHILDREN INTO NORMAL CLASSROOMS

No one can expect children of lower intellectual abilities to function at the same level of accomplishment as children with higher measured intelligence. However, we can expect that the classroom provides opportunity for accomplishment appropriate to the child's level of development. Almost every child should be able to find a meaningful place within the social order of the classroom. Finding acceptance among other children and having the opportunity for normal social intercourse ought to be among the important goals of any program integrating special children into the normal setting.

The Division of Labor

The following observations were made on a girl about 10 years old, with a reading age of six and a half, barely a beginning reader. The children were working on Road Safety Week projects:

> Elisha is in the library corner with another girl, conversing. Her friend goes over to talk to the teacher. Elisha remains in the library corner flipping through the pages of a book. She then leaves the room for a few minutes. Upon her return, she walks across the room, waits to speak to the teacher, then goes back to the library corner, and gets a book. She talks to her friend, while holding the book. Both children walk back to two tables, which are side by side. After a few moments, the friend gets up and walks elsewhere. Elisha looks in her desk for something, then goes over to another table to talk to a boy about his colored pencils. Another boy joins in the conversation. After a few moments Elisha turns away and looks at what several other children are doing at a nearby table. She goes back and talks to the boy about his pencils again. Her friend and several other children are taking paper off a large roll. Elisha helps in tearing the paper off the roll, takes her piece, and goes back to her place. Her friend takes the paper and begins to draw. Elisha goes to the art corner, gets a paint tray, and carefully puts in the powders to make paint. Her friend comes over, and they seem to be consulting about the paints. While Elisha replaces the cans of powder on the shelf, her friend adds water to the powders they have selected. Elisha chats with another child for a while, and then she and her friend pick up some newspapers and carefully lay them out over a table. Before they begin to paint, the two girls take a drawing that the second girl has made to the teacher. The teacher makes some suggestion about the lettering and the composition of the work and the girls go back to modify the poster before they begin painting.

While at first it seemed that Elisha was wandering about the room aimlessly, it soon became apparent that she had teamed up with another girl, and the two children had worked out a division of labor that allowed Elisha to participate in the project. When the two children took the poster to the teacher for correction, it was apparent that the work was presented as that of a cooperating team. Elisha did what she could in the project and was able to share in the completion of a product acceptable in the classroom. We have seen other examples in which a slower child with drawing skills illustrated a project book, while a child with greater conceptual skills did the reading and writing. Stalbow (1975) observed a child who was busily coloring in the border of a complex drawing made by another child. From a social viewpoint, the norms of the class, which encourage children to work together, allow children to work out such a division of labor.

Children Helping Each Other Is Not Cheating

In most classrooms, children can help each other and are encouraged to do so. It is not considered cheating when children work together. The norms allowing cooperation help the child who received assistance to do the work, without making any demand on the teacher. At the same time, the child who gives assistance participates in a responsible and generous social activity. Both children benefit.

The following observation was made of a child who was believed to be somewhat retarded. He started school at a young age, was kept in infant school for an additional year, and was now in a lower junior class. The group had a math assignment, and most children in the room were doing math.

> The boy sitting beside Tom is showing him what to do. He explains carefully and leans over to write something in Tom's book. Tom looks over at the other boy's workbook, while the other boy continues to explain the problem to him. Tom turns back to his own workbook and writes out a problem on a separate sheet of paper. He is working carefully and attentively. The two boys converse about the problems from time to time. Tom's tutor tells him to do a problem and is about to give him the answer. Tom says he wants to work it out for himself. Tom gets up, gets the unifix cubes (a counting aid), and works with them. He continues to work steadily on the problems, using the unifix cubes, for about twenty minutes.

In that instance, Tom worked steadily and had the self-confidence and sense of independence to try to work things out for himself. He did not become overly dependent on his partner. A more dependent child can find that others are *too* willing to help, perpetuating dependence and uncertainty. The following observation was made on a child of borderline intellectual ability.

> Gail is sitting alone at the far side of a table. She is rocking on her chair. Another child approaches her for a moment and then leaves. Gail seems to be watching the observer very intently. Still rocking in her chair, she turns back to her work, talking softly to herself. Still rocking in her chair, she stops working and talks to the two boys sitting across the table from her. She looks back at her work and starts rocking again. One of the boys turns to her and explains what is to be done. She listens, rocks again, and then writes something in her book. Still rocking, she bites her pencil, bites her finger, and then turns back and works at her book for a while. She asks one of the boys for help. He says no, and she talks to him, while rocking. After a while, she gets up, watches what others are doing at an easel, and starts talking to the chil-

dren who are painting. One of the girls who was painting goes back to her desk with her. The girl explains the work to Gail, and then goes back to painting. Gail does the work, sporadically, rocking in her chair all the while.

At the end of the twenty minute observation period, I went over to speak to Gail. At first, I had the impression the work was too difficult for her. I quickly discovered that she was fully capable of doing the coding exercise. She did a number of items correctly, while I was watching, although each time she acted as if she was unsure, and she looked at me to give her cues. When I asked her to work it out herself, she did.

This example suggests that some children may take advantage of the opportunity to receive help, and since other, more capable children are usually willing to assist, the child may learn only to rely on others. A teacher has to be sensitive to the problem and work with that child and with others in the class to limit the assistance to a useful minimum. A teacher can, as this one did, instruct other children to explain the task only, but not to do the task for the more dependent child.

Absorbing Restlessness

The rules in most of the classrooms that we visited allowed all children to move about the room freely, to talk to others, and to vary the activity. The freedom of movement allows some children to discharge a restlessness that would otherwise become disruptive and would require some effort on the part of the teacher to control. As it is, restless movements are absorbed into the complexity of the setting and do not disrupt the work of others. The following observations were made on a boy described as very slow, mildly spastic, having very poor writing and questionable reading skills. He was in an infant class that allowed the children considerable choice of activity, although a certain amount of academic work had to be completed each day.

Jay is holding his book, waiting for his teacher, who is busy with another child. She moves to another child, and he follows her. She then goes to her desk and is immediately surrounded by half a dozen children. Jay goes back over to a table and speaks with two girls, while he looks intently at what they are doing. The two girls are discussing their work as he watches them. They move apart from each other, and he sits at the table that they occupied. He watches two other girls at the table, looks over at the teacher, and starts to talk to one of the girls. He leans over the table so that he can see what they are doing. They talk to each other, but not to him. He watches their work intently, and then says something to one of the girls, who answers him briefly. The girls seem to be comparing their work, discussing what needs to be done, while he watches. Jay points toward their work and says, "square." One girl says, "Don't do that." The girls stop their work and go to the teacher. He sits down, rubs his eyes, and starts to draw in his book. As the two girls sit down again, he picks up a workbook, looks at it, puts it down, and starts drawing again. He looks at the book that the girl is using, points, and smiles. He notices that the remedial teacher has entered the room, and he runs up to her. She talks to him, holds his hand, and pats his face. He goes back to the table and picks up a crayon. The two girls are saying the alphabet. He watches and then says something to one of the girls, who ignores him. A second girl he addresses also ignores him. He goes up to the teacher's desk, fingers the pencils that he finds there, listens to the teacher talk to other children, goes back to his own table, momentarily, and then walks over to where a group of boys are seated. He looks to see what they are doing, points to something on the table, but is ignored. He goes back to his own table, erases some lines on his drawing, and then comes over to me. I spoke to him, found out what he was supposed to be doing, asked him to draw something, and told him that I would help him with the words that he had to write. Jay then went back to his table and set to doing his drawing. In a few minutes he came back to me to show me the words that he had written. After having written four words, he seemed to be finished. He put his writing book away and got out a workbook. He came back to me, showed me the book, then went to his teacher, waiting patiently in the queue of other children who had come up to her. The teacher noticed him and asked him to wait a moment. He did. After she spoke to him, he went back to the table. He studied the workbook, and then he started to color according to the directions. Jay still did not work steadily and was up and down. He got up to get an eraser, went back to work, got up to show his work to me, and then went back to his table again. Finally, he seemed to do the requisite amount of work. He took it up to the teacher to show it to her, and then picked up another book, leafing through its pages by himself.

These observations were made over a span of forty minutes. In this classroom, the children were given a series of assignments to complete during the morning, and when their assignments were completed, they were able to choose other activities. Apparently the child completed the minimum amount of work assigned to him during the allotted time. It is interesting that his restless behavior created no difficulty for others at all. The children seemed accustomed to his ways, and they ignored him or quickly dealt with him if he interfered with them. The teacher, or some other adult, was available to him on his request, and during the entire forty minutes of observation, the teacher did not have to intervene at all. Jay used the teacher much as other children did, to obtain instructions or to have his work corrected, but his restlessness was absorbed into the classroom, and it never required any form of external control. It is doubtful that any more work would have been done in a classroom in which the teacher gave more overt direction to the work. It is virtually certain that his behavior would have required much more of the teacher's attention had the classroom norms allowed less freedom of movement.

Children Accept Each Other

Marie, who was 7 years old, was described as "dim," if not actually retarded. The teacher felt that, if anything, the child's mother was duller than the child. Marie seemed to have learned how to read, but the teacher doubted her comprehension. The child's characteristics immediately brought her to my attention in the classroom. She was impulsive, made large, awkward, sweeping gestures, sat or stood over her work with her body twisted, or had her head tucked under her arm. She sometimes ran or even leaped across the room unexpectedly and suddenly, and she spoke out loudly and inappropriately. One could not avoid noticing that she was different. However, as the following observations suggest, her difference did not lead other children to reject her.

> The children were all taking a weekly test. They were evidently familiar with the procedure. Marie seemed to be looking at the teacher, expectantly. The teacher said, "Ready?", and Marie said, "Off you go." Then the teacher said, "Off you go." Marie waved her arms about and then got down to intensive work on the test in front of her. She pokes her finger at the place where she is working and talks to herself about the work, evidently concentrating. She is bent over the test. After two minutes' work, she gets up and walks over to the teacher, who tells her to do the work again. Marie bends over the test, looks at it intently, does not change anything, and then sits looking at the class. She runs across the room to another child, and then goes back to her place. While the teacher is occupied with other children, Marie suddenly dashes out of the room. (In this school, children are permitted to leave the room and work in the corridor.) Another girl follows her. Marie returns very shortly. Giggling, she gets a notebook out, bends over it very closely, and writes in it for about fifteen seconds. She then runs over to another child, looks at her work, dashes back to her own place, and dashes back to the child once again. She whispers something to the other girl, and then goes back to writing again. Another girl walks over, says something to her, and returns to her place. Marie continues writing, then takes her book over to the teacher, waiting in the queue until the teacher corrects her work. Marie examines the correction, goes to the other child's table, sits down, and writes in her own book. After a little while she returns to her own place, and writes in her book while standing. She gets up, starts to go to the teacher, sits down, writes some more, and then goes to the queue, very intently watching what the teacher is doing with the other children. The teacher looks at her work and corrects it. Marie then walks over to the place where records are kept and makes an entry for herself, while another little girl walks over and talks to her. After she is finished marking the paper, she runs and leaps across the room. She and the other girl take a box of pencils and begin to sharpen them. A third girl joins them, and all three are talking to each other as they work. One girl leaves and a boy joins the remaining two girls. They seem to be discussing pencil sharpening. For some reason, the other girl tells Marie to go away. Marie pokes the girl, and then hugs her, goes away from her, gets her writing book, and goes up to the teacher again. She shows the teacher her book, and the

teacher seems to be giving her directions. Marie gets a pencil, marks her book, goes back to her original seat, and works on the book for a few minutes. Then she gets up, and joins the teacher who is with a small group of children near a typewriter. The teacher corrects her work. Marie goes back to her place, does another item, comes up to the teacher, and has it corrected. Each time she stops for a moment to chat with another child. She keeps up the item work for nearly half an hour, and then at lunch, merrily walks out with a group of three other children, chatting away with them.

Children Socialize Each Other

The opportunity for social interaction may be very important to the child who is different because peers will frequently react in such ways as to let the child know when behavior is inappropriate. At the same time, the give and take of the classroom may encourage a child to learn to be appropriately self-assertive. The following observation was made of a girl in an infant class who immediately stood out as different. She isolated herself during any group activity, her complexion had a pasty whiteness, and her eyes looked red-rimmed. Her teacher said that she had good intelligence, that she did not actively avoid other children, and that she was learning to read very satisfactorily, although she was not well advanced in that skill.

> Sally was seated at a table with four other children working at an assignment. She was rocking back and forth in her chair, and she soon tipped it over. She got up, fixed the chair in place, resumed her work, but soon tipped the chair over again. Once again she went back to work, doing a little work in her workbook, and then leaned over to see what another child was doing. She then went back to her own work, but very suddenly, she leaned across the table and tried to snatch something from a girl. The girl protected her materials by putting her arms over them, and said vigorously, "No, Sally!" Sally subsided and went back to work for a few moments. Suddenly again, she got up, and walked out of my sight. She might have been going to the toilet. One little boy told me, without being asked, that Sally sometimes wet herself. When she returned, she went back to her table, stood beside a boy, and tried to snatch something from him. He protected his property, and then slapped her on the bottom. She subsided once more, sat down in her place, and started working on her book. Shortly afterward, the boy who hit her came over and tried to grab something from her. She wrapped her arms around her papers, screeched at him, and seemed ready to scratch or bite him when he moved away.

It was extremely interesting to observe that she made no reaction at all when children tried to protect their property against her attempts to grab, but she was very active in protecting her own things. Each incident was self-limited; none of the interchanges between children lasted for more than approximately thirty seconds, and the teacher had no need to intervene. The children seemed to be teaching each other about property rights, and this child seemed to be developing some sense of what was right and wrong in her relations with others.

Individualizing Children's Work Patterns

It is not only a matter of finding a place within the social order, which is important, but our observations suggest the children look and act differently depending upon the activity in which they are engaged. If the classroom allows it, it is almost always possible to find an activity acceptable to teacher and child that will productively engage the child for extended periods of time. It is the rules of the classroom, the available materials, and the demands that the teacher inevitably must make of the children that interact with the children's characteristics. One combination allows a child to function and another creates problems for both children and teachers.

Of course, the teacher has an obligation to teach and cannot simply allow a child to do as he pleases. I observed one boy about 10 years old, who was described as a slow learner with an IQ under 90, while he was working in an English workbook. He seemed to follow the pattern of going up to the teacher for directions or for correction whenever he had finished one or two items. The total assignment seemed to be a short one, and when he finished he went to the art corner where he spent all the rest of the morning working on his own project. He took exquisite care in cutting and pasting the parts for a model of a windmill that he was making for a larger project.

His teacher allowed him to spend a great deal of time in art, provided that he completed some minimal amount of other work each day. As their relationship developed, she was gradually increasing the demands that she was making of him. His artwork was not just treated as an escape in this school. The projects he was working on required research to obtain appropriate models; the headmaster demonstrated the value that he placed on the boy's work by putting on a one-man art show, exhibiting the boy's work to the whole school.

As another example, I observed a teacher spend 15 uninterrupted minutes working individually with a child. Afterwards, the boy went out to the art corner, where he did very little except to watch others and daydream. When I asked him what he was doing, he told me that he had difficulty deciding on what he was going to draw. He made a false start, while I watched, tore up the paper, spent another half-hour thinking, and finally, just before lunch, he completed a respectable drawing of a dinosaur and a tree.

The teacher told me that the child would not do any work without the immediate presence of an adult. The 15 minutes of intensive individual work satisfied her that he had completed his basics for that day. She did not feel any need to keep him working at another task. Moreover, she felt it was better to let him alone to make up his own mind, even if it seemed as if he were wasting time, because she was concerned about promoting his dependence by telling him what to do and by prompting him to work.

The teacher was able to give him the individual attention that he needed because she was part of a team of three teachers who worked with about 80 children, vertically integrated in age from seven to eleven. The other two teachers were well able to take up the work of responding to the other children. In general, the norms of the classroom encouraged independent work, with minimal supervision throughout most of the day.

Activities to Integrate the Child

It is not only important to find activities that allow children to perform normally in the classroom, but it is also helpful to move children toward activities that enable them to become an integral part of the group.

In one classroom, a boy was working very diligently at a typewriter. The teacher had identified him as a nonreader. In fact, the teacher had been told by the boy's parents that he would literally vomit if forced to read. The child had been given the task of preparing a stencil, containing word lists that other children in the class would be using. Although the child was unable to read, he was able to match letters on a typewriter keyboard with those on a word list and slowly copy each word.

I was in that classroom for approximately one hour, and I did not see the child so much as move off his seat, even though the rules of the class allowed the children to move freely throughout the classroom. Another child, working on something completely different, would look over his shoulder every now and then and offer suggestions or help him to find his place in the list. That nonreader was dealing with symbolic materials, was making letter discriminations, and was dealing with letter combinations. The task that he had been assigned was a real one, since others in the class would be using the materials that he was producing. He had a place in the classroom and could feel that he was making his contribution even though he was a nonreader at that time.

Art, Concrete Experience, and Learning

When drawing and painting are employed in the classroom as a recreational device, children may be absorbed in what they do, but the experience is often separated from other learning. In many of the classrooms that I observed, arts and crafts were an intimate part of the business of teaching and learning. The children observe, study, read, write, construct, draw, and paint about real objects. Immediate experiences become the occasion for a lesson that employs several modalities of learning and allows children to participate at their own levels.

One room contained an earthworm farm and a number of project books about various facets of earthworms. The project originated when the teacher noticed that a large number of earthworms were on the sidewalks, after being forced above ground by the heavy rain. She immediately set the children to gathering the earthworms. Some children had the assignment of mapping the area around the school, dividing it into square yards, and counting the number of worms that were found in each square yard. Other children graphed the numbers of worms that were obtained. In subsequent days, the children read about earthworms, observed them in their tank, wrote about them, and drew and painted them. The project had been created spontaneously, and the teacher said that she stopped it after a week or so, when she sensed that the children had lost interest in it.

In another school, during the summer hornets had built a large nest over the entrance to the school. All of the children saw the hornet's nest when they arrived for classes. An exterminator was called, and after he safely removed the nest, he gave it to the headmaster, who seized the moment to create a project. The headmaster, who also taught, sectioned the nest and accumulated books and charts about flying insects. The hornet's nest was the focal point for a science and nature study project that included drawing and painting insects and their habitats. I observed one boy with spina bifida seated at an easel for an entire morning, painting a bee, working from a textbook. The teacher took the work very seriously, and at one point discussed with him the relative size of the wings and the body, the number of segments that he had included, the number of legs, antennae, and so on. Other children used the hornet's nest to observe shapes and drew geometric forms based on their observations of the hive. Some made cuts of these forms and used them for block printing. In other words, the artwork was fully integrated into the teaching program, just as the teaching program was integrated into the immediate experiential environment of the children.

Do Special Children Work in Regular Classes?

I have emphasized the ways in which restlessness can be absorbed in the classroom. I have mentioned only a few of the many examples of highly concentrated work that was observed in many children designated as slow, retarded, or as having emotional problems. Stalbow's (1975) observational data showed that children designated as special did, in fact, work less and concentrate less well than those designated as normal. However, the difference, while statistically significant, was modest, and many of the special children had work scores in the range of normal.

The special children tended to wander in the classroom a greater proportion of the time, and they tended to spend more of their time in transitional activities, such as getting or putting away materials or sharpening pencils. Such activities are all legitimate within the classroom. While the children may use these activities as excuses to avoid the more difficult symbolic work, they also do reading, writing, and arithmetic, but to a somewhat lesser degree than normal. Stalbow observed special children doing symbolic work in 46 percent of her observation intervals, and she observed normal children working in reading, writing, or arithmetic about 62 percent of the time. Special children do not avoid the work completely by any means, but they tend to make more use of the other options that the freedom of the classroom provides.

Few of the classrooms that we observed allowed the children absolutely free choice. According to the teachers, the median amount of choice time is about 25 percent of the day, limited to a set of activities designated by the teacher. In all the classrooms, all of the children had academic work that they were required to do. In these classrooms, instead of keeping the child in his seat, squirming uncomfortably or daydreaming, a child is permitted to move about and interact socially. Since classroom norms legitimized such movement, their behavior is not disruptive in the context of the classroom.

THE CLASSROOM TEACHER'S PERSPECTIVE

Most, but not all, of the teachers that I spoke with were in favor of the policy of maintaining retarded and emotionally disturbed children in the normal classroom.

Benefits

The teachers uniformly spoke about social benefits accruing to the special children. They were very much aware of the stigma that is associated with attendance at special schools or special classes. A few said, "After all, what would they learn from *other* disturbed children?" They felt that better social relationships were promoted when a child remained in a normal school. Some saw the presence of special children in the normal classroom as an opportunity for the social training of the normal child. Other teachers indicated that they felt it useful that children discover their own level in normal competition with their peers.

Few of the teachers felt that it was necessary or advisable to protect the children from failure, and several said that they allowed children to try things even when they knew the child would fail, as long as the child wanted to try. In the case of physically handicapped children, teachers encouraged natural behavior as much as possible. For example, the teacher of a child born with a deformed hand had encouraged the child to use her arm as naturally as possible, and not to hide the deformed hand. It was my impression that the child was very much at ease and not at all self-conscious. In another instance, I witnessed an interesting exchange between a child who walked only with the aid of a walker and a normal child who offered to get something for him. The child with the walker very casually rejected the offer and went to get it for himself. The whole episode seemed to me to be very natural and easygoing.

Costs

Teachers had two objections to the policy of integration. These objections were voiced nearly uniformly. The first objection was that special children required an inordinate amount of time from the teacher. The second objection reflected the teacher's professional conscience and the relative isolation of the classroom from other professional resources. Teachers said that the special child was deprived of an opportunity for greater progress in the smaller classes and from the specialized knowledge and techniques that the trained, special class teacher would employ. Some seemed to feel guilty that they were not able to give the child all that they felt was desirable, in terms of time, individual attention, and remedial educational experiences. In this sense, the special child was experienced as a burden, but I found no teacher who explicitly said that it was not the regular classroom teacher's responsibility to work with such children. Headmasters voiced much the same sentiments as the teachers.

The objection based on time seemed to have several components. For one, if a child was considerably slower than the rest, the teacher would have to prepare special work cards, ditto sheets, etc., just for that child, increasing the teacher's preparatory time. The teachers did not feel that resources were available for this purpose. The problem of finding special materials seemed to be reduced considerably in the fully vertically grouped classrooms, since a very wide range of materials was present at all times.

In addition to the need to prepare special materials, the question of time breaks down into several other issues. A great deal of the instruction in all classrooms, whether formal or informal, is done through workbooks and other prepared materials meant to be self-teaching. In most of the classrooms that I observed, the teacher rarely taught concepts to the whole class or engaged the whole class in question and answer recitation. A good deal of the teacher's time was spent in starting children off on work, and then correcting the work in individual sessions, which rarely lasted more than a minute. Boydell's systematic observations of Leicestershire classrooms bears out my impression of many Oxfordshire classrooms (Boydell, 1975). Children come up to the teacher one at a time. They wait in a queue or in a little group around the teacher until it is their turn. The teacher examines their work, comments on it, asks questions about it, or explains what is to be done and how it is to be done. Children with adequate reading ability and with good comprehension quickly grasp what is required and proceed to do the work.

In general, since children work individually, and at individually determined rates, I rarely saw children who could not do the work that was expected of them. However, it did seem to me that the directions in some of the workbooks in math and in English or in reading comprehension were complicated or unclear. I usually found that I could start a child working with a minimal explanation of what needed to be done, once I understood it myself. Slower children had more difficulty in reading and understanding the instructions. Such children were more dependent upon the teacher for directions and explanations. Many of the slower, more immature, and more dependent children tended to do a single item, go to the teacher for correction, go back to their seats, do another item, come back for correction, and so on. In some instances, teachers encouraged such a pattern. In other instances, it was a natural consequence of the child's difficulty in working intensively without immediate feedback.

Observational Data

Stalbow's (1975) observations revealed that special children indeed had more contact with teachers than normal children in the same classrooms. The number of work contacts with the teacher per hour was somewhat greater for special children than for normal children, but the difference was not statistically significant. Special children also received more disciplinary comments and more directions to get back to work than did normal children. Stalbow's sample included children of normal intelligence who were considered emotionally disturbed. The disciplinary contacts were of low frequency in any event, averaging about 2.5 per hour of observation per special child. Her data indicated that disciplinary contacts were somewhat more frequent with children of average or better intelligence who were considered emotionally disturbed than they were with children classified as borderline or as retarded.

In reviewing these observations, there is little question that having special children in the normal classroom requires that the teacher make some effort to work with the special child. The special child may well take somewhat more time, even in a situation in which instruction is highly individualized. It was not my impression that the amount of time that each special child required was necessarily inordinate. However, a conscientious teacher wishes to do his best for each child, and a conscientious teacher has the problem of deciding what is the best use of teaching time. It was my impression that those teachers who emphasized the social and emotional development of their children were somewhat less concerned about the time, while those who emphasized the academic, intellectual aspects of the work were more concerned with time. I believe that in a school with an emphasis on individual standards of accomplishment, in which the headmaster and other teachers are fully supportive of work with special children, teachers perceive the additional time not as burdensome, but as an opportunity to give to a child. The self-starting quality of work in the open classroom can help a teacher work with special children without feeling guilty that he is taking away from others.

Team Teaching as an Aid to Individualization

Team teaching seemed to be another method of enhancing the opportunities for individualized instruction and meeting the time problem. However, many teachers and headmasters reported that teams were difficult to organize and difficult to maintain. Almost all said that it was a question of "personalities." I did observe several teams of two and three teachers that seemed to be working very well. The teachers planned together, and the children moved freely through the space that the team utilized. Beginning teachers found this pattern very helpful, once they understood how it worked.

True teaming in this fashion allowed teachers to plan individual and small group time for a variety of purposes. Most of the time, the children were engaged in individual work, with all three teachers available to provide assistance or to correct work. Children usually approached the teacher who they considered to be theirs, and small group work was conducted by a teacher with his own group. However, groupings frequently cut across "home" teacher lines. If a teacher was occupied, any child was welcome to approach another teacher for assistance. When one teacher took a small group of six into a quiet room to read poetry, the other two teachers supervised the remaining 60 children in the larger area.

Teaming worked well when the children were given a great deal of responsibility for individual activity. As far as I could tell, it worked very well in fully age-integrated (vertical or family) groups. It was my impression that the team teaching offered the teachers the greatest flexibility in the ways in which they could use their time and in the way that they could devote themselves to individual children. It seemed to have great potential for integrating children at all levels into the same working environment.

Paid ancillary personnel and unpaid volunteer helpers are also used to work with children. Attitudes toward such paraprofessional helpers vary considerably, school by school, and classroom by classroom. Most teachers welcome aides, but some teachers are concerned about the implications, for the profession and for the children, of having untrained people doing the work of teachers. At a conference I received the distinct impression that the group of teachers and headmasters who were present believed that paid aides were the most vital resource that enabled them to work with special children in the schools. They provided the necessary pair of extra hands to allow the teacher to work with other children or to concentrate on the special child.

LIMITATIONS

Not all children could be maintained in the regular class, despite the best efforts of the staff and of the supportive services. Three examples follow of children who had to be excluded. The children seem to represent the major types of failure, and they indicate that some special facilities will always be necessary for some children.

An aggressive child who engages in dangerous actions sometimes requires controls that the school cannot provide. A child whose repertoire included fire-setting and whose aggressiveness brought complaints from the surrounding community was eventually referred for residential placement. The school had tried to work with him for a year, but there was no improvement. His conduct was wearing on all concerned and none of the teachers felt that they could work with him. Even if such a child does develop a relationship with a teacher, if his aggressive conduct spills over into the community, the school can do nothing about that. On occasion, such a child will fight with others, bully them, or steal from them. The school then has a responsibility to protect the other children of the community. In this instance, all concerned, including the child guidance authorities, agreed that the child would be better off in a more controlled setting.

A second child was placed in a residential setting due to the instability of his home. The parents had separated and there was a total lack of support at home. The child might well have continued in the school if he was placed with foster parents in the same catchment area, but the school cannot be expected to work with a child when the home fails to provide a minimum of care and stability.

A third child, with an IQ of 54, was referred to a residential school after a year's trial because the staff felt that the child had little or no understanding of anything that was going on. She rarely, if ever, participated in school work. From the staff's viewpoint, she was simply occupying space, and no effort on their part had shown the least sign of influencing the child.

It is my impression from discussions with headmasters and teachers that some indication that the school is doing something for the child is necessary to maintain motivation to work with the child. Any sign of responsiveness or of improvement, or any special skill or talent that enables a child to find a place in the school, will make it much easier for teacher and headmaster to continue the effort. A young child who frequently soiled herself was tolerated by the teacher and the class despite other very odd behavior because she had improved in response to demands and because she evidently had learned to read and write readily. In another instance, a headmaster told me that he kept a child in school whenever there was any sign at all that the child could participate in any aspect of the school's program. He told me of one girl who did very little academic work, but she held a valued place in the school because of her athletic abilities. She participated in the school's sports program, and other children appreciated her abilities. It is when there is no evidence of progress, nor evidence of constructive participation in any activity, that it is in the best interest of all to refer the child to a special setting. I was impressed that a fairly wide range of difference could be tolerated, if the teacher set a tone of support. However, if a child had odd ways, set himself apart, or was a nuisance and destructive, it was much more difficult to gain acceptance for the child from the teacher and from other children.

Parental desires represent another critical element. Many parents prefer that the child remain in a normal setting and will resist efforts to evaluate or to refer children to a special class or to a special school. In other instances, parents feel that placement in a special class or special school is desirable. On occasion parents will press for such placement even if the school is willing to work with the child. Sometimes the child is more difficult to manage at home than in school, and the child is experienced by the parents as a burden that they can no longer bear. In such instances, unless there is other support for the family, it is difficult to dissuade parents from such a course of action.

CONCLUSION

It appears that a great many, if not most, children who have special educational problems can be maintained in the open classroom. Flexibility in attitude and a structure that supports individualization of instruction seems to make it feasible to maintain most children. It is almost always possible to find activities and ways of working that enable each child to remain productive. I am of the impression that the children benefit socially in the sense that they are not labeled, and they do interact cooperatively with other children in a variety of ways. There is no indication that the children do any better in terms of learning to read, write, and do arithmetic, yet there is no indication that they do any worse than they would in any other situation (Gomes, 1973). In some instances, the children receive the benefit of recognition for real accomplishments that are competitive. Both the normal and the special child learn about personal limitations. Participating in a normal social setting with its usual demands helps the person who is different to learn about those demands and about the consequences of failing to meet appropriate social norms.

In my observations, the other children, by and large, seemed accepting of the special children, and the teachers also reported the same. However, I did not really ask the normal children how they felt about the special children, nor whether they played together outside of school. Pitt's (1976) review of the literature indicates that there may well be public acceptance and private rejection. We must also take into account cultural characteristics of British society that may make it easier for special children to be accepted. Moreover, there are many aspects of the educational tradition in England (e.g., the age-grade structure and lack of defined curriculum) that support individualization. Those elements are not present in American schools. Nonetheless, it is my opinion that teachers can create a climate in which the special child is accepted. Done well, the open form of education provides the classroom with an organizational context in which individualization can take place, and the appropriate values and behavioral norms can be established. British education cannot be transposed to the American scene, but we certainly may learn about the principles that can be applied.

ACKNOWLEDGMENTS

I am indebted to Mr. John Coe of the Oxfordshire Schools, who made the arrangements for me, to Mr. Francis Backhouse, Headmaster of Longfields School, Bicester, who helped me to understand the program in his school, and to the many headmasters and teachers who generously gave me time and information. Seymour B. Sarason and Samuel Brownell of Yale, Heidi Wolfstetter-Kausch of SUNY Buffalo, and Samuel Meisels provided criticism and comments that were very helpful in rewriting an earlier draft of this paper.

REFERENCES

Bennett, S. N., and Jordan, J. 1975. A typology of teaching styles in primary schools. Br. J. Educ. Psychol. 45:20–28.
Blatt, B. 1976. This crazy business: Leadership in mental retardation. In: R. B. Kugel (ed.), Changing Patterns in Residential Services for the Mentally Retarded. 2nd Ed. President's Committee on Mental Retardation, Washington, D. C.

Boydell, D. 1975. Teacher-pupil contact in junior classrooms. Br. J. Educ. Psychol. 45:313–318.

Central Advisory Council for Education (England). 1967. Children and Their Primary Schools. 2 volumes (Plowden Report), HMSO, London.

Gomes, L. A., Jr. (ed.) 1973. The integration of children with special needs into regular educational programs: An annotated bibliography. Boston College Division of Special Education (mimeographed), Boston.

Levine, M. 1976. The academic achievement test: Its historical and social functions. Am. Psychol. 31:228–238.

Pitt, L. B. 1976. Mainstreaming: A Critical Review of the Literature. Unpublished Ph.D. Qualifying Paper, Department of Psychology, SUNY, Buffalo.

Sarason, S. B., Levine, M., Goldenberg, I. I., Cherlin, D. L., and Bennett, E. M. 1966. Psychology in Community Settings. John Wiley & Sons, Inc., New York.

Stalbow, S. 1975. A comparison of the behavior of problem children and normal children in an informal primary school classroom. Third Year Psychology Project, Department of Experimental Psychology, Oxford University.

A Developmental Approach for Preschool Children with Special Needs

Bernard Allen Banet

There are two basic approaches to the design of individualized educational programs for young handicapped children — the diagnostic/corrective approach and the developmental approach. Programs based on the pedagogical logic of diagnosis and correction assume that the major purpose of early educational intervention is to identify areas in which the child shows a deficit in relation to his age-peers or a lack of consistency in his own performance. Testing often provides the data for educational "prescriptions" in the diagnostic/corrective mode. From information about the child's deficits, specific objectives can be developed that represent steps toward remediation of the deficit. Sometimes information about the etiology of a particular handicapping condition is used in making educational plans or "prescriptions," or the technology of behavior modification may be used by the special education interventionist. Incentives or "reinforcers" may be systematically used to motivate the attainment of objectives.

Diagnostic/corrective interventions typically assume not only that the child must be motivated by adults (therapist, teacher, parents) but that he must be "taught" new skills in a direct, didactic way. Often the teaching is done in clinical sessions where a special educator persistently and patiently drills the child in a particular skill. Diagnostic/corrective logic is linked to the assumptions that underlie the entire field of special education. Such assumptions have given rise to the existence of separate professional specialities within special education and to the procedures enacted into state and federal law by which children must be categorized according to diagnostic labels before they can receive special education services.

In contrast, programs based on the logic of "developmental validity" primarily attempt to promote learning experiences that exercise and extend developmentally emerging abilities, that expand the learners' interests and long-term plans, and that are optimally timed for ease of learning and retention.

A developmental approach has elements that are analogous to "diagnosis" and "prescription," but the individualized programs that evolve in a developmental program do not start with an analysis of a child's deficits. Rather, educators seeking to implement developmentally valid programs for handicapped children identify the child's status on a developmental continuum and provide experiences that permit the child to exercise emerging abilities that in most cases the child will be strongly motivated to use. A developmentalist identifies the experiences that challenge and help the child practice broadly generalizable skills that are typical for children at that particular developmental period. It is assumed, at least as an initial strategy, that the child can take a very active role in defining for himself the appropriate developmental match between his skills and the learning activities in which he engages. In other words, a developmental approach need not substitute highly specific developmental-sequential information for highly specific behavior-deficit information. The child, as well as the adult, has a role in planning and selecting activities.

This chapter describes the High/Scope Cognitively Oriented Curriculum as an example of a developmental approach in early childhood special education. This chapter presents the historical background and basic goals and strategies of the High/Scope model. Some important child outcome data are also presented.

THE HIGH/SCOPE APPROACH

The Cognitively Oriented Curriculum is a framework for early childhood education derived from Piagetian principles and developed by the High/Scope Educational Research Foundation under the leadership of David P. Weikart. The Curriculum originated in one of the first early childhood intervention programs of the 1960s, the Ypsilanti-Perry Preschool Project, and has evolved as an early childhood model used in the High/Scope demonstration classrooms, as well as in preschool, infant, and elementary programs in many locations throughout the world (Weikart et al., 1971; Hohmann, Banet, and Weikart, 1979).

The High/Scope Foundation has completed a four-year cycle of work funded by the Bureau of Education for the Handicapped. The Cognitively Oriented Curriculum has been used with an integrated group of handicapped and nonhandicapped children in High/Scope First Chance demonstration preschool classes in Ypsilanti, Michigan. High/Scope

Foundation staff have been working with teachers in several states in order to evaluate the curriculum's usefulness as an inservice training vehicle in special education preschool programs.

In the demonstration classroom in Ypsilanti, one third of the children are handicapped as defined by criteria used by the Michigan Department of Education, which indicates eligibility for school services under Michigan's mandatory special education legislation. The handicapped children served by the project were also screened on criteria relating to the probability that they would be mainstreamed, or integrated, into regular classrooms in later schooling, since the purpose was specifically to demonstrate a program that could make an important difference in children's later school careers. The High/Scope First Chance project serves children who are labeled as mentally retarded (educable or trainable), language impaired, physically or otherwise health handicapped (e.g., epilepsy, scoliosis, cerebral palsy, muscular dystrophy, stroke, heart disease), hearing impaired, or emotionally disturbed. At centers in Michigan, New Jersey, Ohio, Virginia, and Maryland the High/Scope model is being used with a very broad range of children, including some youngsters more severely handicapped than most in the Ypsilanti program. The teacher-child ratio in the Ypsilanti classroom has been 1:7 with two professional teachers in charge of each classroom.

High/Scope's work with handicapped preschool-age children is an outgrowth of universally applicable developmental principles. The view that certain handicapping conditions are *developmental delays* may be one very effective general strategy within a framework that is based on developmental universals. For example, such an approach assumes that the best way to promote growth in a 4-year-old child who is two years behind his peers in intellectual and verbal development is to provide the rich variety of concrete experiences and accompanying language activities that one provides for a nonhandicapped 2-year-old. Attempts to target certain narrow behaviors that appear more age-appropriate for a 4-year-old may only result in very narrow learning, not generalizable to other skills and not matching the child's motivational inclinations.

For a child who is not neurologically impaired, but shows developmental lags because of sensory or motor limitations, the educator's task is to mobilize the child's existing resources toward achieving developmentally appropriate intellectual and social competencies. These skills may be channeled in different ways and through different modalities. For example, communication for a deaf child may include experiences with signing rather than experiences exclusively with oral language, but the experiential base that provides interesting things to talk about, a reason and an invitation to communicate, must be present. This set of active experiences should be basically the same for the deaf child and the hearing child and the same for the language impaired child and the child with "normal" language.

Teachers in a Cognitively Oriented program focus on experiences that pertain to developmental processes, rather than on behavioral outcomes. Such experiences are *key experiences*. These are the classes of active experience that cognitive developmental theory suggests are involved in the mastery of the developmental tasks of the preschool-age child. These key experiences are used to plan activities for groups of children, as well as to provide a way of thinking about individual children. They are called 'experiences' rather than 'goals' in order to emphasize for teachers the many different ways in which each experience can occur in the life of a child. This is more useful than thinking of experiences as *attainable* concepts that are to be checked off and perhaps never returned to.

We try to maintain a balance of teacher initiation and child initiation. The child makes an explicit plan each day, and the adult helps the child to formulate and to carry out that plan. Adult interactions with children often occur in the context of helping a child examine the ways of accomplishing his plan.

To create an environment where the key experiences are likely to occur and where children can plan a variety of activities, the High/Scope framework suggests a room arrangement and a daily routine specifically designed to encourage active learning. Such an environment has a variety of work areas or interest centers (a block area, an art area, a dramatic play or "house" area, and an area for small manipulative materials). The routine is structured to permit a variety of modes of interaction with peers and adults: small group activities, outdoor play, whole class games, and musical activities. At the heart of the day is the *work time,* in which children make a plan, carry out their chosen activities in the various interest centers, and then discuss and represent their activities. The routine is maintained consistently so that children can operate within a predictable timeflow from day to day.

Adults are encouraged to develop very general strategies in order to provide an optimum match between a child's classroom activities and the appropriate key experiences. These very broad strategies are exactly the same for handicapped and nonhandicapped children.

GENERAL STRATEGIES SUPPORTING CHILD DEVELOPMENT

Extending Concrete Experiences Through Language and Representation

The cycle of children's experiences begins with concrete materials and physical involvement, both sensory and motoric. Very young children or children who are still functioning primarily at the sensorimotor level may continue to function at this concrete level. Those who are able to use more abstract mental abilities are encouraged to extend their active, concrete experience via representations in a variety of modes, including language. Relating representational activities to concrete events or experiences is viewed as important, even when children are able to deal with the concept or event on a more symbolic level. Representational activity may be channeled by the teacher, but the specific content and style of the representation is not dictated by the adult. The key experiences most relevant for this basic strategy of extending active, concrete experiences through language and representation are grouped as follows:

Active Learning

Exploring actively and with all senses
Discovering relations through direct experience
Manipulating, transforming, and combining materials
Using large muscles
Taking care of own needs
Choosing materials
Acquiring skill with tools and equipment

Language

Conversing about personally meaningful experiences with adults and
    peers
Describing (and listening to others describe) objects, events, and rela-
    tions
Expressing feelings in words
Having one's own spoken language written down by an adult and read
    back
Having fun with language: rhyming, making up stories, and listening
    to poems and stories

Representation

Recognizing objects by sound, touch, taste, and smell
Imitating actions
Relating pictures, photographs, and models of real places and things
Role playing, pretending
Constructing models out of clay, blocks, etc.
Making drawings and paintings

Some children with special needs are still functioning at the sensorimotor level when they are 3 years of age or older. For these children, as well as for others with less severe delays, the basic manipulative/

exploratory activities are the most developmentally appropriate. There is no attempt to extend these activities immediately into experiences that require high level (i.e., more abstract) symbolic or representational processes. Thus, for a developmentally delayed or intellectually impaired preschool-age child, we provide readily transformable materials, such as water, sand, and finger paint. Of course, these materials are used by all preschool-age children, but the special needs child may engage in different activities with the materials, and the teacher's responses and questions are based on the way in which the child interacts with the materials. A good learning environment encourages children to interact with materials in diverse ways, according to their developmental level, rather than imposing one way to use the materials. Two examples are discussed.

> A normally developing 4-year-old child will use sand to make "roads" for toy cars. A child still functioning at the sensorimotor level will be interested in filling and emptying containers of sand, but not in using the sand to represent something else.

> While a 4- or 5-year-old can make playdough from a picture-recipe chart, measuring the flour and water and salt and oil with measuring cups and spoons, a child who is developmentally 2 years old will enjoy manipulating the ingredients and transforming them into dough, but will not be able to decode the chart. In the same work/play group, a child with a hearing impairment might assist with some of the steps that require fine motor coordination (such as pouring) or quantitative concepts (using measuring cups).

The self-confidence and excitement of being able to contribute to the final result is very important to all children. Open-ended materials and activities give validity to many different contributions and results.

For children with language delays or impairments, the active concrete experiences provide a context and a reason to talk with others. In the course of such experiences, peers can act as both models and sources of reinforcement. Asking other children for materials or equipment or describing what one has accomplished to the teacher are ideal ways for the child to utilize the language that he is learning. This is language that is purposeful, social, and generalizable outside the classroom. Language in the speech clinic too often is removed from real experiences and from the need and joy of communication, and therefore it may not generalize to home and school situations. Encouraging a wide variety of representations, not just verbal representations, means that children whose language lags behind their general cognitive development have a number of ways in which to make their feelings and ideas clearer: through art media, role play/pantomime, dance and movement, and construction with blocks or carpentry tools and wood. This richness of materials and diversity of possibilities makes it possible for a child with sensory or perceptual deficits to find alternative means of initiating active transactions with the environment and with peers. The hearing impaired or visually impaired child is given incentives to interact with materials and with people; these children are invited by the environment to use *both* their impaired sensory channels and their normally functioning ones.

Adopting a Problem-Solving Orientation

A second basic strategy, which complements active-concrete learning and extension through language and representation, is a strategy of helping children to define goals, to discover problems in the process of trying to attain goals, and to explore and evaluate alternative solutions to a problem, whether it is a problem involving objects or people. It is exciting for teachers and parents to see this problem-solving orientation developing in young children. It is all the more exciting when the orientation is seen in special needs children.

Children experience a daily routine in the Cognitively Oriented Curriculum that asks them to make plans and choices. They learn from this routine that they can accomplish something if they first make a plan, and by making this plan they also learn that they have explicit choices and alternatives. We have seen this approach generalized from the classroom to the home. We create environments in which teachers and parents learn that it is their job to help children encounter interesting (and solvable) problems.

> An emotionally disturbed boy, labeled hyperactive by some, exhibits long periods of focused attention and purposeful activity, as he makes an airplane out of wood at the workbench. He chose to go to the workbench and he decided that he wanted to make an airplane. The teacher helped him think about the materials, tools, and procedures that he would need. Later, at "recall time," he drew the airplane and dictated a story about it in which he described what he did when the glue was not strong enough to hold the wings on the plane.

Providing choices and a rich variety of developmentally appropriate materials is an alternative to the kind of environmental restriction conventionally prescribed for handicapped children. The notion that special needs children require stimulus-lean environments may have evolved as a way of getting children to attend to highly structured tasks that are not developmentally appropriate, and hence not interesting. This would explain why children seem to become "distracted" by other stimuli in such an environment.

The belief that special needs children require extrinsic reinforcements for participating in learning activities may have grown out of settings that provide developmentally inappropriate activities. In most cases where children have been able to participate in a Cognitively Oriented preschool program, it has been possible to find activities that are intrinsically motivating. The systematic use of social reinforcers has also been unnecessary, since these rewards occur naturally in an open preschool environment. The systematic record-keeping and scheduling of reinforcements by the teachers has not been required. The children derive a sense of accomplishment from carrying out their own plans, rather than from pleasing the teacher.

Expanding from Here and Now to There and Then

An approach that stresses active learning and choices supports intellectual growth in many ways. Representation and conversation are two examples. That is, in the process of talking about experiences and representing them in several modalities (actions, drawings, models, etc.) children consolidate their comprehension of events and build analytic and creative skills. Children learn about relationships and pay increased attention to the structure of objects and events. A basic strategy used by teachers in the Cognitively Oriented Curriculum is that of expanding conversation and representational activities from the here and now to more remote events and places. This begins to occur as children become more capable of dealing with the past, the future, and spatially distant realities. This strategy is part of an expansion of learning from things to relationships, comparisons, and quantification. Some of the key experiences that contribute to this expansion are the following:

Spatial Relations

Fitting things together and taking them apart
Rearranging a set of objects or one object (folding, twisting, stretching, stacking, tying) and observing the spatial transformations
Observing things and places from different spatial viewpoints
Experiencing and describing the positions of things in relation to each other (in the middle, on the side of, on, off, on top of, over, above)
Experiencing and describing the direction of movement of things and people (to, from, into, out of, toward, away from)
Experiencing and describing relative distances among things and locations (close, near, far, next to, apart, together)
Experiencing and representing one's own body (how it is structured, what various body parts can do)
Learning to locate things in the classroom, school, and neighborhood
Interpreting representations of spatial relations in drawings and pictures
Distinguishing and describing shapes
Distinguishing between *some* and *all*

Seriation

Comparing (Which one is bigger (smaller), heavier (lighter), rougher (smoother), louder (softer), longer (shorter), taller (shorter), wider (narrower), sharper, darker, etc.)

Arranging several things in order along some dimension and describing the relations (the longest one, the shortest one, etc.)

Number Concepts

Comparing number and amount (more/less, same amount, more/fewer, same number)

Comparing the number of items in two sets by matching them up in one-to-one correspondence

Enumerating (counting) objects, as well as counting by rote

These experiences and concepts are an important bridge between physical encounters with the world and the kinds of abstract reasoning skills that are necessary for success in school. When special education programs attempt to teach academic skills (alphabet recognition, clock or calendar reading, simple arithmetic) before the child has mastered the underlying spatial or temporal concepts upon which these skills are based, the result can only be frustration for the child, or superficial or rote learning. Often academic skills are introduced to developmentally delayed children with the thought that the children will look normal if they can write their names, appear to understand the calendar, know right from left, etc. Rather than drill concepts not understood by the developmentally younger child, it makes more sense to provide the foundation upon which such concepts can later emerge more easily. For example, building up expectations about the flow of time in the daily routine (planning time, work time, cleanup time, recall time, etc.) is a useful step toward mastery of clocks and calendars. Similarly, grouping materials in categories and making them easily accessible can enhance children's understanding of their environment. An organized daily routine and classroom environment can provide the predictability and stability that all children need if they are to be comfortable in an environment that invites choices and creativity.

The general strategies and key experiences described above are being used with all types of children, not just handicapped children. Thus, the Cognitively Oriented Curriculum has been shown to be a framework that can serve as a basic vehicle for teachers working with integrated groups of handicapped and nonhandicapped children. The High/Scope Preschool and other programs around the country that use this model have demonstrated that a model that strives for developmental validity rather than remediation and attainment of specific objectives through didactic teaching can best help to create learning environments that are both least restrictive and most facilitative.

EVALUATION FINDINGS

The quantitative evidence that is available to demonstrate the effectiveness of a developmental approach is striking because it includes longitudinal followup research:

Educable mentally retarded children who attended the first preschool program that used the Cognitively Oriented Curriculum (The Perry Preschool in Ypsilanti, Michigan) scored significantly higher than a nonpreschool control group on achievement tests given at the end of eighth grade (Weikart, Bond, and McNeil, 1978).

Children in the Cognitively Oriented preschool classes in Ypsilanti have consistently shown impressive test gains on IQ-type pre-to-post testing. In one study, children with an average IQ of 80 on the Stanford-Binet at the beginning of the year demonstrated an average 24-point IQ gain by the end of the program and a sustained gain of 15 points 5 years after the conclusion of the program (Weikart, Bond and McNeil, 1978).

Findings from the 1975-76 school year show that the handicapped children in the High/Scope Preschool experienced important gains (Banet et al., 1976). Pre- and post-testing with the McCarthy Scales of Children's Abilities revealed that the children, as a group, advanced 2.02 months in mental age for each month in which they attended the High/Scope First Chance Demonstration Preschool. The gains of the variously handicapped children were equivalent to those of their non-handicapped peers.

These findings suggest that developmental preschool programs can produce measurable gains that endure over many years. These findings are as powerful a validation of the developmental approach as are any outcome data that have been reported for other approaches in the preschool intervention literature.

CONCLUSION

The Cognitively Oriented Curriculum is one of many approaches that serves young handicapped children in "open" environments. Continued research should clarify the applicability of developmental versus diagnostic/corrective models, as well as issues relating to the structure of environments for young handicapped children. It is our strong belief that effective, developmentally appropriate programs for normal children and for special needs children will be remarkably similar.

REFERENCES

Banet, B., Rogers L., McDonald, B., Matz, R., Ispa, J., Bixby, S., Alder, S., and Flores, I. 1976. Program Performance Report, High/Scope BEH Demonstration Preschool Project (OEG-0-74-2720). High/Scope Educational Research Foundation, Ypsilanti, Mich.

Hohmann, M., Banet, B., and Weikart, D. P. 1979. Young children in action: A manual for preschool educators. High/Scope Educational Research Foundation, Ypsilanti, Mich.

Weikart, D. P., Bond, J. T., and McNeil, J. T. 1978. The Ypsilanti-Perry Preschool Project: Preschool years and longitudinal results through fourth grade. Monograph no. 3. High/Scope Educational Research Foundation, Ypsilanti, Mich.

Weikart, D. P., Epstein, A., Schweinhart, L., and Bond, J. T. 1978. The Ypsilanti Preschool Curriculum Demonstration Project: Preschool years and longitudinal results. Monograph no. 4. High/Scope Educational Research Foundation, Ypsilanti, Mich.

Weikart, D. P., Rogers, L., Adcock, C., and McClelland, D. 1971. The cognitively oriented curriculum: A framework for preschool teachers. University of Illinois, Urbana, Ill.

An Environment for Everyone
Autistic and Nondisabled Children Learn Together

Peter Knoblock
Ellen B. Barnes

JOWONIO: THE LEARNING PLACE

Background

Jowonio, The Learning Place,[1] is a community school for nondisabled and severely emotionally disturbed children. Created in 1969 as an alternative to regular public school, Jowonio served as an open program in which a child could receive a personal and individualized education. Because there were few alternative programs in the area, the school received referrals of children who demonstrated learning and adjustment problems in school. In an open program where structure can be varied and many authority issues, such as power struggles between children and teachers, can be obviated, children in difficulty could be accepted and responded to. In 1975, parents of young, severely disturbed children and the school staff wrote a proposal for a fully integrated therapeutic program; the New York State Department of Mental Hygiene responded by assigning four staff positions to the school.

At the present time, Jowonio, The Learning Place, serves children 3 to 9 years of age. One-third of these children are severely emotionally disturbed, while two-thirds are so-called typical children. The children are grouped into "family group" classrooms with an age range of three years. While there is one lead teacher per classroom, there is approximately one adult for every three children because the school uses master's level interns and undergraduate student teachers from Syracuse University and

---

[1] Jowonio, in Onondaga Indian language, means "to set free."

207

volunteers as additional staff. All children at Jowonio are thought of in developmental terms, and their programs are based on a clinical model of assessment, program planning, implementation, and evaluation. The diagnostic and teaching approach known as Developmental Therapy, developed by the Rutland Center in Athens, Georgia (Wood, 1975), is used in assessing and planning for the special children. Active and open learning approaches are used with all children. A major emphasis of the program is the design of developmentally integrated experiences. The program includes a systematic evaluation component and efforts to maximize parent involvement.

This chapter explores our definition of open education as it relates to special education. It describes in detail the ways in which teachers and children have enacted a number of open education practices and concepts within the context of a therapeutic school climate for both handicapped and nonhandicapped children.

OPEN EDUCATION AND SPECIAL EDUCATION

The term *open education* is one of those educational approaches that has been greatly misunderstood. Few seem to feel neutral about it, most are either for it or against it. In general, the "it" is what has confused professionals and lay persons. For many people, open education is similar to an ink blot. People look at it and see many things — most of which they do not like. For others, open education came and went before they had a chance to really grasp what was involved. The popular news magazines wrote the obituary of open education in 1974 when the "back to basics" movement claimed to be replacing open education as the educational method of choice. The articles essentially stated that the country had tried "it," and open education had failed to teach children basic skills. A still smaller number of individuals have always practiced open education and will probably continue to do so.

Some educators viewed open education as one of a vast array of educational innovations, joining a list including programmed instruction, performance contracting, competency-based instruction, computer-assisted instruction, and so on. For those educators it was something to try, and if it "worked" then they would use it. Needless to say, it did not work out for those individuals, nor should they have assumed that it would be a satisfactory approach for them. After all, it must be realized that no approach or educational method can survive on its own. Each approach, particularly an interactional approach, such as open education, requires skillful application by a person who is aware of its power and limitations.

We have never thought of open education as one of those new educational approaches to be tested and discarded if it does not produce results. In the first place, it is not new — it is only repeatedly discovered, modified, and put on the shelf for another generation to rediscover. The results are not dependent on the explicit methodology of open education, but are dependent on the ways in which adults and children together act on the values and beliefs implicit in this approach and in the manner in which they translate them into practice.

Cremin (1961) has written an incisive account of the progressive education movement in this country and has traced its history and development. Cycles and reverberations of particular approaches keep reappearing in slightly different forms. Open education owes its development to this recurring history of educational practice and to a number of individuals who view their work as child-centered. Thus, some of the most fully articulated, open education programs are being implemented by teachers of very young children. Similarly, open education has also appealed to special educators who have traditionally had a strong interest in individualization and have more recently begun to focus on issues of normalization.

As with most relationships, certain ground rules must be established, and such is the case if open education and special education are to build on each other. It may be instructive to begin by identifying some of the misconceptions concerning open education that may exist in the minds of special educators.

Misconception 1 "Proponents of open education believe in allowing children to do what they want to do at all times." While there is a strong interest on the part of teachers in helping a child use his time wisely and constructively, open education is *not* a laissez-faire approach, giving complete control of the classroom experience to the child. Neither does it allow for complete control by the teacher. Ideally, a partnership can be worked out between teacher and children so that the learning plans that a teacher has for each child can be enacted in a climate of safety and trust.

Misconception 2 "Open education does not contain within its philosophy or methodology a way for skill development to become a priority." This is a particularly important issue for all special education teachers who are confronted daily with children who have major learning problems. There is absolutely nothing inherent in the philosophy or methodology of open education that precludes focusing on a child's skill needs. What is different about open education's response to skill development is that it focuses on fostering children's involvement in the learning process. The development of a competent, skilled, and independent learning child is the foundation of open education. What may also be different about the open education approach is its unwillingness to unduly fragment children, i.e., to consider their learning problems as isolated parts. Open educators prefer to view the child as a whole being and to see learning problems that are usually interconnected with all aspects of the child's development. In our setting, a child's learning plan always encompasses a broad range of behaviors and skill areas, e.g., behavior, socialization, communication, and (pre)academics. Within each area a child may have a particular problem, such as a short-term memory deficit, and this is planned for and responded to in specific ways. However, our experience has taught us that particular learning problems usually cut across several areas of functioning. For the open educator, the question is not whether to focus on a child's learning needs, but how to structure a child's learning experience so that the child can be active, involved, and can experience himself in positive ways.

Misconception 3 "Isn't it true that a child's future education and transition into other programs can be jeopardized by spending time in an open education setting?" The answer is no, as long as care is taken to respond to both the affective and cognitive needs of the child. The research on this point is equivocal. There are studies that report children making gains in social skills while maintaining appropriate cognitive gains. Other studies depict a range of findings — from no differences between children in open settings and traditional classrooms to gains in social skills over academic skills, and so on (Gardner, 1966; Spodek and Walberg, 1975). Once again the classroom teacher is left with contradictory findings and must proceed on the basis of his professional judgment about what kind of learning environment is most conducive to a child's growth.

Misconception 4 "Open education principles and methods cannot be applied to special education, since many children with special needs require a high degree of structure." What is misunderstood here is the enormous amount of planning and designing of a child's program and school day that takes place in an open setting. It is here that an open education teacher's commitment to individualizing the instructional program for each child becomes central. No assumption is made that all children can or should respond to the same structure (which includes openness, freedom, limits, controls, restrictions, reinforcements, and so on). The task of the teacher, family, and, to the greatest extent possible, the child is to determine what structure(s) responds best to the particular needs of the child. The critical issue is that "structure" is not an "all or nothing" concept in open education. For example, an elementary school built in Toronto was designed as an open education setting. Rather than have fixed rooms and walls, sections of each floor were partitioned by movable walls, bookcases, etc., to allow for modification when necessary. Of particular interest was the way in which the staff had designed each floor. They recognized the readiness and ability of different children to respond differently to openness. Thus, the floor plan allowed some areas to be more architecturally open than others, and some areas were more confining and smaller, having desks and small work tables. No stigma was attached to those children who were assigned to a particular area. The goal was to assist each child in becoming more independent and, if possible, to function in more open spaces. However, some children with specific/special needs remained in the contained space and experienced the other spaces only under more controlled conditions.

Fortunately, most programs that espouse an open education orientation implement it in a variety of ways. When responding to many children with special needs it is not possible or desirable to maintain a doctrinaire attitude about any one approach. For example, one of the basic tenets of open education, in particular, and therapeutic teaching with severely disabled children, in general, is to foster as much independence as possible. In our language development training approach with autistic children we strive to help the child become more independent, but this long-term goal is often accomplished by directing the child through a step-by-step language development program in which the teacher is quite active in the early stages, with the goal in mind of fostering more active involvement by the child as initial skills are gained.

OPEN EDUCATION APPLIED TO EMOTIONALLY DISTURBED CHILDREN

In our setting for nonhandicapped and severely emotionally disturbed children we have identified two major factors that contribute to our understanding and practice of applying open education in a therapeutic school program. These are: 1) the fostering of maximum participation on the part of everyone in the learning environment, and 2) the designing of an environment that combines structure and warmth.

Fostering Maximum Participation

The notion of maximizing the participation and activity level of everyone in a learning environment is a basic tenet of both open education and therapeutic educational approaches. In our setting many of the special needs children are labeled severely emotionally disturbed, and, more specifically, autistic or "autistic-like." In most instances they are withdrawn and experience major difficulties in relating to other children and adults.

For autistic children the major goal is to help energize them as much as possible. In our opinion, the ideal way to go about such a complex task is to have teachers behave in an active and intrusive fashion. When we apply this notion to the nonhandicapped children in our setting, it is just as relevant. By fostering a high activity level we can facilitate more peer interaction and can work toward our ultimate goal of a caring environment in which the participants share with each other and feel some responsibility for one another. Finally, by encouraging the activity level of teachers, they too have a way of expressing their skills and interests. As mentioned earlier, it is important to eliminate the myth that open classroom teachers stand by passively while children whirl giddily about the room. According to our definition, an open education setting is open to the teacher, as well. Indeed, in an open education setting a premium is placed on the inclusion of all parties — children, teachers, and families. Although the process is complex, the potential value to the child is enormous.

This notion of a high activity level for children and teachers has been discussed by Bussis and Chittenden (1970) and lends encouragement to the notion that there are aspects of open education that are quite central to our work with special children. Figure 1 shows the contributions of the teacher and of the child in each of four instructional approaches. The activity levels or contributions of teachers and children are high within an open education setting.

This is particularly relevant for us — for both our special and nonspecial needs children. One of the assumptions concerning the value of integrated settings lies in the potential for the positive peer modeling that nondisabled children can have on disabled children. This assumption is being tested in our classrooms by encouraging children to talk with each other, to play games, to be active, and to initiate, rather than simply to react to what is placed in front of them. In essence, we hope that children will come to feel a degree of psychological ownership of the environment and thus be responsible not only for what happens to them but for what happens to others as well.

Building in Structure and Warmth

As we discussed earlier, there is a structure to everything. Structure is seen in the attitudes, activities, schedule, beliefs, and practices that are found in an environment. In the broad area of educating severely emotionally disturbed children, a variety of studies and articles have begun to highlight the importance of establishing a clearly defined structure that com-

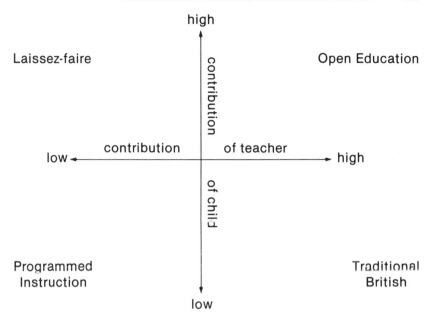

Figure 1. Double classification scheme based on extent to which (1) individual teacher and (2) individual child is an active contributor to decisions regarding content and process of learning (Adapted from Bussis, A. M., and Chittenden, E. A. 1970. *Analysis of an Approach to Open Education.* Educational Testing Service, Princeton, N. J.).

bines warmth and caring in order to facilitate child change (Barnes and Knoblock, 1973; Knoblock, 1973). In the past there has been an attempt in psychotherapy research to prove which method of therapy best facilitates client change. Today, the proponents of various classroom methodologies for teaching disturbed children are attempting to conceptualize and document their approach (Rhodes and Tracy, 1972), but it is likely that change is best accounted for by particular variables or dimensions of a method, rather than any one particular method. We have come to see that an environment for children who are as disturbed as ours are can find a balance between planning *for* and planning *with* a child.

We conceive of structure on a continuum, and no two of our disabled children require the same amount. What each does require is a high degree of planning. The ultimate goal is to move each child toward independent functioning. We see this process as developmental, for teachers as well as for children. Not every teacher begins with a clear idea of how to help children become active learners. As adults, we work with each other to change in this direction. However, whether we are discussing children or teachers, the dimension of treating each other with respect, warmth, and caring is central. We have had teachers on our staff with a strong behavioral interest who radiated incredible warmth. Hence our disclaimer early in this section that methodology may be only one factor, and teacher behavior and personality the other forces, of importance. The strong humanistic core to open education supports a teacher in seeing each child as a whole person, one who has dignity and who commands respect without having to earn it.

OPEN EDUCATION AND INTEGRATION

As with every learning environment, we have continuously modified our ideas and integration strategies. A dramatic example of this has been our shifting notions of how to design an appropriate schedule for a child that both fosters integration and responds to his need for particular assistance. The issues of scheduling, grouping, and programming are discussed in the following sections.

Scheduling of a Child's Day

For the purposes of clarity, our discussion of scheduling is separated from grouping issues, but in practice the two topics are related. Initially, we hoped to schedule a special child's day so that he spent as much time as possible with the other children in the group. If a child needed one-to-one attention, it was usually provided for him in the classroom. This decision was made in part only on philosophical grounds. The reality of having a limited number of staff available will often determine what and where activities will occur. As our program developed, we became more and more comfortable with efforts to intrude into the life space of some of our special children. After all, a number of them manifested behavior that seemed designed either to remove themselves from contact with others or to prevent the adults from coming close. As we observed and worked with some of our more withdrawn children, it seemed increasingly clear that *we* would have to make the decision for the child that our world was worth taking part in.

As we developed our approach it seemed that openness and intrusion were not mutually exclusive. Howes (1974) presents a chart in which he outlines the levels of decision-making in a classroom, ranging from teachers making unilateral decisions to pupils developing the options and teachers serving as resources. We believe that in order to move toward our ultimate goal of fostering more independent behavior, it is absolutely necessary that we engage special children, and this may require heavy input on the part of the teacher.

We use a teaching framework known as Developmental Therapy (Wood, 1975). This model is based on the application of teacher interventions geared to a child's developmental stage of functioning. At the earliest stage, a sensory stimulation approach is called for, and a high intrusion level on the part of adults is dictated by the child's needs. For children at this stage we developed a high intrusion schedule. One example is the following:

Intensive Stimulation Times	Family Group Involvement
9:30–10:30 Individual work	9:00–9:30 Group activity
11:00–12:00 Small group work	10:30–11:00 Snack
12:30–1:15 Individual work	12:00–12:30 Lunch with group
	1:15–2:30 Group games, singing, trips

Special needs children, who can spend more time profitably with nonhandicapped children, will have a schedule that balances time in and out of the family group.

James is a child who is focusing on and imitating other children, although he is seriously delayed in both language and other cognitive skills. His weekly schedule, shown in Figure 2, is an example of integration during skill times, as well as social times, keeping some periods for one-to-one or small group stimulation in areas like language. In an individualized program like ours, the schedule must be equally well thought out for each of the children. Each child's day is arranged for maximum learning. The major difference for nonhandicapped children is the greater range of grouping possibilities in which they can participate.

Criteria for Grouping Special and Nondisabled Children

Although in the final analysis decisions regarding grouping children are the result of a clinical process, we do adhere to a number of guidelines.

1. *Cross-age groupings*   We are committed to mixing the ages of children and utilizing the concept of family grouping (Ridgway and Lawton, 1965) in which there is a range of three years in each group. The advantages are many: children of varying developmental abilities can be placed together in a less stigmatizing manner (e.g., a 5-year-old special child and a 3-year-old nonhandicapped child may be involved in many of the same tasks), children can serve as helpers or tutors to each other, and none of us really spends our time exclusively with others our age.

2. *Placement of High Responders*   Our experience has led us to identify a number of children who respond with great caring and skill to the special children (and usually to adults and other children as well). We have been studying their behavior through classroom observation, using both observational checklists and specimen recordings (narrative field notes of behaviors and interactions). It is interesting to note that a child's

Figure 2. The Weekly Schedule: Meeting the needs of a special child within an integrated classroom. (This schedule was developed by Valerie Fenwick.)

	Monday	Tuesday	Wednesday	Thursday	Friday
8:45–9:00	Buses Arrive	Buses Arrive	Buses Arrive	Buses Arrive	Buses Arrive
9:00–9:30	Individual Skill Time	Individual Skill Time	Individual Skill Time	Individual Skill Time	Individual Skill Time
	James in play therapy at community facility (+)	All children at group table where the focus is working independently. For James tasks center on extending academic and problem-solving abilities.	Same as Tuesday	James in play therapy at community facility (+)	Same as Tuesday
9:30–9:50	Free Choice Time	Free Choice Time	Free Choice Time	Free Choice Time	Free Choice Time
	James arrives at school from therapy at 9:50	James makes choice within limits. Involvements would fall into the following three categories: 1. Relationship building with significant adult. Emphasis is on sharing trust and on stimulation.	Same as Tuesday	James arrives at school from therapy at 9:50.	Same as Tuesday

Time					
	Controlled Movement Skills Group / Social Studies / Science Group	2. Play with considerable adult support. Relationship building with other children. 3. Play with minimal adult support — alone or with other children	Dramatic Movement	Controlled Movement Skill Group / Social Studies / Science Group	Controlled Movement Skill Group / Social Studies / Science Group
9:50–10:30	James participates in the first of these groups where those developmental movement skills defined in his program are stressed	Snack	Entire class involved at this time in "acting out" various situations/roles, also involved in moving to music. James strongly supported by significant adults	Same as Monday	Same as Monday
10:30–10:45	Snack	Immediately after snack all children prepare for and move to university pool for swimming	Snack	Snack & Swimming	Snack

continued

Figure 2 — continued.

	Monday	Tuesday	Wednesday	Thursday	Friday
10:45–11:15	Meeting	Swimming	Meeting	Swimming & Meeting	Meeting
	Monday meeting involves entire class in problem solving through cross-sensory-processing. Refinement of abilities in the five sensory areas stressed.		Wednesday meeting involves whole group in planning for trip in the afternoon and in sharing news and problems.	Immediately after movement group James and two other children prepare for and move to university pool for swimming. Others eat snacks and participate in meeting related to self-expression and group process.	Friday meeting involves whole group in a related sensory experience or pictorial expression.
11:15–12:00	Play Skills Group Math Groups	Swimming	Play Skills Group Math Groups	Swimming (+) Math Groups	Play Skills Group Math Groups
	James participates in the first of these groups where play sets are defined and taught, play skills are developed and spontaneous play is encouraged and extended. A variety of open-		Same as Monday	James and two other children return from swimming at 12:00	Friday play skills group stresses developmental movement skills which facilitate among children free play in a gross motor sense. Interactive games are stressed.

ended materials is used. Individual and group interaction are emphasized.

Time	Monday	Tuesday	Wednesday	Thursday	Friday
12:00–12:30	Lunch	Lunch	Lunch	Lunch	Lunch
12:30–1:15	Language Stimulation Group (+) Reading Groups	Language Stimulation Group (+) Reading Groups	Trip	Language Stimulation Group (+) Reading Groups	Language Stimulation Group (+) Reading Groups
	James and two other children with similar language delays meet regularly at this time to work on broadening both receptive and expressive speech and more general language abilities, i.e., reading. Socialization as well is held to be an important goal here.	Same as Monday		Same as Monday	Same as Monday
1:15–2:00 (whole group activity)	Gym (obstacle course)	Cooking	Trip	Free-Choice Time	Singing

continued

Figure 2 — continued.

	Monday	Tuesday	Wednesday	Thursday	Friday
2:00–2:30	Writing Time	Writing Time	Writing Time	Writing Time	Writing Time
	All children at group table working in some fashion on written expression. James is learning letters and refining the eye-hand coordination needed to make them on his own. Underlying these tasks is the still more all-encompassing goal of teaching the symbolic significance of letters and written words. Additional time is spent on pictorial representation as well.	Same as Monday	Same as Monday	Same as Monday	Same as Monday
2:30–2:45	Children board buses and depart	Children board buses and depart	Children board buses and depart	Children board buses and depart	Children board buses and depart

(+) indicates times *not* integrated for James

response level may vary from one year to another. One of our children, 3½ years of age, appeared to be a natural-born therapist. The next year she was mostly focused on herself and did less reaching out and responding to others. Her own needs were salient, and developmentally she seemed to have different priorities. We are careful not to lock a child into a position where he always has to be responsive — a burden for anyone. In arranging our groups we selectively place responsive children when we know about them, but only if the placement seems appropriate for them as well.

3. *Placement Using Friendship Patterns*   Twice each year we administer a sociometric test to all of our children. It consists of sorting color photographs of each of the children in a family group. Each child is seen individually and his responses are tape-recorded. Based on this accumulated data and ongoing observations, we are able to determine which youngsters express themselves and act on some mutual basis for a relationship. In placing children in a particular group, we put those together who have already formed some relationship, and, if possible, we may keep them together beyond one year.

4. *Matching Child with Teacher's Style*   Perhaps the most important consideration is the matching of a child's needs with a teacher whose style and skills respond directly to those needs. We realize that the literature is filled with statements about the importance of teacher flexibility (Hunt, 1966), and we agree. However, the reality is that some teaching styles and some children's behaviors and needs can be matched to facilitate child change.

In selecting our staff we have looked for teachers with diverse skills and backgrounds. Just as there exists a range of activity levels for children, the same is true for teachers. On this dimension alone, teacher activity level, many grouping decisions can be made. For example, if we have a group in which several children are very withdrawn and functioning on a sensorimotor level, it is important to have a teacher who is able to intervene dramatically with those children. Of course, this does not mean that the needed intrusion is solely the responsibility of one teacher. There must be additional support so that others share this responsibility. It is asking too much of one person to interact constantly with a severely withdrawn child (or any child) without the assistance of others.

PROGRAMMING

The programming decisions made by adults are of critical importance in meeting the needs of individual children and in fostering integrated social interaction between disabled and nondisabled children. By programming we refer to the provisioning of the environment and to the content and structure of the activities that are presented to children. The classrooms in our setting are highly stimulating and rich in materials — consumables, games, books, and toys. They represent an economy of plenty. We think of materials in two different ways: a) generic materials that can be used in a variety of ways at different developmental levels (e.g., blocks, cuisenaire rods, water play equipment), and b) specific materials that are chosen to meet the needs of individual children in terms of their skills (e.g., reading, language, play) and developmental level.

Within each room, staff members have designed spaces to evoke the appropriate use of materials (e.g., reading lofts, messy corners). There are also spaces for low stimulation, either within the classroom or in an adjoining room. We are challenging the assumptions about environmental stimulation that many professionals make about severely disturbed children (Cruickshank et al., 1961). Thus, rather than reducing stimulation in general, we try to identify each child's specific needs for limiting visual and auditory stimuli.

The content and structure of activities varies according to scheduled times, child's perceived needs, and teacher interest. We focus on affective, cognitive, and social needs with all children. As mentioned earlier, our program has a very wide range of children in it. It requires creative planning to develop experiences, which can include this wide range of children, and at the same time respond to children's particular needs. This is accomplished through developmental activities that all children enjoy, such as singing, cooking, and eating, and clay, sand, and water play. Flexible materials also facilitate integration; for instance, children can use cuisenaire rods in many ways and degrees of complexity, including building, sorting, and matching, and representing mathematical processes. Thus, within an integrated group of children sitting at a table, children working at their individual level with rods can talk about what they are doing, as well as feel a part of the group experience.

Teachers consciously set up activities that require several children to work together. Examples include murals, the rocking boat, and alphabet games. The teacher may also specifically ask some children to help others with particular tasks. "Partners" are a common phenomenon, and peer teaching and helping is actively reinforced for all children. A nonhandicapped child's willingness to approach a disabled child is monitored and reinforced by teachers throughout the year.

Social-emotional objectives are of critical importance for all children, but particularly in a program that includes children whose primary area of disability appears to be in their affect and relationships. The focus on feelings occurs constantly in the multitude of classroom interactions, but it is also structured into the program by teachers as a legitimate activity. Each family group meets daily for a group meeting. The format varies from a greeting time to a "magic circle," but the focus is the feelings of individual children and adults or the group interaction. These meetings offer an opportunity for feelings to be raised that relate to the wide range of children in the room. For instance, in one class children talked about how they felt when someone pulled their hair at a time when this behavior was creating tension in the group. These meetings offer an opportunity for all children to be viewed as participants. Each child is encouraged to speak, and disabled children who cannot speak may be interpreted for by other children or adults. This group time is also a time for celebrations — birthday parties, holidays, and special visitors; all children are included and celebrated.

Teachers play a crucial role in the acceptance and successful integration of disabled and nondisabled children. By their words and behavior, teachers demonstrate their respect and caring for each and every child in the school. Children seem to feel valued, and in turn can respond positively to others. Children model the teachers' words and behaviors with each others. Teachers offer explanations for behavior and suggest ways in which to deal with the behavior of others. They support growth of all children at different levels. For example, teachers offer congratulations and delight when a child first drinks independently from a cup, or when another child reads a page in a book or writes his name for the first time. Teachers intervene when children are upset, which demonstrates to all children that adult support will be there when they need it. In contrast, teachers recognize the importance of allowing, even encouraging, children to resolve their own conflict situations. This is particularly important in an integrated program if the disabled children are to be seen as peers by the other children. Our teachers frequently facilitate such interaction by prompting nonhandicapped children to use particular interventions with the special children. For example, at first we noticed that some children were addressing questions to teachers that were intended for children. A child might ask his teacher if Johnny wanted a cookie, instead of asking Johnny. This frequently occurred when a child was involved with one of his nonverbal or less verbal peers. In such a situation we typically respond by suggesting that he ask the child directly. In other instances a teacher may model a way to stop aggressive behavior and may have other children utilize the same approach.

TEACHERS' PERSONAL GROWTH

In our view, the dimension of personal growth for teachers and other staff members is central to an open and integrated setting. At our school we focus on this in a number of ways. First, each team of three staff members meets on a regularly scheduled basis at least three afternoons each week. At these meetings children's programs are reviewed, and teacher behaviors and interactions are discussed. An effort is made not only to allow feedback to be given and received, but to have it done with skill and care. The giving and taking of feedback does not occur automatically — it is risky, particularly with people who work so closely with one another and who are as interdependent as our teachers, because of our program and scheduling.

For feedback to occur, there must be someone willing to initiate it. In each classroom the lead teacher has assumed this as one of her responsibilities. As these discussions and relationships develop, a teacher may ask to have a particular activity or plan reviewed. This can be accomplished by the lead teacher or by another staff member in the room. It is also possible to have someone who is not a member of the classroom staff observe specific behaviors or activities.

The primary feedback strategy is one of making certain that each person feels a sense of support and can relate to a specific person and/or group. Each family group has a support person (administrator, resource teacher, or parent worker) who meets with them at least once a week with her own agenda or one that is provided by the teachers in the family group. The lead teachers and/or paid staff meet weekly, as do the student interns.

One of the critical issues of teacher development is the relationship between teacher flexibility and teacher personal growth. A long-range goal for our teachers is that they develop a repertoire of skills and behaviors that will allow them to select the most appropriate intervention, depending on the needs of a child. To facilitate the attainment of this objective, we utilize a framework developed by Hunt (1966) in which he conceptualizes a hierarchy of skills needed by a teacher and a range of interventions needed to respond in facilitative ways.

We have had any number of potential "mismatches" between a child's behaviors and the available style of a teacher. In one instance a very soft-spoken and rather passive teacher was faced with a 7-year-old boy who was very active both verbally and physically. The boy was easily disoriented and tended to feel overwhelmed by his thoughts and feelings unless his entire day was predictable. His teacher's own lifestyle tended to be more easygoing. As the teacher began working with this child, it became obvious to everyone involved that intense structuring of the child's school day would be needed. This meant that discrete time blocks and activities would have to be developed and adhered to on a daily basis. At one point the teacher verbalized: "This is a very hard thing for me to do — to be this organized and systematic — it's damn hard!" Having recognized both the child's needs and his own style, the teacher was able to modify his own behavior and radiate the appropriate behaviors. Sometimes the behaviors that need to be changed are more superficial, such as using a clearer, more dramatic voice quality, but other times there may be major discrepancies between teacher styles and children's needs. The important point is that teachers should also be seen as capable of change and growth. We strongly urge a support system for teachers, as well as for children, so that all persons in a learning environment may feel safe to explore personal issues and grow in skills.

EVALUATION

Efforts are made at Jowonio to evaluate both individual child progress and the degree to which children are integrated. Child progress is assessed through the use of the Developmental Therapy Objectives Rating Forms (DTORF), which are also used to establish treatment objectives for each child (Wood, 1975). Teachers keep either daily or weekly records on specific activities and objectives. Children are rated every eight weeks on the DTORF and changes are noted in the objectives that are mastered. There are two formalized progress reports per year to parents, with an updated learning plan prepared every eight weeks to adapt to the revised goals in the Rating Form checklist. Children are periodically videotaped. These videotapes serve as records of child growth and as sources for feedback to staff.

Integration is traced through the expressed attitudes and behaviors of the nondisabled children toward the disabled children. Sociometric measures and individual interviews, using photographs of the children in each family group, give data about attitudes. From this material it appears that the nondisabled children do not perceive the disabled children as qualitatively different than themselves; the unusual behavior of disabled children (aggression, screaming, ritualisms, etc.) is treated as one aspect of an individual, rather than as the whole person. Children are direct and descriptive about what they do not like about a child ("He pinches to get your attention"; "He wrecks my buildings"), as well as what they do like ("He's fun to play with"; "He likes me"). They perceive changes in other children and state them in matter-of-fact terms ("He doesn't hurt people much anymore"). They have developed explanations for the unusual behavior that some of the special children exhibit ("He's mad cause he has to do his work"; "He doesn't want nobody to eat his food"; "He's saying that because he's trying to talk, and he doesn't know what words to say").

Observations using an observational instrument, the "Systematic Who-to-Whom-Analysis Notation" (Swan, 1973), and specimen recordings provide additional data on the degree of social integration in the family groups and the kinds of interactions that occur between students. In the preliminary analysis it appears that the majority of the interactions between disabled and nondisabled students are positive (positive attending, cooperation, affection). In addition, in the rooms where teachers made strong efforts to integrate children, the special needs children interacted more frequently with a greater number of nondisabled children.

Our evaluation procedures are designed to be used in a formative way — to provide feedback to teachers so that programs can be modified. We have also tried where possible to combine evaluation and record-keeping procedures to minimize the teacher workload.

PARENT INVOLVEMENT

As a parent-initiated school, a basic premise of our program has been that parents must be involved in their child's school experience. This involvement has now been mandated as part of Public Law 94–142, which requires that parents participate in the development of the Individual Educational Plan for their child. We attempt to stimulate parent-school communication on a variety of levels through regular parent-teacher contact (notes, phone calls, home visits, classroom observation), a full-time parent worker, and group meetings for informational, educational, and social purposes. Our goals for parent contact include the following: gaining and giving information about child behavior and needs, identifying goals and objectives of the school program, developing a consistent approach both at home and at school regarding learning and behavior issues for the child, providing emotional and advocacy support to parents, teaching and supporting parents in home training of their child, offering opportunities for parent education and growth, and offering opportunities for socialization as adults and as a family.

We feel that parent support of the school is a critical factor in a venture as unique as ours. As far as we know, no one in this country is integrating autistic children to the extent that we are. In addition, clinically programming for children labeled severely disturbed or autistic is very problematic; no one really has the right answers about effective long-term interventions. It is crucial that parents know what is going on with their child at school and that they feel comfortable with both the people and the programming. Every day counts with severely involved children, and we must work in concert — home and school — to be sure that the time is used as effectively as possible. The families of our children have many ongoing needs, including behavior management help and someone to talk with who knows and values their child and can relate to the difficulties of having an autistic child. We try to respond to these needs to the extent that we can.

In addition to the support of parents of disabled children, the school must have the interest and support of parents of nonhandicapped children. Parents of nondisabled children must feel comfortable with the program that is offered to their children, and they must be willing to have their children in a school that enrolls severely disabled children and that is committed to innovative approaches to education. The parents of nondisabled children have maintained an active interest and support for the school. When interviewed, parents of nondisabled children all mention the individualized nature of the program, the warm personal quality of the teacher-child and child-child interactions, and the exposure that their children were receiving to a wide range of individual differences as reasons why they enrolled their children at the school.

SUMMARY

This chapter reviews the philosophical basis and fundamental program elements of an open education school program that serves severely disabled and nondisabled children together. The most unique aspect of The Learning Place Program is its attempt to fully integrate severely handicapped children (labeled autistic, "autistic-like," severely emotionally disturbed) and, at the same time, to provide for them and for the nonhandicapped children an exemplary individualized, clinical program. Evaluation procedures and parent involvement are also discussed. In our program we are attempting to document our efforts and to disseminate material and information to others who are interested in the integration of a wide range of children. We believe that a quality program can be developed that integrates severely disabled children and nondisabled children in an open learning environment. We encourage others to try such an approach.

REFERENCES

Barnes, E. B., and Knoblock, P. 1973. Openness and Advocacy: Teacher attributes and behaviors for mainstreaming children with special needs. In: N. Kreinberg and H. L. Chow (eds.), Configurations of Change: The Integration of Mildly Handicapped Children into the Regular Classroom. Far West Laboratory for Educational Research and Development, San Francisco.

Bussis, A. M., and Chittenden, E. A. 1970. Analysis of an Approach to Open Education. Educational Testing Service, Princeton, N. J.

Cremin, L. A. 1961. The Transformation of the School: Progressivism in American Education 1876-1957. Vintage, New York.

Cruickshank, W. M., Bantzen, F. A., Ratzeburg, F. H. and, Tannhauser, M. T. 1961. A Teaching Method for Brain Injured and Hyperactive Children. Syracuse University Press, Syracuse.

Gardner, D. E. M. 1966. Experiment and Tradition in Primary Schools. Methuen & Co., London.

Howes, V. M. 1974. Informal Teaching in the Open Classroom. Macmillan Publishing Company, Inc., New York.

Hunt, D. E. 1966. A model for analyzing the training of training agents. Merrill-Palmer Quarterly 12:137–156.

Knoblock, P. 1973. Open education for emotionally disturbed children. Except. Child. 39:358–365.

Rhodes, W. C., and M. L. Tracy (eds.), 1972. A Study of Child Variance. Vol. 2. Interventions. University of Michigan, Ann Arbor.

Ridgway, L., and Lawton, I. 1965. Family Grouping in the Primary School. Ballantine Books, Inc., New York.

Spodek, B., and Walberg, H. J. (eds.) 1975. Studies in Open Education. Shocken Books, New York.

Swan, W. W. 1973. An observational instrument based on the objectives of a special education curriculum. Presented at the Division D, AERA Annual Meeting, February, New Orleans.

Wood, M. M. (ed.) 1975. Developmental Therapy: A Textbook for Teachers as Therapists for Emotionally Disturbed Young Children. University Park Press, Baltimore.

Open Education and Young Children with Special Needs

Impact and Resources

Evaluation in Open Classrooms
Emergence of a
Qualitative Methodology

George E. Hein

In reality, every [statement of fact in natural science], however true it may be, is true only relatively to the means of observation and the point of view of those who have enunciated it. So far it may be depended upon. But whether it will bear every speculative conclusion that may be logically deduced from it, is quite another question.

T. H. Huxley,
quoted in Charles Darwin's autobiography

The field of special education is undergoing a revolution. Children in need of special services are receiving increased attention as part of the broad social movement that recognizes the rights of various constituencies. The Hobbs report (1975), with its careful analysis of the problems of special education and the difficulties of labeling children, attests to the concern for treating each child as an individual with unique strengths and potential and for the adjustment of educational programs to the needs of the child. The passage of comprehensive special education legislation in many states and the passage of Public Law 94-142, The Education for All Handicapped Children Act, add official status to the movement to value all children, to adjust education to their needs, and to move toward accepting differences without considering them defects.

These concerns are similar to those that have been raised by proponents of open education. Indeed, Harman (1975) has argued that the impact of Chapter 766 (special education legislation in Massachusetts) lies in educators recognizing that "*All* Children Are Special," and that some basic tenets of open education — recognition of differential rates of growth in children, recognition of diversity among children, need for individual curriculum, and teaching to a child's strengths — must become part of the educational plan for all children, including those who receive special services.

The growth of open education in the United States in the past ten years has made proponents of that movement aware of the fact that the traditional forms of assessment and evaluation were not adequate to their goals. Within open education, as within education in general, there has been a re-examination of evaluation theory and procedures and the development of new ways of assessing children and evaluating programs. These approaches are particularly relevant to the newer perspectives concerning children with special needs. This chapter summarizes the open education experience in the hope that it can prove useful to special educators.

My intention is to provide a coherent viewpoint concerning educational evaluation that will be helpful to all practitioners who are concerned with best serving every child. Some of the work cited is specifically associated with open education practice, while other theoretical statements and applied procedures are part of the general development of educational research and evaluation during the last few years. For this general work, I have chosen examples that illustrate a particular qualitative pattern. No effort has been made to provide a comprehensive survey of all work on assessment and evaluation during the last decade, nor to present points of view that are inconsistent with an open education perspective.

OPEN EDUCATION AND EVALUATION

History

In the 1960s a new educational approach began to gain adherents in the United States. Unlike the curriculum reform movement of the 1950s which essentially was an effort to change the subject content within the existing context of schooling, this newer movement challenged the very structure of the school and the way in which all aspects of education were carried out. The open education movement, as it came to be called, raised serious questions about teaching, learning, curriculum, room arrangement, the goals of education, and the grouping of children. In short, it suggested a whole new philosophy of education.

As open education programs developed, initial attention was focused on implementation: teachers began to familiarize themselves with materials, practitioners traveled to England to observe informal classrooms, there was increased interest in Piaget and the field of child development, and teacher centers were established where teachers and parents could discuss educational issues, explore "hands-on" work, and participate in workshops.

In the early days of heady experimentation, evaluation issues did not have a high priority. The educational reforms of the 1960s were not always well understood, and many assumed that traditional evaluation methods would automatically show the advantages of any new approach. Others viewed the educational reforms primarily within the context of larger social reforms. As long as the educational reforms were part of the effort to create a more just, prosperous, and joyous society, it did not appear fundamentally important to examine the nature of the reforms. However, as funds and enthusiasm for educational reform diminished, questions about the value of reform became more important.

It became clear to advocates of open education that the ways in which evaluation was being carried out were simply not appropriate to the issues raised by the open classrooms. The kinds of answers that could be derived from the evaluation questions that were being asked did not match the goals of the reformers. In subsequent sections traditional educational evaluation, its limits when applied to open education prac tice, and some of the alternatives that are being developed are discussed.

The initial enthusiasm for open classrooms has diminished, yet thoughtful implementation of open education practice continues. Classroom teachers, schools, and a few school districts continue to develop sound programs that take into account the perspectives of open education. At the same time, these practitioners are addressing the inevitable evaluation questions: How good is this approach? What does it accomplish for children? How much do they learn? Which is better, open or traditional education?

Traditional Styles of Evaluation

In American education there are essentially three types of approaches to evaluation; that is, three ways in which data have traditionally been gathered to assess the impact of education on individual children, or on classrooms and schools. These approaches are: standardized achievement tests, the application of previously developed behavioral instruments, and research studies from within the educational community. Each of these has a set of assumptions and an associated tradition that have proved to be insurmountable obstacles as attempts are made to apply them to open education programs.

Standardized Achievement Tests   It has become almost fashionable to attack the standardized testing industry and the use of such testing in the schools. The critique is necessary as the use of tests continues to increase, and tests still remain the most powerful arbiters of "successful" educational practice in this country. Any report on reading scores in a school system is local news, and reports of national trends, such as a de-

cline in SAT scores, is instant national news (as are the various and contradictory reasons that are put forward to explain the decline).

Standardized achievement tests are based on two assumptions: first,
that there is some body of knowledge, existing independent of the learner,
that can be classified and organized. The aim of the test is to find out how
much of the standard information and concepts each learner has acquired, regardless of the circumstances of testing, learning, life situation,
background, etc. The second assumption is that knowledge can be
organized in such a manner that the total quantity of this knowledge has
some value, and all individuals who are tested can be classified linearly
along a continuum with reference to the amount of this knowledge that
they possess. Thus, it is possible to establish a "normal" distribution and,
by using this distribution, to speak of any child as reading in the top 95th
percentile or reading as well as half the children in the country or reading
1.7 years below grade level.

Advocates of open education strongly stress that knowledge is not an
independent entity, but it depends on the learner and his or her interaction
with the world. They reject the notion of a clear classification of knowledge. In its place they urge that specific facts or vocabulary words for different learners should be related to the learner's interests and local surroundings. Finally, since open education advocates argue forcefully that
the ability to express one's knowledge depends a great deal on the occasion in which one uses it, the whole approach of standardized achievement testing is not compatible with open education. In a paper that com-
pares various aspects of open classrooms and the testing situation,
deRivera (1973) has pointed out how the two are incompatible:

1. *Open classroom*   Children are encouraged or at least allowed to
   share, to converse, to help one another.
   Testing situation   No talking, no sharing, no helping one another.
2. *Open classroom*   Children exercise and demonstrate their knowledge and skills in many different modes: verbally, by action, dramatics, writing, etc.
   Testing situation   The children's response mode is limited to
   reading, listening, and marking. Knowledge and skills which they are
   used to exercising in one mode have to be translated to the mode of
   response that fits the test.
3. *Open classroom*   Generally, flexibility is such that children can
   finish most tasks they begin and can go on to something else when
   finished. Children can move around the room.
   Testing situation   No moving on to the next task when finished,
   often not enough time to finish a task. Children must remain seated at
   a desk.

4. *Open classroom*   Children generally work at many different tasks, so that comparisons are not easy and competition is not encouraged.
   Testing situation   Children work on the same task at the same time so that comparisons are facilitated.
5. *Open classroom*   Each child is viewed as a complex, unique individual, having strengths and weaknesses, but each is essentially qualitatively different from others.
   Testing situation   Quantitative differences between children are important, qualitative differences are lost. Success is defined by others' failures. (The 60th percentile means that 60 percent of the children in that grade score below.)
6. *Open classroom*   The child is given learning experiences designed to develop a self-image of a competent, effective, successful person. This is considered an important attitude for effective learning.
   Testing situation   The very children (those who are weakest in skills) who need the support of a positive self-image in order to continue learning are discouraged and frustrated by failure.
7. *Open classroom*   Thoughtful, critical thinking is encouraged.
   Testing situation   Often random guessing is a more successful strategy than thoughtfulness since the tests are limited in time. Thoughtfulness is not rewarded.
8. *Open classroom*   Intrinsic motivation (i.e. learning for learning's sake) is considered the most effective motivation for long-term learning.
   Testing situation   Extrinsic motivation (i.e. learning for some outside reward) is encouraged; learning in order to pass the test. [deRivera, 1973, p. 7]

A secondary issue that is derived from the critique of standardized testing concerns the shortcomings of these tests. Oscar K. Buros, longtime editor of the prestigious *Mental Measurements Yearbook,* has recently repeated his view that "most standardized tests are poorly constructed, of questionable or unknown validity, pretentious in their claims, and likely to be misused more often than not" (1977, p. 9). It has been shown repeatedly, by both professional and lay analysts, that questions are ambiguous, misleading, simply impossible to answer, or supplied with false answers in the key. Several critical analyses are contained in an issue of the *National Elementary Principal* (Houts, 1975). Critics have also documented that the curriculum reform movement of the 1950s had a profound *non*effect on the standardized tests used in schools. Project Torque (Schwartz, 1975; Taylor, 1977) has analyzed current tests in mathematics and has concluded that almost all of the questions deal with simple computation and with the ability to read. There are no references to the "new" math, which presumably had influenced the content of school texts, nor do the tests adequately assess mathematical concepts. Finally, widely used tests are often anachronistic and contain glaring biases. For example, the Detroit Tests of Learning Aptitude (Baker and Leland, 1935), which are still used very widely, include pictorial material that is stylized and out of date. Boys and girls are all Caucasian and neat in appearance, with the girls wearing dresses and the boys usually in shirts and ties. Adults may wear fashions of the 1920s, and a man is pictured in an American-made convertible, a car that has not come from Detroit assembly lines since before some of the children who are taking the test were born. Yet, on one subtest children are asked to describe "What is foolish, what is silly about the picture" with the correct answers being "coat on backwards, buttons in back" and "steering with face toward rear."

Previously Developed Behavioral Instruments   A second approach to the evaluation of educational programs has involved the application of previously developed research tools to classroom settings. A broad range of behavioral instruments is available to analyze what takes place in classrooms. A fine collection of these instruments is found in the 15 volumes of *Mirrors of Behavior* (Simon and Boyer, 1965). Unfortunately, most of these instruments are based on a view of the classroom and of education that is not applicable to the open education approach. Just as the standardized achievement tests have a traditional view of knowledge, so the observational instruments presume a traditional view of classrooms: they see the classroom primarily as a place where the teacher is the instructor, where direction, the determination of curriculum, and other class activity is primarily transmitted through the teacher, and where there is an easily codified set of expected student behaviors. Major characteristics of open education programs, such as student initiated curriculum, student-student interaction as a basis for learning, and true individualization, are not included as categories on most of the instruments. Hence, these important aspects of classroom life, which must be examined in order to begin to understand what is happening in open classrooms, are not amenable to study using these standard instruments.

Research in Education   Many studies have been carried out in open and other classrooms based on the prevailing models of research and evaluation in education. These studies usually are of the form in which one variable is isolated to measure its effect on a single or very discrete set of student behaviors, and some form of experimental or quasi-experimental design is employed to ascertain whether the variable does indeed effect a particular result. Does the use of a different basal reader result in higher levels of achievement on the standardized test? Does a flexible schedule increase independent reading?

Again, the *form* in which this research (or evaluation design, as is often the case for program evaluations) is carried out, usually precludes a significant answer to the questions raised by open education. The notion that one particular factor can be isolated from its surroundings, analyzed, controlled, and examined for its effect in the absence of other effects, is questionable on two grounds. First, performing this kind of research entails certain theoretical assumptions that proponents of open education simply do not share. Primary among these is the assumption that human lives can be analyzed into discrete components and the effect of one component can be studied in the absence of and without considering its interaction with other factors. Second, even if this rather simplistic view of life were correct, it is questionable whether any natural setting, that is, a classroom with real children, can approach this ideal. The actual events in schools are such that it is almost impossible to establish a controlled experiment where everything except the desired variable is kept "equal." Sometimes ethical problems get in the way of scientific methodology (for example, is it ethical to deny some children treatment?), other times logistical problems intervene (the teacher from experimental group A is reassigned to control group B in the middle of the experiment), and sometimes just the usual diffusion of information and the open character of the public school setting interferes with the canons of laboratory science. (Teachers from control and experimental groups share information, children leave one class for another, or the promotion of a key staff member shifts the emphasis of a program.)

All things considered, the methods of traditional classroom evaluation that are available appear to be unequal to the task of developing sound evaluations of open classrooms. Existing studies that try to assess open education using typical educational research approaches make this clear. In some instances students in open classrooms performed very well on standardized tests, in other instances there were no significant differences. For example, analysis of the psychological impact of open education in many settings showed positive, insignificant, and negative effects (Horwitz, 1976). Taken in the aggregate, studies of open classrooms mainly demonstrate *no* effect on children, but the very nature of large-scale norm reference tests is such that individual program differences are not likely to show up significantly. The tests are designed to conceal individual program effects. For example, the goal of most test designers is to devise questions that "differentiate" well and are likely to have close to half of the children in the entire sample answer correctly and half answer incorrectly. A question that differentiates for only one kind of population, or between a small group of students who have a special experience and the vast majority of the rest of the school population, is likely to be rejected during the preliminary trials of test items because either too few or too many of those tested answer correctly.

Perhaps the best evidence of the inability to develop meaningful evaluations of open education (as well as of several other classroom approaches) using traditional evaluation tools is contained in the results of the recent national Follow Through evaluation (Stebbins et al., 1977). As the program progressed and this major national research effort was implemented, there was increasing pressure for "results" and for information about which educational approach was the best, or at least, which group of approaches was most successful. Tens of millions of dollars were spent on evaluation, and every child in the program was repeatedly tested with a battery of standardized instruments.

The methodology and the results of the evaluation program have been subject to severe criticism (House et al. 1977), and it is essentially impossible to decide what the "results" of the program have been. The two most striking conclusions from the available data are: first, the differences between individual communities, which tried any educational approach, were much greater than the differences between educational approaches. Thus, standardized test scores for children from districts that implemented open education approaches differed more among themselves than the set of scores differed from a group of districts that implemented a more traditional educational program.

Second, the programs that followed an instructional format and a curriculum that was similar to the evaluation tools used showed higher results on the evaluation than those programs that did not. When the programs gave instruction that was very similar (both in content and in form) to the tests that were used for evaluation the children scored higher on the tests than they did when the programs were far different from the tests in both content and form. Precisely the same problem is posed in the first section above: traditional testing is not suitable for evaluating open education.

The recognition of this mismatch between traditional evaluation procedures and the goals of open education practice essentially led to a crisis in the open education field. In 1972, at the initial meeting of the North Dakota Study Group on Evaluation some participants argued that work had to be modified so that programs would show up better on traditional measures. Others suggested that traditional measures and forms of evaluation should be reformed and improved. If only the standardized achievement tests were better, more representative of a wider subject area, and less prejudicial, then they would be useful for open education evaluation. Still others argued that what was needed was a whole restructuring of evaluation, a new look at the enterprise and its relation to educational practice.

In response to the crisis three approaches to restructuring evaluation in open education were identified:

1. An exploration of theory and its relation to educational practice
2. An examination of past practice to discover relevant examples of evaluation work
3. The development of new methods (or the revival of older ones) that provide meaningful evaluation possibilities for open classrooms

The remainder of this chapter discusses these three topics.

Evaluation Theory and Educational Theory

During this century, educational research and evaluation (as well as other social sciences) have been dominated by the quest for quantification and by the goal of developing social sciences, which have the same legitimacy as the physical sciences. The early research of Thorndike and other behaviorist-oriented educational researchers was devoted to developing a cumulative body of knowledge in education that would have the same predictive power, certainty, and causal interrelation as the physical sciences. The model that was employed was late nineteenth century physics, a model that has been severely questioned in recent years. The education community's preoccupation with experimental design, with "objectivity," with stress on simple measureable properties, and with the search for linear causal chains emerges from this tradition.

Scientific Method   Other scientific models could have been chosen as the model for education. As is the case with other disciplines, the field might have been divided between practitioners who followed the "experimental model" design style of research and those who patterned their work after other, equally viable and successful research strategies. For example, in the field of biology, parallel research traditions that examine the relationship between structure and function have existed for centuries. One approach to this field has been to examine living organisms and to try to understand how they behave from the examination of their constituent parts. For example, the early studies of anatomy and Harvey's discovery of circulation of the blood fall into this group followed, after the invention of the microscope, by the splendid work on detailed structure: tissue, cell theory, microanatomy, etc. Later in the nineteenth century, as analytic chemistry techniques became available, biologists and chemists studied the biochemical structure, or composition, of living organisms and began to understand some functions in terms of their underlying molecular chemistry. Finally, in our own century further technical progress, such as the discovery of x-ray crystallography and electron microscopy, has resulted in a further expansion of understanding of structure and function: we now know about genetic codes, molecular aggregates in cells, composition of protein, enzymes, hormones, etc.

Yet, fruitful as all this work has been, it has covered only a fraction of biology. Any understanding of how organisms function or behave always includes another critical component: the direct study of behavior in its natural setting. Again, there is a long tradition of natural history, classification, study of fossils, breeding experiments, and, in the nineteenth century, the remarkable natural history observations that led Darwin to his revolutionary theory of animal behavior. Since Darwin, there have been the ethology studies of Tinbergen, Lorenz, Von Frisch, and many others, as well as work by Jane Goodall on chimpanzee behavior and a host of similar natural history studies concerning ecology, behavior, adaptability, etc. For a further discussion of this tradition, see Hein (1976).

This latter tradition is clearly different from the analytic activity described above; it has been enormously fruitful in enriching our knowledge of the world around us and is undeniably recognized as part of the overall scientific enterprise. The first of these three points is important for us here: the work in these fields can all be described as a form of "watching and wondering" (as it has been called by Tinbergen), and thus is strikingly different from the "experimental design" model of molecular biology, and of most work in educational research.

Qualitative Methodology   In the last few years, a number of educational researchers have argued that this second style of research has some place in education (see Wilson, 1977; Mehan, 1978). Characteristically, work in this mode does not result in numerical data and thus has been described as qualitative methodology. The goal of this kind of work is not so much to discover a simple causal connection, but to describe and explain phenomena in the context in which they are found; and to try to develop a general idea of why something happens, considering the factors that affect activities in the natural world.

Recently, a number of educators have pointed out the need for qualitative research and evaluation studies and various terms have been coined, including *illuminative* (Parlett and Hamilton, 1976), *interactive* (Stake, 1967), and *expressive objectives* (Eisner, 1969), to describe evaluation approaches. Bronfenbrenner (1976) has called for an *ecological* perspective on educational research. Although theoretical writers vary in the details of their analysis, certain common themes emerge that provide an appropriate framework for evaluation work supportive of open education.

First, all writers recognize that there are different paradigms for doing evaluation or research, and work in one tradition cannot be judged by the standards of the other tradition. Most of Charles Darwin's work cannot be described as experimental research following "good" research design, nor can it even be classified as fitting into one of the "quasi-experimental" designs described by Campbell and Stanley (1963). This does not render his work and his conclusions invalid, it simply suggests that he was following another tradition. Darwin's conclusions have a different kind of validity and they provide us with a different type of information and insight into nature than do, for example, Mendel's experiments with generations of peas.

Similarly, the knowledge about classrooms and children's learning gained from observational studies, interviews, or other "informal" evaluations can be valid even if these materials do not produce statistically significant numerical data. They may or may not be valuable in terms of other criteria.

Second, research and evaluation studies in the qualitative mode have certain attributes in common. The researcher follows some general theory and has some general framework into which the data that are collected must fit. This framework is not a single testable hypothesis, but it is a general set of hypotheses that make up a position, for example, a theory of personality or a concept of how children learn. The reason for expanding a working hypothesis to include a more general framework is that qualitative methodology deliberately makes room for the observation of surprising or unexpected phenomena. The evaluator does not set out to test a single hypothesis, but sets out to gather data within a framework to obtain any information that may be relevant to a general issue. In terms of child assessment, the evaluator will not try to isolate only the child's ability to differentiate beginning word sounds, but while interested in that problem, the evaluator will also consider the child's general response to the testing situation, the child's surroundings, interaction with others, etc.

Setting is an important part of qualitative methodology (hence, Bronfenbrenner's term, *ecology* of education). Any research or evaluation performed in the qualitative tradition must take into account the surroundings of the work and should discuss the results in terms of the setting. For example, Cazdan (1974) has argued that the best way to assess children's language ability is through *concentrated,* rather than *contrived,* encounters. She believes that any test situation (one in which the examiner knows the answers to the question asked the pupil) is contrived and gives a distorted view of children's language. Instead, she urges concentrated, natural conversation as a measure of language ability. Of course, the concentrated encounter must be described in terms of its setting.

Another component of qualitative methodology is the stress on the subject's participation in the evaluation or research and the need to obtain the subject's views, where possible. Along with this is the recognition of the role of the experimenter (or evaluator) in any results. The traditional approach to the problem of experimenter intrusion (experimenter bias) is to try to make the situation as impersonal as possible. Thus, a typical testing situation places a tester and a child (often strangers to each other) in a bare room, with the tester reading a script or protocol and engaging in little interaction with the child being tested. The alternative, advocated by the qualitative method, is to recognize that even such stylized controlled encounters have a biasing effect on children. Thus, standardization is considered less important than a description and recognition of the evaluator's role. The intention is not to render the situation neutral, but to find a place for the person in research, to set up certain rules of behavior, and also to ensure that the role of the person is known, reported, and understood.

Finally, since qualitative research stresses the need to consider a number of interacting factors, there is a concern that these factors be considered simultaneously. The goal of qualitative research is not to find simple linear chains, but to unearth the complex of causes, interactions, and interdependencies that determine any situation. Thus, the methodologies that are used are deliberately developed to respond to these complexities. Fortunately, the qualitative style has been used for decades, not only by biologists, but by a whole range of social scientists, anthropologists, sociologists, and others. Through their efforts a whole host of field methods have been developed, described in the social science literature, and are available to educators (for example, see Glaser and Strauss, 1967; Filstead, 1970).

The alternative, qualitative evaluation and research methodology, is particularly appropriate for open education assessment. Open education stresses the need to view a child as a whole being within his or her environment and to develop a curriculum that takes into account the external and internal forces that impinge on a child. Open education advocates capitalizing on occasional events and on having curriculum grow and spread from experiences. Superimposed on all this day-to-day spontaneous and holistic character is an over-arching theory of child development and social interaction. The apparent openness is simply the individual variation within a general conceptual framework. Any evaluation that focuses on simple causal connections, on recording specific regularities of behavior, may find only chaos. However, evaluation that permits immersion in the situation and accepts diversity at the individual level within a general scheme can both discern patterns and can describe events in a way that meets the canons of scientific objectivity and interpersonal reliability.

Historic Practice

While proponents of open education have criticized and rejected current evaluation practice, there has been an effort to review previously developed methods for evaluating children's learning and to look into the literature of the past to find antecedents for present work. Two major trends can be identified that are relevant to current needs. These are the influence of Piaget's research methodology and the revival of a serious child study movement.

Piaget   Interest in child development is growing rapidly in the United States, and teacher education has begun to include a major component of work in this area, after decades of relative neglect. The most powerful force in this field has been Jean Piaget. His conclusions, but more important his methodology, contribute significantly to any understanding of ways to carry out the evaluation of children's learning. Current texts stress Piaget's stages of development, his insight into children's learning, and the wealth of data that he and his colleagues have collected. The most striking aspect of his work is the style in which it is carried out. It varies so drastically from the formal standards of the traditional educational research model that in the 1930s Piaget's work was dismissed in this country as not rigorous enough to be significant. For example, his methods were described as "a subjective approach to the analysis of child behavior little removed from ordinary literary speculation" (Pratt, 1933).

The basis of Piaget's methodology is a clinical interview technique in which the interviewer not only asks questions, but also probes the responses, modifying the interview in accordance with the child's answer. The goal is not so much to survey what a large number of children do or how they respond under standard conditions, rather it is an attempt to find out what is in the mind of each child, by extending in depth the questioning or the material that the child has available. Piaget's first work with children in 1920 illustrates the method. He was employed to standardize some English test items on French children but, in his own words:

> Now from the very first questionings I noticed that though Burt's tests certainly had their diagnostic merits, based on the number of successes and failures, it was much more interesting to try to find the reasons for the failures. Thus I engaged my subjects in conversations patterned after psychiatric questioning, with the aim of discovering something about the reasoning process

underlying their right, but especially their wrong answers. [Evans, 1973, p. 118]

Since that time, Piaget has stressed the exploration of the meaning behind acts and the need to examine not just a response, but to find out why the response is given. Of course, this approach is in sharp contrast to the requirements of standardized diagnostic testing, in which the examiner's behavior is strictly delineated and the aim is to try to present the test situation in the most impersonal and standard fashion possible. It is revealing to contrast the Piagetian interview with an American version, modified to fit the standardizing conditions for administering and scaling a diagnostic test. In the following excerpt from *The Child's Conception of the World* the interviewer (I) probes to discover the meaning behind a child's (C) response at a critical stage in which the child's ideas are confused:

MART (9;5)
I: What does the moon do whilst you are walking?
C: It follows us and then it stays still. It's we that move and the moon gets nearer us all the time we're moving.
I: How does it follow us?
C: It stays still and it's we who come nearer it.
I: How did you find that out?
C: When you pass in front of houses you don't see it any more, you only see the wall.
I: Then what did you decide?
C: That it hadn't moved.
I: Why do you think it followed you?
C: I made a mistake; when there wasn't a house there it was all the time in front of me.
I: Why does it move?
C: No one makes it move! It's in the same place all the time. [Piaget, 1929, p. 214]

A sample from the specific verbal instructions in the *Concept Assessment* kit (Goldschmidt and Bentler, 1968), designed to assess children's understanding of a typical Piagetian task, is:

Look. I am putting these blocks here.
Now tell me. Is there as much wood here as there, or does one have more? Why?
O.K. Let's do something else. [p. 1]

As a research tool, the Piagetian interview, although qualitative, is a formal instrument. In Piaget's laboratories, interviewers are trained for a year before they are permitted to gather data. The use of the method throughout the world and the general agreement about stages of children's intellectual development derived from such work attest to both the reliability and the validity of this method. The clinical interview becomes both an evaluation tool and a source of diagnostic information for a teacher that is beyond the reach of most formal diagnostic testing.

Child Study   Another major branch of past work that is of interest to adherents of open education is the whole field of child study through observation and documentation. The tradition of this research is long and distinguished. It developed at the same time that the testing movement began, and the usefulness of research from systematic observation of children as an evaluation tool has been stressed repeatedly by those close to classrooms and teaching.

A particularly useful collection of information is contained in the recently reprinted Bulletins of the Bureau of Educational Experiments (Winsor, 1973). The Bureau was a private organization that later evolved into the Bank Street College of Education. The bulletins, published just after the first world war, stressed the need for the scientific study of children, as well as the need to document what was happening in the many experimental schools that were operating at the time. One bulletin, entitled "School Records, An Experiment" stresses the need for careful documentation and observation in order to develop a curriculum that was suitable for individual needs. The writer stresses that only the teacher, the person who knows the child and works with the child, can fully understand children's responses and can fully evaluate the significance of children's actions. "Even an expert stenographer [today we would use a tape recorder] loses much of the significance of the byplay because nobody but the teacher understands its implication" (Winsor, 1973, p. 212).

The headings of various subsections illustrate the concerns of the classroom research of that time: "Concrete illustrations are necessary to a school record," "What the children are achieving is shown only in the responses of the children themselves," and "Records which show school progress must show processes of growth in the school." Other points stressed are: that in order to understand an individual, his or her behavior in a group must be recorded as well as his or her own work, and that only longitudinal records can fully describe emotional states and children's overall growth and development.

Very similar approaches are discussed in *Ways of Studying Children,* a manual for teachers by Almy (1959) based on materials prepared a generation ago by Ruth Cunningham and associates at Horace Mann-Lincoln Institute, Columbia University. The manual emphasizes that observation in the natural setting is the basis for understanding children. The teacher who wishes to assess children and to provide suitable learning opportunities for them must engage the children, ask them about themselves, study them in groups, and study the way in which children express themselves.

Only a small portion of the assessment work in the Almy manual involves formal testing, and this testing must be interpreted in the context of the broader knowledge of the children gained from the informal, qualitative methods.

The two publications mentioned here are only a sampling of the broad literature of the child study movement. They are particularly relevant to the development of open education evaluation because they were written for teachers and by teachers to assist other practitioners. The publications point out what educators in the field have recognized for some time: that the best judge of individual children is the person who has worked with them the most, that the best setting for evaluating children is the natural one of the classroom in which they live and work, and that the best record of their strengths and weaknesses is the documentation of the work that they do. Starting with these ideas, open educators have developed a number of particular approaches to evaluation that are described in the next section.

DEVELOPMENTS IN OPEN EDUCATION EVALUATION

Since standardized achievement testing and formal assessment were not considered appropriate to evaluate open classrooms, alternative models had to be developed. This work has begun, and a number of interesting results have emerged. In particular, a number of relatively straightforward methods have been found to provide much needed information.

School Evaluations

In evaluating the Cambridge Alternative Public School, Engel (1977a; 1977b) developed a number of direct tests of reading and mathematics. One test involved asking the children to read a story written by children. Another test was a math test that involved manipulating blocks to determine if the child had acquired basic math skills. To describe these tasks is to relate only a fraction of the story. An important aspect of this evaluation of children's progress in school was the *process* of developing the evaluation. All constituencies at the school were involved, including parents, teachers, administrators, and children. The tasks that were chosen were known to all and understood by all. Thus, one benefit from developing the evaluation instruments locally was that it allowed the whole community to participate. Accordingly, it led to a clearer understanding of what any evaluation could or could not do. A second aspect of the evaluation was that the skill assessment tasks were only part of a wider evaluation effort, which included classroom observation, questionnaires, work samples, teachers' statements, and child interviews. There was no need to develop a complicated or standardized reading test because the skill assessment task was only part of a wider "battery" that gathered data from a range of sources and over a range of experiential domains.

A similar approach was employed by Olson and collaborators assessing work at the Marcy Open School (Olson, 1973, 1974), a public school in Minneapolis. Again, the emphasis is on a series of rather simple activities that, when taken as an aggregate, provides a picture of a child or a school's progress. Olson points out that the goals of evaluation must match the goals of the program, and, therefore, in assessing a program that advocates a personalized curriculum and the experiential and holistic nature of learning, the evaluation of the school must also be based on personalized evaluation, experiential nature of the evaluation, and holistic evidence for evaluation.

Within this framework, assessment procedures include questionnaires, observations, checklists, samples of work or of records, interviews, teachers' records, meeting notes, sociograms, and an assortment of other materials. For the assessment and evaluation of individual children, any two or three of these methods may be sufficient; for larger program evaluations, a collection is usually needed. In her *Handbook of Documentation,* Engel lists (and illustrates) the following forms or records:

THE CHILD
1. Reports to parent
2. Periodic samples of paperwork in all areas (including drawings, maps, etc.)
3. Photographs of large-scale and three-dimensional work
4. Math and reading skills checklists
5. Self-assessment essays, questionnaires, or transcribed interviews
6. Lists of books read
7. Assessments of reading level and/or "reading biographies"
8. Lists of outside interests or activities
9. Single child observations, descriptive accounts, and recordings
10. Teacher's notes and comments
11. Child-kept records

THE CLASSROOM
Any of the above documents can be included or summarized here. Also:
1. Time activity charts
2. Collations of individuals' spontaneous choices
3. Transcribed tapes of class discussions
4. Sociograms
5. Curricular flow charts or other diagrams
6. Maps of room arrangements
7. Lists of materials and activities
8. Observations in one classroom activity area
9. Teachers' journals

10. Schedules
11. Plans
12. Descriptions of adult interactions
13. Summaries of skills assessments
14. Summaries of specialists' programs
15. Lists of class trips
16. Parent notes or comments
17. Special projects
18. Teacher interviews transcribed
19. Self-evaluations by teachers
20. Teacher time charts
21. Directives, bulletins, or standard forms

THE INSTITUTION

Any of the records listed under "The Child" and "The Classroom" that seem relevant could be included here. In addition, these materials can be re-ordered to give a more general perspective (a summary of all the field trips taken during the year, a collection of curriculum diagrams, a statistical breakdown of children's spontaneous choices throughout the school) or description of special programs (school-wide music program, new math lab materials). Also:

1. Lists of courses attended by staff members during the year
2. School calendars
3. Parent interviews and questionnaires
4. Notes by principals
5. Excerpts from minutes or summaries of staff meetings
6. Agenda, excerpts, or minutes from parents' meetings
7. Memoranda
8. Publicity
9. Reports on buildings, grounds, and maintenance
10. Role descriptions
11. Staff lists
12. Time budgets for principals
13. Whole school activities
14. Maps of the buildings
15. Summaries of records (attendance, fire drill, finances, budget, etc.)
16. Lists of visitors
17. Notes or reports on the school and community; volunteer help
18. Summaries of directives from the school department or district
19. Notes or reports by principals on special problems
20. Notes on special programs and educational innovations
21. Statistics on children
22. Rules and regulations
23. Time budgets for specialists
24. Photographs of the buildings
25. Photographs of special events
26. Follow-up reports from other schools
27. Notes, reports, etc. by consultants or advisors
28. Statements of theory, goals, and assumptions [Engel, 1975, pp. 5-7]

The examples above focus on "informal" approaches to evaluation and on methodologies that are devised for particular situations in such a way that they cannot be transferred to another setting without modification. However, work has begun on the development of qualitative instruments that can be used across programs and that approximate more closely the kinds of methodologies that are suitable for large-scale research and evaluation projects, but still take into account open education principles: concern for the entire situation, the events within their surroundings, interest in process, as well as outcome, and respect for each child as a unique learner. An example of such methodology is the BRACE instrument developed at Bank Street College of Education (Bowerman and Mayer, 1976), which includes training procedures and helps teachers to analyze the behavior and verbal communication of children in such categories as adult intervention, the structure of classroom interactions, children's behavior patterns, etc. The objectives of the system are:

> To sensitize teachers and paraprofessionals to their own patterns of communication and class management. To study individual students' language and behavior. To assess the learning environment, the quality of interaction within it and students' language and behavior in relation to specific educational objectives. To help teaching staff establish their own specific objectives for change and assess their progress towards those objectives. [Bowerman and Mayer, 1976, p. 1]

Other Examples

Three specific examples of qualitative methodology that illustrate the kind of approaches that are possible and document the interrelationship between evaluation and other aspects of teaching and education in general are of particular interest.

The Prospect School, North Bennington, Vermont An intensive use of qualitative methodology is provided by the Prospect School, North Bennington, Vermont, and its founder and director, Patricia Carini (1972, 1973). Since its founding in 1965, the school has devoted itself to a detailed program of evaluation and research based on careful record keeping and the systematic collection of children's work. The school recognized that the recording of process had to use qualitative methodology and had to be carried out over time. A significant collection of materials has been gathered, including:

Children's work (e.g., drawings, photos, etc.)
Children's journals
Children's notebooks or written work
Teachers' weekly records

Teachers' reports to parents
Teachers' assessment of children's work in math, reading, and activities
Curriculum trees
Sociograms

Not only is the data collection systematic, but it is based on a carefully developed research design (Carini, 1972) intended to gather data on:

Experimental investigations of the thinking process
Longitudinal definition of developmental stages
Longitudinal assessment of the impact of the innovative learning situation
Modification and qualification of developmental stages
Objectification of the continuity and transformations of affective and thematic content in the reorganization of successive developmental stages

However, a more recent offshoot of this work has been its extraordinary ability to be useful in a wider school context. The whole process of administering the school and making decisions about children and curriculum has been affected by the availability of careful documentation and the resulting knowledge concerning the children. The work has provided the basis for curriculum decisions, for reports to parents, for developing hypotheses about child development, and for description and diagnosis of children.

Furthermore, the methodology has been of service in developing a model for teacher training and teacher development. Both the data that have accumulated over the years and the methodology developed during that period have been helpful to individual teachers and clusters of teachers in various public school settings in increasing their understanding of children and of curriculum possibilities, and in furthering their own insight into the teaching/learning process. By immersing themselves in the methods developed at the Prospect School, teachers have been able to combine documentation and evaluation with self-renewal and growth as professionals.

Collaborative Research with Teachers Another approach illustrates the effort among open education practitioners to integrate evaluation methodology with other aspects of teaching. The early childhood group at Educational Testing Services (Bussis et al., 1976) has developed a style of research that involves teachers as partners in the work, that uses the teacher's insights and special knowledge of children to generate new data and, at the same time, to give the teacher information that is useful for his or her particular situation. The group is currently engaged in a collaborative project on reading in which teachers and teacher advisors collect data such as reading samples, pictures, and other information on specific children, in an effort to discern the various ways in which children learn to read, to document the process of learning of specific children, and to provide the collaborating teachers with insight into ways of teaching and meeting the needs of individual students. The project reflects the ETS group's belief in the need for research and evaluation work, which is an integral part of the activity that is being studied and thus involves all the constituents as contributing members.

Exploring Children's Concepts Through Language   The effectiveness of qualitative analytic evaluation methods for teacher training is further illustrated by research that has been carried out by Churchill and Petner (1976) in a public school system.

They went into classrooms and recorded children's spontaneous speech while the children engaged in such activities as building with blocks, working in the sandbox, or conversing at the lunch table. They then prepared transcripts of the children's conversations and analyzed them with the teachers, examining the content for clues concerning children's cognitive levels, learning styles, and other information about the children's knowledge of concepts. They combined naturalistic observation with assessment data on individual children and used this combination as a means for helping teachers increase their knowledge of both children and assessment tools. Petner (1976) describes it as identifying four kinds of experiences that were felt to be useful to teachers and paraprofessionals in making assessments of their students' needs and progress. These experiences include:

1. Have teachers participate in an active learning process by confronting objective data, analyzing it for meaning, and reflecting on its implication for the classroom.
2. Train teachers in naturalistic observation and assist them in translating observations into practical curriculum plans.
3. Help teachers develop a theoretical base to underlie and give broader meaning to observations of children.
4. Explore the methods for the systematic recording of observations and events that reveal children's interests, strengths, levels of understanding, and academic progress, as a guide for planning and for assessment of the evolving classroom curriculum.

Again, the emphasis is on combining evaluation with a means of feeding back the evaluation information to teachers so that it can be of assistance to them.

CONCLUSIONS

Although the range of approaches to evaluation in the above examples is clearly great, some general conclusions concerning evaluation in open education can be drawn.

1.   Qualitative evaluations tend to use methods that can be analyzed for the reasons behind the answers. Instead of the statistical detail of standardized test scores and rating scales of diagnostic assessments, open educators favor the kind of tools that can provide clues about how a child's mind works. Thus, every effort is made to make accessible to the evaluator the process that the child uses in arriving at his or her answers. In each of the examples given above, important components of the evaluation are data collected from teachers and parents who have actually worked with the child. Much of the material collected by the evaluator is gathered in one-to-one interaction with the child, and includes not only the child's response, but also the child's approach to the task and what the child actually does. The importance of this approach is highlighted in a study by Meier (1973), who presented New York City school children with items from the Metropolitan Achievement Test and asked them to discuss the items with her. She noted that many of the children's wrong answers stemmed not from their inability to read, but from social and cultural differences between the children and the testmakers.

2.   The relationship between assessor and "client" is a major difference between the quantitative and the qualitative models. Open education evaluations are often conducted by a participant observer — a person who has an interest in the program, who attempts to understand the children and the staff, and who feels a responsibility to uphold the integrity of the program. Of course, such involvement (which may be true also of "outside" evaluators) carries with it responsibilities for a critical stance and for honest reporting. This issue, which also affects traditional evaluators, has been discussed in social science literature (see Filstead, 1970).

3.   The concern with observing phenomena within a framework leads open education evaluators to gather data from different sources and to use a range of instruments. They are unlikely to rely on a single measure, a single test, or, for that matter, a single observation or interview to reach a judgment. The recognition of the complexity of situations carries with it the safeguard of requiring various sources of information and various types of instruments. Any teacher who has received a report on a child in his or her classroom who was tested on a single occasion by a stranger using a limited battery of instruments knows the importance of tempering the results of such evaluations with other information about the child.

4.   An additional property shared by most qualitative evaluations is that the conclusions derive directly from the descriptive data. Thus, the information is in a form that is readily accessible to parents, teachers, and other decision makers.

5.   The application of qualitative approaches can be frustrating and trying during the course of an assessment or evaluation. The person gathering the data, collecting the interviews and amassing the information is usually flooded with material, much of which may appear to be of little value by itself. There are no comforting norms with which to compare, few statistical measures to perform, and sometimes no apparent value in individual items (a property that is shared with many standardized, quantitative procedures). However, the cumulative amount of information gathered, when analyzed, examined, and interpreted, can provide a surprisingly full picture of a child or program. Small items that appear at first to have little meaning become powerful when they indicate consistently recurring behavior on the part of an individual or program or when they correlate to show consistent trends or patterns.

The validity of qualitative approaches is dependent on this congruence of data from a variety of sources. Individual measures cannot usually be compared to a standardized norm, but the collection of different types of information requires that the data show an internal consistency, e.g., that the results of teacher ratings, parents' assessment, and evaluators' testing of a child be consistent with each other. Those who have undertaken qualitative evaluations have repeatedly found that concerns about validity, expressed by teachers and administrators, disappear when the totality of evidence reinforces itself and a coherent picture of a child or a program emerges from the data. In those cases where serious discrepancies occur in the various sources of data, the lack of agreement usually brings to light some particular educational problem.

SUMMARY

All evaluation involves judgment and decision, and therefore all evaluations are controversial and subject to dispute. However, too much of traditional evaluation practice has become divorced from the major purpose of education — providing appropriate quality education for *every* child. In striving to make evaluation "scientific" and objective, we have often made it obscure, with results that are incomprehensible to parents and with procedures that leave no opportunity for participation by classroom teachers. The methods that have been developed recently by advocates of open education strive to re-unify evaluation and teaching and to provide comprehensive and substantial data that can be understood by all and can be used to make practical decisions about the education of children.

Open education practice has many similarities to contemporary approaches to the education of children with special needs. In both instances, educators, considering the capabilities of a student, are concerned with fitting educational practice to the needs of the individual and in developing the fullest potential of each child. The approaches to evaluation discussed in this chapter are directly applicable to assessing the education of children with special needs.

Ultimately, the persons who should benefit most in education are the children. In deciding on evaluation strategies and specific instruments, we have to ask ourselves which approaches best serve the children who are our responsibility. The qualitative methodology described here and the specific examples derived from it are the best current hope for providing individual, thoughtful, and truly analytic evaluations of each child as an individual. Whether used in open or traditional classrooms, with handicapped or nonhandicapped children, this style of evaluation provides the basis for designing the most helpful educational setting for all children.

ACKNOWLEDGMENTS

I wish to express my gratitude for the encouragement, advice, and helpful criticism provided me in the preparation of this chapter by my friends and colleagues Posie Churchill, Cynthia Cole, Jeremy Cott, Brenda Engel, Susan Harman, Bonnie Leonard, Sam Meisels, Deborah Meier, and Jeanne Speizer.

REFERENCES

Almy, M. 1959. Ways of Studying Children. Teachers College Press, New York.
Baker, H. J., and Leland, B. 1935. Detroit Tests of Learning Aptitude, Pictorial Material. Bobbs-Merrill Company, Inc., Indianapolis.
Bronfenbrenner, U. 1976. The experimental ecology of education. Educ. Researcher 5:5–15.
Bowerman, G. W., and Mayer, R. S. 1976. The Brace System for Staff Development. Bank Street College of Education, New York.
Buros, O. K. 1977. Fifty years of testing: Some reminiscences, criticisms, and suggestions. Educ. Researcher 6:9–15.
Bussis, A., Chittenden, E., and Amarel, M. 1976. Beyond Surface Curriculum. Westview Press, Boulder, Col.
Campbell, D. T., and Stanley, V. C. 1963. Experimental and Quasi-Experimental Design. Rand McNally, Chicago.
Carini, P. F. 1972. Evaluation of an innovative school. In: D. D. Hearn, J. Burdin, and L. Katz (ed.), Current Research and Perspectives on Open Education. ERIC Clearinghouse on Early Childhood Education, Urbana, Ill.
Carini, P. F. 1973. Taking account of progress. Childhood Educ. 49:350.
Cazdan, C. 1974. Concentrated amd contrived encounters: Suggestions for language assessment in early childhood education, mimeograph, Cambridge, Mass.

Churchill, E. H. E., and Petner, J. 1976. Children's Language and Thinking: A Report on Work-in-Progress. North Dakota Study Group on Evaluation, Grand Forks, N. D.

deRivera, M. 1973. Academic achievement tests and the survival of open education. Education Development Center News 2:7.

Eisner, E. W. 1969. Instructional and Expressive Objectives: Their Formulation and Use in Curriculum. AERA Monograph Series on Curriculum Development, no. 3. Rand McNally, Chicago.

Engel, B. 1975. A Handbook of Documentation. North Dakota Study Group on Evaluation, Grand Forks, N. D.

Engel, B. 1977a. One way it can be. Today's Educ. 66:50–52.

Engel, B. 1977b. Informal Evaluation. North Dakota Study Group on Evaluation, Grand Forks, N. D.

Evans, R. I. 1973. Jean Piaget, The Man and His Ideas. E. P. Dutton, & Co., Inc., New York.

Filstead, W. J. (ed.) 1970. Qualitative Methodology: Firsthand Involvement with the Social World. Markham Publishing Co., Chicago.

Glaser, B. G., and Strauss, A. L. 1967. The Discovery of Grounded Theory, Strategies for Qualitative Research. Aldine Publishing Company, Chicago.

Goldschmidt, M. D., and Bentler, P. M. 1968. Concept Assessment Kit. Educational and Industrial Testing Service, San Diego.

Harman, S. 1975. All children are special. Notes from Workshop Center for Open Education 4:15–27.

Hein, G. E. 1976. The science of watching and wondering. Urban Rev. 9:242–248.

Hobbs, N. 1975. The Futures of Children. Jossey-Bass, San Francisco.

Horwitz, R. A. 1976. Psychological Effects of Open Classroom Teaching on Primary School Children: A Review of Research. North Dakota Study Group on Evaluation, Grand Forks, N. D.

House, E. R., Glass, G. V., McLean, L. D., Walker, D. F. 1977. No Simple Answer: Critique of the "Follow Through" Evaluation. Center for Instructional Research and Curriculum Evaluation, Urbana, Ill.

Houts, P. (ed.) 1975. Special issue on achievement tests. National Elementary Principal 54:4–101.

Mehan, H. 1978. Structuring school structure. Harvard Educ. Rev. 48:32–64.

Meier, D. 1973. Reading failure and the tests. Workshop Center for Open Education, New York.

Olson, R. A. 1973. A Value Perspective on Evaluation, mimeograph, Minneapolis, Minn.

Olson, R. A. 1974. Marcy Open School, 1973–74 Goal Evaluation. SEA Internal Evaluation Team, Minneapolis, Minn.

Parlett, M., and Hamilton, D. 1976. Evaluation as illumination: A new approach to the study of innovative programs. In: G. V. Glass (ed.), Evaluation Studies, Review Annual 1. Sage Publications, Beverly Hills, Cal.

Petner, J. N., Jr. 1976. Evaluation in proper perspective. Urban Rev. 9:248–257.

Piaget, J. 1929. The Child's Conception of the World. Routledge, Paul and Kegan, London.

Pratt, C. K. 1933. The neonate. In: C. Murcheson (ed.), A Handbook of Child Psychology, 2nd Ed. Clark University Press, Worcester, Mass.

Schwartz, J. L. 1975. Math tests. National Elementary Principal 54:67–71.

Simon, A., and Boyer, E. G. 1965. Educational Mirrors of Behavior. Vol. 1 and subsequent volumes. Research for Better Schools, Philadelphia.

Stake, R. E. 1967. The countenance of educational evaluation. Teacher's College Record 68:523–540.

Stebbins, L. B., St. Pierre, R. B., Proper, E. C., Anderson, R. B., and Cerva, R. T. 1977. Education as Experimentation: A Planned Variation Model. Vols. IV A–D. Abt Associates, Cambridge.

Taylor, E. F. 1977. The looking glass world of testing. Today's Educ. 66:39–44.

Wilson, S. 1977. The use of ethnographic techniques in educational research. Rev. Educ. Research 47:245–266.

Winsor, C. 1973. Experimental Schools Revisited. Agathon Press, Inc., New York.

Assessing the Effectiveness of Open Classrooms On Children With Special Needs

Anthony S. Bryk
Samuel J. Meisels
Martha T. Markowitz

Open classrooms are educational settings based on a highly differentiated or individualized level of interaction between teachers and children. Although popular accounts paint a permissive picture of open classrooms, open education should not be associated with a maturationist or laissez-faire view of education in which the teacher is a passive facilitator of information and the child controls the learning experience. Open education also should not be identified with a view that holds that the teacher or the curriculum determines what the child must learn *a priori*. Rather, in open classrooms, teachers and children are joint contributors to decisions regarding the process and content of learning (Bussis and Chittenden, 1970; Bussis, Chittenden, and Amarel, 1976). This approach does not entail an explicit agreement between teacher and child on every issue of classroom control and decision-making. However, it does assume that the teacher's decisions regarding pacing, sequence, materials, and setting will be largely influenced by the information generated by the child in the classroom environment.

The effort to create an environment that is interactive on several levels poses problems for the teacher in planning classroom activities,

Preparation of this chapter was supported in part by Grants G00-75-00230 (Learning in Integrated Classrooms) and G00-77-02886 (Evaluation Methodology for Early Childhood Special Education Programs) from the United States Office of Education, Bureau of Education for the Handicapped. The chapter represents a collaborative effort on the part of the authors.

establishing individualized goals and objectives, and creating developmentally appropriate curriculum. In certain respects, the educational program for each child in an open classroom is unique. This factor compounds the problems of evaluation in open education and poses a dilemma. Since open classrooms are so highly individualized, it may not be possible to subject them to standard program evaluation efforts; yet, without evaluation, the essential interactive character of the open classroom is put in jeopardy and its potential widespread applicability is seriously limited.

This chapter explores the issues that surround the evaluation of the effectiveness of open educational programs for young children. In particular, it focuses on developmentally oriented open classroom programs that enroll young children with special needs. Such programs present methodological challenges that cannot be met by standard evaluation paradigms. Our purpose is to introduce an alternative approach and to describe its implementation in a mainstreamed open educational program consistent with developmental principles.

OPEN EDUCATION AS A DEVELOPMENTALLY
APPROPRIATE SETTING FOR CHILDREN WITH SPECIAL NEEDS

The relevance of open education to children with special needs has been discussed in other publications (Meisels, 1976, 1978). In general, the essential variables of open classrooms that have been described in these writings consist of: 1) a classroom environment prepared in accordance with certain specialized conditions, 2) extensive opportunities for child initiation and activity in the classroom, and 3) teacher activity and intervention of an interactive type. These three major variables are discussed briefly.

Environment   The open classroom is an "information-rich" environment. It is an environment intended to transmit and generate information to children and adults. The classroom is usually set up as a workshop, dominated by interest areas. These areas include centers for reading, writing, math, science, artwork, blocks, water play, and dramatic play. Often the interest areas accommodate more temporary pursuits, such as a science museum, an incubator, a circus project, cooking, or even a print shop. Unlike the traditional classroom, desks and chairs do not occupy most of the space. In the open classroom, desks are replaced with unassigned, small tables that can be moved to locations where they are needed. There is no formal locus of learning in the classroom; learning takes place wherever something of particular interest to a child happens to be and/or where a systematic interaction between teacher and child can be implemented. Thus, such classrooms rely on a wide variety of materials that are accessible to teachers and children. These classrooms also rely on an environment and an educational program that encourage children to explore the wealth of available options, but do so in a way that transmits information to the children and to the adults working with them.

Children's Interests and Initiative   Open classrooms provide children with numerous opportunities to engage their curiosity and to utilize their initiative in the process of learning. This exercise of children's interests and initiative is basically an information-generating and information-transmitting activity. As such, it is an essential aspect of the teaching process in open classrooms. The potential for discovery is present at all times for children in open classrooms, yet such discoveries are not necessarily random, nor are they restricted to the subjective experiences of individual children. In the act of discovery one can recognize what might be termed "unaided" or unmediated discoveries, such as when a child learns about the properties of magnets, the working of an equal-arm balance, or the mixing of colors. Other unaided discoveries could include the teacher finding out who can read, how the classroom can be rearranged to create a certain feeling in one part of the room, or what conceptual problem is standing in the way of a child's learning to add. "Aided" or mediated discoveries also abound: one child is taught by the teacher how to read the word "home," and he then makes generalizations about other words with silent e's; or the teacher discovers a new use for a classroom material after watching children play with it, and then talking about it with them.

Thus, for the teacher, the provision of freedom of choice means that he must carefully examine the choices made by the child, as well as the way in which the child chooses. This is the only way that the teacher can acquire the information that he needs to direct his own behavior. If the environment is not sufficiently ambiguous or does not contain a wide enough variety of choices, the children will not be able to choose, and the teacher will have insufficient information. As Hawkins (1974) points out, lacking information, the teacher will not be a very good diagnostician of what the children need. Not being a good diagnostician, he will be a poor teacher. He will be a poor teacher because he will not have had adequate basis for making his choices: choices of goals, materials, timing, strategy, and attitude.

Teacher-Child Interactions   In open classrooms that are developmentally oriented, teachers actively intervene in children's learning. Such intervention can be considered interactive with the child's needs and abilities to the extent that it relies on and makes use of information acquired previously by the teacher. This information forms the framework for the teacher's contribution to the child's activity. Among the data that the teacher tries to collect and use are observations about children's styles of conceptualization, their ability and way of making choices, their peer associations, their family history, their cognitive skills and knowledge, their self-perception, their attitude toward achievement, their dependence on authorities, and their curiosity, creativity, attitudes, feelings, and moods. Some of this information is acquired through direct interviewing and questioning; however, most of it is obtained from careful observation of the ways in which a child questions and interacts with the classroom environment and its inhabitants.

Developmentally Oriented Classrooms

Open education is an approach that is based on information acquired by the teacher from the child's interactions with the physical environment, from the environment determined by other children, and from the environment created by relationships with adults. In consequence, educational decision-making is highly deliberate, although highly differentiated. Such an approach is consistent with a cognitive-developmental view of education (see Kohlberg, 1968, 1972; Kohlberg and Mayer, 1972; Kamii and DeVries, 1977). As stated by Kamii and Derman (1971), the cognitive-developmental view considers teaching to be:

> a method that helps the child make his own discoveries by asking the right question at the right time. The "right" question is in precise harmony with what the child is thinking about at the moment. The "right" timing allows him enough time to integrate and consolidate a new discovery before the next question is introduced. [p. 145]

No teacher can be "right" all the time with all the children with whom he is working. However, the developmentally oriented teacher is seeking to bring about the acquisition of irreversible structures in children, rather than immediate and short-term gains. Such lasting change is dependent on a highly individualized program that focuses on the specific needs of individual children and that is informed by a sound theory of growth and development.

Open Education and Special Education

It is in this perspective that developmentally oriented open classrooms must be viewed when considering their relevance for children with special needs. In the past, most handicapped children were enrolled in educational programs that did not focus on their individuality and their interactive relationships with animate and inanimate environments (see Johnson, 1962). However, in the open classroom handicapped children are exposed to a setting that fosters and encourages interactivity. Children are encouraged to manipulate objects directly, to try new experiences, and to reorganize old ones. Children are permitted opportunities to engage in a variety of relationships with their peers and to engage in a learning process that is directed, but not wholly determined, by their teacher. Activities and experiences in such classrooms have multiple objectives rather than binary, or right or wrong, outcomes. Learning is immediate and direct, rather than mediated through rules and rote explanations. Moreover, where the process *and* the content of learning are critical features of the educational approach, as is true of open classrooms, progress is defined in individual terms, rather than through some specification of a common terminus or objective to be achieved by each and every child.

The Eliot-Pearson Children's School

This approach to working with handicapped children has been implemented in several programs described in this book. In this chapter illustrations concerning the impact of open classrooms on children with special needs are drawn from the Eliot-Pearson Children's School at Tufts University.

Eliot-Pearson is an integrated, or mainstreamed, preschool and kindergarten. Approximately 20 percent of the 90 children, who are ages 3 to 6, have mild or moderate handicaps. A wide variety of handicapping conditions is represented in the school population. The program at Eliot-Pearson has been described by Meisels (1978), but it is further clarified in later sections of this chapter. Principally, it is a program that stresses activity, experience, and a systematically adaptive role for the child vis-à-vis his environment, peers, and teachers.

Educational programs that follow such principles bear some striking similarities to each other, in terms of congruence of objectives, implementational strategies, motivational rewards, and fundamental growth and learning theory. Such an approach supports activities with multiple objectives and is highly appropriate for children who require a variety of specialized learning experiences and opportunities for expression. Nevertheless, such an approach is exceedingly difficult to subject to standard types of evaluation design.

PROBLEMS IN UTILIZING TRADITIONAL EVALUATION
STRATEGIES TO EVALUATE THE IMPACT OF OPEN CLASSROOMS

The treatment-control group paradigm dominates the practice of program impact evaluation. This approach is based on statistical principles of experimental design. Typically, one or more experimental or program groups is compared with a control group or with pre-existing information on a control condition. Average outcome differences across the groups are considered by adherents of this model to be an appropriate summary measure of program impact. This basic strategy is utilized whether one is investigating a single outcome (e.g., ability to read at a specified level) or an extensive array of developmental variables. In the latter case, one would simply examine a series of mean differences across groups for the set of outcome variables.

In recent years numerous ethical, social, political, and logistical problems have been encountered in the many applications of this basic approach (see Riecken and Boruch, 1974; Bryk, 1978). Several substantive difficulties in the application of this approach have been raised by Hein (1975) and Stodolsky (1972; 1975). This situation is further exacerbated by the highly individualized nature of programming that is required in order to be responsive to the special needs of the handicapped child who is enrolled in a developmentally oriented open classroom.

In the open classroom, the actual sequence of classroom activities and experiences cannot be defined *a priori*. Rather, the educational experience for a particular child can only be specified in the dynamic interaction of the program with the child. Nevertheless, this does not entail that such program activities must be idiosyncratic. Every teacher operates within a general framework from which individualized educational programs are derived. In every open classroom there exists a set of implicit or explicit program objectives. However, the open classroom teacher has no expectation of implementing all of these objectives with every child, nor of implementing them at the same rate or in the same way. This is particularly true of children with special needs, all of whom present such different needs and abilities that no single curricular sequence and structure could be appropriate.

For example, the program at Eliot-Pearson is drawn from a broad set of developmental objectives that fall within four major domains: personal/social, gross motor, fine/perceptual motor and cognitive/language. Specific objectives within each of these domains are listed below.

PERSONAL/SOCIAL

1. To develop the ability to express one's feelings
2. To accomplish successful separation
3. To develop a sense of independence and self-confidence
4. To increase impulse-control and ability to accept limits
5. To increase the level of attention and involvement in activities
6. To improve the ability to make transitions, follow classroom routine, and make self-regulated choices

7. To develop the ability to feed oneself
8. To develop the ability to be generally independent in toileting
9. To develop a positive self-image
10. To develop trust relationships with teachers
11. To increase the ability to make a friend
12. To increase positive interactions with peers
13. To acquire skills of group participation

GROSS MOTOR

1. To develop the ability to hop, skip, balance, and climb stairs
2. To improve body awareness
3. To develop the ability to throw and catch a ball
4. To increase coordination and agility

FINE/PERCEPTUAL MOTOR

1. To develop the ability to cut with scissors and to use drawing implements
2. To improve skill in writing and printing activities
3. To develop the ability to discriminate among shapes and figures
4. To increase the ability to work with manipulative materials, e.g. puzzles
5. To develop the ability to button, zip, tie, and dress oneself

COGNITIVE/LANGUAGE

1. To increase exploration and mastery of a broad repertoire of curriculum experiences
2. To increase the ability to differentiate between reality and fantasy
3. To acquire readiness information, e.g. colors, street names, etc.
4. To develop the ability to match, classify, and seriate
5. To improve pre-reading and early reading skills
6. To develop the ability to understand numbers and to perform simple addition tasks
7. To develop the ability to understand and follow directions
8. To acquire auditory memory skills
9. To stimulate expressive language usage
10. To improve clarity of speech (articulation, pronunciation)
11. To develop the ability to name common objects correctly
12. To learn to use pronouns and prepositions correctly
13. To develop proper syntax and sentence construction

Taken as a whole, these objectives represent the macro-structure of the Eliot-Pearson program. Different subsets are drawn from these objectives in order to meet the needs of individual children. The individual differences between children also determine the type of implementational strategies utilized for each objective. The following two cases briefly illustrate how such a common set of program objectives can be utilized to meet the needs of children with very different abilities and problems.

CASE 1: BECKY

Becky, who is nearly 6 years old, is enrolled in an Eliot-Pearson classroom with 17 other children, 4 and 5 years of age. Becky is an only child. Her father is employed as a machinist, and her mother does not work. When she entered the program she displayed bizarre expressive language, inappropriate social behavior, and an unusual sensitivity to distractions and irrelevant details in her environment. In addition, Becky was lacking in confidence in her gross motor activities and showed poor fine motor coordination when manipulating objects and when drawing. In general, Becky tended to perseverate and to become absorbed in a fantasy world unless she was directed and focused by her teacher. Becky also required constant encouragement in order to continue to develop cognitive skills.

A subset of objectives from the set of general program objectives was selected for emphasis with Becky. The individual objectives are shown in Table 1.

CASE 2: JONATHAN

Jonathan, who is nearly 5 years old, is enrolled in an Eliot-Pearson classroom with 18 children, 4 to 5 years of age. Jonathan has one younger sibling. His parents are separated, and his mother is at home. Jonathan is physically unable to walk. When he started school, he was learning to use a walker in order to maneuver himself about the classroom.

Jonathan is a self-assured, even-tempered child who easily engages in play with other children. Initially he needed assistance in moving his body to a seated position in a chair. Gross motor activities constituted an area of heavy emphasis throughout the year.

Jonathan's fine motor and manipulative skills were age-appropriate, but he needed encouragement to engage in printing and drawing activities. Jonathan also required assistance in the acquisition of cognitive skills. He did not know the names of shapes or how to count beyond the number three. He was unable to perform one-to-one matching tasks or to differentiate between the smallest and largest object in a group. In the area of language, he had difficulty naming common objects and using simple prepositions appropriately. He also had difficulty in articulating certain consonant blends, and he needed encouragement to engage in general conversation.

Objectives that were selected for Jonathan are listed in Table 2.

These two cases demonstrate how children who exhibit differing needs and abilities are provided with different, although overlapping, sets of objectives. These objectives are then utilized in the formation of appropriate classroom programs. In general, the individualized character of the Eliot-Pearson program yields a differentiated profile of emphasis within the overall set of program objectives. Figure 1 lists each of the program objectives and shows its level of emphasis across the entire population of 18 handicapped children enrolled at Eliot-Pearson in 1977–78. Note that only two of the 31 program objectives were emphasized with every child. Thus, the relative importance of these objectives and the corresponding implementational strategies utilized varied considerably from child to child.

The highly individualized approach represented in Figure 1 presents significant problems for the standard treatment-control group paradigm. Even if one were to assume an ideal situation in which there was substantive program effects for each child, as well as reliable and valid quantitative assessment of these individual gains and a perfectly matched program and control group, it would still be unlikely that one would obtain evidence of significant program impact, as defined by statistically significant mean differences across groups. A highly individualized program can be effective without all of its subjects moving in a particular direction on all dimensions within a single evaluation time frame.

This uniformity constitutes the implicit assumption of all traditional univariate and multivariate analysis methods. The large-scale investigation of the effectiveness of open classrooms by Bennett and his colleagues (1976) is subject to this criticism. In individualized programs the search for mean differences across groups in a variable-by-variable fashion is often futile. There is usually considerably less statistical power than might appear on the basis of total sample size since each variable is only relevant for a small subset of cases at any particular point in time.

However, the problem of applying the standard evaluation paradigm to developmentally oriented programs is even more complex than that which is revealed by the insensitivity of the "mean differences across groups" indicator of program effectiveness. Even if it were possible to measure short-term gains with perfect validity for each individual on each program dimension, a problem of interpretation would still exist. In the absence of a detailed assessment of the needs of the individual child, and an account of the program "intentionality" or focus over the recent short term, it is impossible to place a value on the outcomes or conclusions yielded by the standard methodology.

For example, two 4 and one half year old children with special needs, enrolled in the same preschool program, may participate in standard pro-

Table 1. Case 1: Becky — Objectives

Personal/Social	Gross Motor	Fine/Perceptual Motor	Cognitive/Language
[a]1. To develop the ability to express one's feelings.	[a]1. To develop the ability to hop, skip, balance, and climb stairs.	[a]1. To develop the ability to cut with scissors, and use writing and drawing implements.	[a]1. To increase exploration and mastery of a broad repertoire of curriculum experiences.
2. To accomplish successful separation.	2. To improve body awareness.	2. To improve writing/printing abilities.	2. To increase the ability to differentiate between fantasy and reality.
3. To develop a sense of independence and self-confidence.	4. To increase coordination and agility.	4. To increase the ability to work with manipulative materials.	3. To acquire readiness information.
4. To increase impulse-control and ability to accept limits.			7. To develop the ability to understand and follow directions.
5. To increase the level of attention and involvement in activities.			8. To acquire auditory memory skills.

9. To stimulate expressive language.

6. To improve the ability to make transitions, follow classroom routines, and make self-regulated choices.

9. To develop a positive self-image.

10. To develop trust relationships with teachers.

11. To increase the ability to make a friend.

12. To increase positive interactions with peers.

13. To acquire skills of group participation.

<hr>

aThese numbers correspond to the Program Objectives listed on page 262–263.

Table 2.   Case 2: Jonathan — Objectives

Personal/Social	Gross Motor	Fine/Perceptual Motor	Cognitive/Language
[a]7. To develop the ability to feed oneself.	[a]1. To develop the ability to balance and to climb stairs.	[a]2. To improve skill on writing and printing activities.	[a]1. To increase exploration and mastery of a broad repertoire of curriculum experiences.
8. To develop the ability to be generally independent in toileting.	2. To improve body awareness.	3. To develop the ability to discriminate among shapes and figures.	3. To acquire readiness information.
10. To develop trust relationships with teacher.	3. To develop the ability to throw and catch a ball.		4. To develop the ability to match, classify, and seriate.
	4. To increase coordination and agility.		5. To develop pre-reading and early reading skills.

6. To develop the ability to understand number and to perform simple addition tasks.

8. To acquire auditory memory skills.

9. To stimulate expressive language usage.

10. To improve clarity of speech.

11. To develop the ability to name common objects correctly.

12. To learn to use pronouns and prepositions correctly.

aThese numbers correspond to the Program Objectives listed on page 262–263.

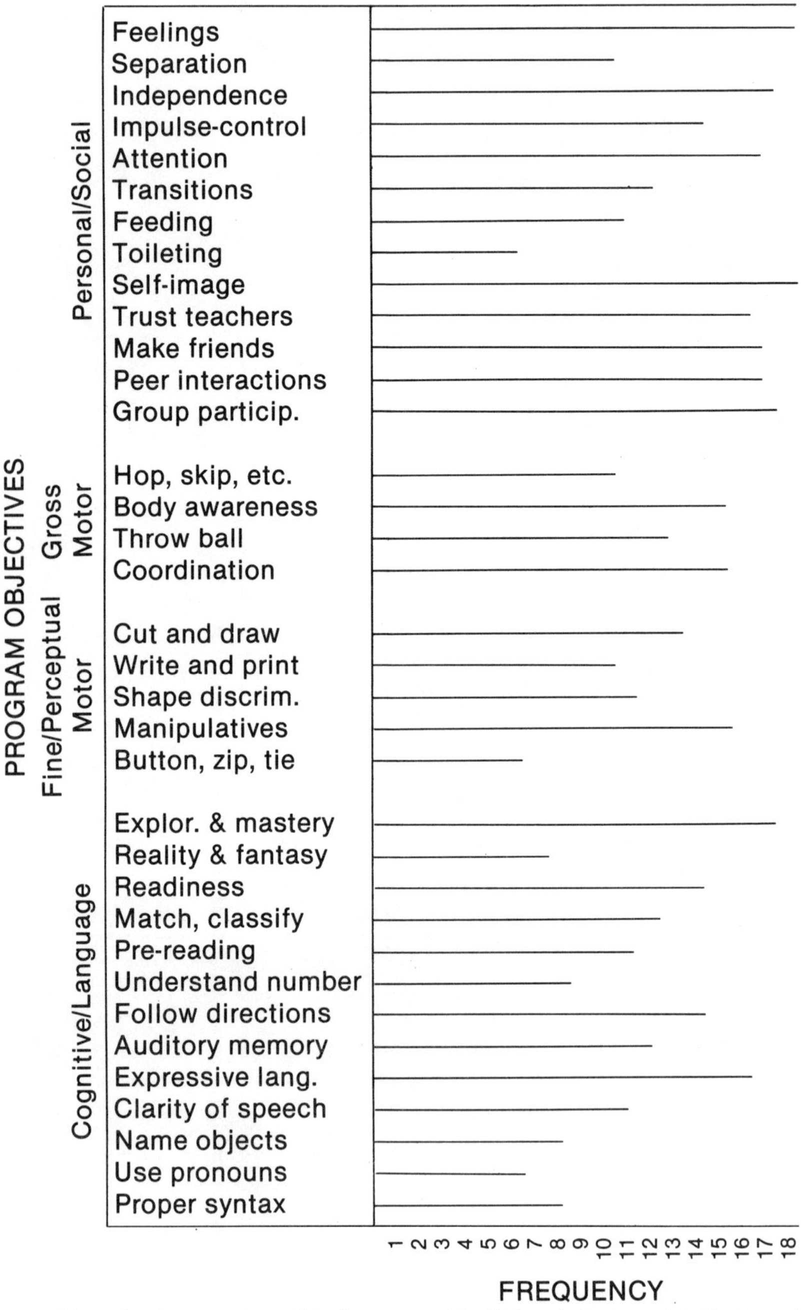

Figure 1.   A comparison of the frequency with which each program objective is emphasized for children with special needs enrolled at the Eliot-Pearson Children's School (N = 18).

Table 3.   Pretest and posttest data collected using McCarthy scales.

| Case I (perceptual motor strong, gross motor skills weak) | | | | |
| | Pretest | | Posttest | |
Skills	Raw score	Index score	Raw score	Index score
Perceptual Performance	46	60	47	50
Gross Motor	16	31	32	40

| Case II (Perceptual motor weak, gross motor skills strong) | | | | |
| | Pretest | | Posttest | |
Skills	Raw score	Index score	Raw score	Index score
Perceptual Performance	15	30	36	39
Gross Motor	44	63	44	56

gram evaluation activities. For the first child, Case I, the needs assessment determines that the child is strong in the perceptual motor area, but weak in gross motor functioning. The short-term focus for this child is in the latter domain. For the second child, Case II, an opposite needs assessment and instructional emphasis emerges. The program focuses for a short term on improving perceptual motor skills. Pretest and six month post test data using the *McCarthy Scales of Children's Abilities* (McCarthy, 1972) is collected on each of the children as shown in Table 3. Significant progress takes place in the gross motor domain for Case I. In the period of six months the child has gained almost a standard deviation (s.d. = 10.0) on the index score. The child's perceptual motor skills have remained steady. The posttest index score of 50 is equivalent to average performance of children at this age. Educationally, this would be considered a successful program experience. Similarly, for Case II there is meaningful progress in the perceptual motor area, again a gain of almost a standard deviation, while gross motor performance remains adequate for this age.

However, if all that one examines is the individual pre/post index score gains for the two cases, the results are quite different:

	Perceptual Performance	Gross Motor
Case I	− 10	+ 9
Case II	+ 9	− 7
Average	− 0.5	+ 1.0

As suggested earlier, examination of mean gains indicates no dramatic effects. Further, while the data on individuals suggest some gains for subjects in some areas, the aggregate scores do not present a particular pattern. These scores reflect pseudo-negative effects (i.e., an individual short-term "loss" that is of no educational or clinical significance) counterbalancing important positive gains that are attributable to deliberate program activity.

In short, these considerations lead to the inescapable conclusion that there are important inconsistencies between the basic assumptions of the treatment control group paradigm and the reality of individualized open classroom experiences for special needs children. Clearly, the evaluation methods that are utilized must be carefully fitted to the nature of the program under study. For any strategy to be responsive to the complex structure of the open classroom, it must focus on individual growth — too much is concealed in average differences. Further, it must examine individual progress in the full context of the individual case. Information on individual gains is often uninterpretable if removed from the context of the individual needs assessment and the resultant instructional efforts.

TOWARD A SINGLE-CASE EVALUATION STRATEGY

Appropriateness of Single-Case Experimental Methods

Most effectiveness questions for developmentally oriented open classroom programs take place at a micro-level of activity. Although there are some questions that derive directly from the generic structure of the program and can be projected onto every individual child (e.g., Are handicapped children interacting with peers as often as nonhandicapped children? Do handicapped children utilize the same strategies for obtaining teacher attention as their nondisabled peers?), most cannot. Most questions concerning effectiveness require an examination of the impact of the educational program developed in interaction with the specific needs of an individual handicapped child. Thus, the problem that arises is how to study program impact in an individual case.

One alternative that merits consideration is the $N = 1$ research design methodology. Recent efforts (Hersen and Barlow, 1976; Krathochwill, 1978) have advocated more extensive use of this approach in research on clinical and educational settings. These designs have seen extensive use in basic research in special education (see Dukes, 1965; Baer, Wolf, and Risly, 1968; Yates, 1970; Blackman, 1972; Guralnick, 1973; Kazdin, 1973; Edgar and Billingsley, 1974; and White, 1977).

There are two main versions in current use: the reversal (ABA or ABAB) design and the multiple baseline design. From the perspective of evaluating developmentally oriented open classrooms, the reversal design is inappropriate since it is highly intrusive to the instructional process. It requires that teachers alter their interactions with the handicapped child for research rather than instructional purposes, and it assumes that there is no carry-over of the treatment effect across period reversals.

Multiple baseline designs appear more promising. The multiple baseline design involves the successive application of the treatment to a number of subjects who are being monitored continuously on the dependent variable. A treatment effect is inferred if behavior changes occur only upon application of the experimental variable. This approach makes less intrusive demands on the instructional process, it does not require large numbers of subjects, and it does not require that a control group of children be excluded from the program. It has been suggested (Guralnick, 1973; Wynne, Ulfeder, and Dakof, 1975) that this approach is particularly well suited for highly individualized programming in a mainstreaming context.

The difficulties in applying this approach to evaluating the effectiveness of developmentally oriented, open classroom activities are subtle. The difficulties are derived from the shared control that characterizes the instructional process and from the developmental perspective on child growth, which views functioning as a system of interrelated skills set in a long-term framework. First, the multiple baseline design assumes that the evaluator can control the onset of the treatment to meet data collection needs. However, in open classrooms the "treatment" is ever present and the child may engage himself before the adults initiate treatment, or even without their knowledge.

Second, as a result of the shared control in open classrooms, there is only limited predictability that the program, as actually experienced by the child, will follow any *a priori* pattern or sequence. In fact, the environment that the handicapped child experiences in an open classroom is not fully defined until he enters that environment. The child has impact on his peers and his teacher, and they have impact on each other in turn, creating a new set of relationships with their own boundaries and constraints. It is within this newly created organization that the child's program begins to unfold. Even if the program is highly purposeful, attempting to optimize development for the handicapped child, it is taking place within a framework whose future structure is only predictable in part.

Third, although there is clarity and purposefulness in the long-term goal structure for a program such as Eliot-Pearson, that is, competence in each of the basic developmental areas, there are numerous short-term routes that can be followed in the achievement of this desired end. From an educational perspective, each route may be equally successful. Thus, even if one comprehensively assesses an individual child's needs, no unitary instructional strategy or specific set of short-term objectives may be apparent.

In short, the multiple-baseline approach is an experimental strategy. As with all experimental methods (see Sutherland, 1973), it is predicated on the applicability of principles of prediction and control. In a traditional teaching situation where the teacher exercises primary control and in which instruction follows a predetermined sequence, experimental strategies are feasible as long as the teacher is willing to transfer that control to the evaluator. However, open classroom settings involve only modest levels of predictability and controllability. There are important differences between the characteristics of the open classroom experience and those educational settings that are typically subject to the basic behavioral research paradigm. These differences have significant consequences for the choice of an appropriate research methodology.

A Naturalistic Single-Case Approach

In the absence of an appropriate experimental mode for examining the effectiveness of open classrooms on individual, handicapped children, we have developed a naturalistic strategy for examining individual child progress over the course of an academic year. Due to the limited utility of *a priori* individual child goals, the strategy begins with a goal-free orientation (see Scriven, 1972) focusing on a simple documentation of an individual child's needs as they unfold in his initial experiences within the program.

This raises an immediate question of what can be admitted as evidence of child progress in the identified areas of need. Measurement issues represent a major concern in the evaluation of many different types of social programs. Some (see Patton, 1975) have argued that because of the generally primitive state of quantitative assessment, impact studies assess effectively only a narrow band of experience under restricted conditions. When we apply inadequate measures, Hein (1975) has argued that we almost assure that open classroom programs are not favorably evaluated.

It is necessary to reconsider the wisdom of a purely empirical perspective. The quantitative information that can be collected provides, at best, a highly segmented picture of open classrooms. We propose to use such data as evidence to be combined with information gathered from a more qualitative/clinical perspective. In attempting to provide a rich picture of the individual case, we adopt a *mixed multiple measure strategy*. For example, in examining the effectiveness of the Eliot-Pearson program in achieving its objectives with individual children, we employed both quantitative measures, such as the *McCarthy Scales of Children's Abilities* (a standardized norm-referenced evaluation instrument), a classroom observational instrument, criterion-referenced checklists, and qualitative strategies, such as clinical observations, structured and unstructured staff and family interviews, and regular program clinical notes.

A matrix that relates program objectives to potential sources of evidence concerning progress toward these objectives is presented (Table 4). This matrix serves as a heuristic, since not every cell will be available on every child, and even if filled, the cells may not contain much useful information for a particular child vis-à-vis a particular objective. This is particularly true for some of the qualitative techniques, such as clinical observations. Nevertheless, the matrix is a useful planning device for examining the individual case, since it suggests sources of information and indicates program objectives on which there is little or no information.

Although no single measure in this array may be individually strong, several measures taken together can create a total picture that reliably documents individual child progress over time. As a child develops, certain patterns consistent with this growth should emerge across the multiple measures. One may think of this approach as a set of windows, each providing a slightly different view of the same phenomenon. This chapter presents an actual case as an illustration of this mixed multiple measures approach for assessing child progress.

However, beyond simple strategies for documenting individual progress, a naturalistic single-case methodology must also consider two other issues:

1. To what do we attribute the progress that we document?
2. Is this documented progress meaningful or educationally significant?

We examine the causal attribution question first; the second question is discussed later.

Attribution of Effect

It is impossible to obtain absolute causality in social science research. Attached to all of our "knowledge" is a measure of uncertainty, reflecting the inadequacies of our theories and research strategies, and the inherent complexity of basic social phenomena. Even the perfectly conducted, randomized treatment-control group study provides only probabilistic evidence about treatment effectiveness. In contrast, anecdotal documentation of child progress constitutes weak grounds on which to make causal assertions about program impact. Even if the evidence concerning child progress is strong, plausible alternative explanations exist for such progress (e.g., a natural growth spurt). In the naturalistic study of a single case, it is not completely possible to counter every alternative explanation of observed progress. It is useful to attempt to catalogue for each case the possible explanations and to assess the subjective likelihood of such alternatives from the perspective of the various participants in the process (e.g., parents, teacher, evaluators). However, a demand for absolute evidence is a demand for absolute causality (see Cronbach, 1975).

In focusing on the plausibility of the program impact hypothesis, we propose to examine the causal theory of action apparently operating in each case. According to Patton (1978), such an evaluation model requires that we make explicit the assumed causal relationships in the chain or system of objectives for the individual child, construct a means-end hierarchy, specify the validity assumptions that link the two together, and identify and collect appropriate data to examine the "goodness of fit" in the individual case.

We have organized the actual implementation of this causal theory of action evaluation model in terms of a sequence of questions that should be asked about each case:

A. Program as Planned
    1. From an examination of the individual educational plan and available diagnostic data, what would be appropriate goals and objectives for this case?
    2. If the program is effective for this child, what kinds of progress, stated *a priori* by parents, teachers, program directors, and developers, should we expect to witness?
    3. What kinds of program strategies would constitute reasonable means toward this end?

Although the information acquired from the responses to these questions is insufficient for the utilization of a goal-based evaluation model, the meaningfulness of any observed child progress must be examined in the context of the recognized special needs of the individual child. Without this base of data on the program as planned, it is difficult to make judgments concerning program effectiveness.

B. Assessment of Child Progress
    4. What evidence is there that the child is making progress?
    5. Is the documented progress consistent with the assessment of the child's needs and *a priori* expectations about progress?
    6. What other possible explanations for observed progress are tenable (e.g., maturation, effects of other programs in which a child may participate, other activities on the parents' part, etc.)?

Here we employ the mixed multiple measures strategy to assist in determinations about progress. While careful assessment of *a priori* goals (from the data concerning the program as planned) is emphasized, progress should be monitored in each of the major developmental areas.

C. Program as Experienced
    7. From the teacher's perspective, what is the program intentionality (i.e., what is it trying to do and why?) as it actually unfolds over time?
    8. How does an outside observer characterize the child's experience in the program?
    9. Is there congruence between the program as intended by staff and as experienced by the child?
   10. To what degree are the experiences of the child a likely result of direct teacher behaviors, the general structure of the environment, or chance aspects of the setting, not subject to control by any method or individual?
   11. What theoretical base or philosophical assumptions are re quired to establish the validity of the linkage between documented "means" (program as delivered) and documented "ends" (assessment of child's progress)?

These questions strike at the core of our investigation of the plausibility of the causal theory of action for the individual child. Answers to these questions can establish a basis for forming conclusions about the activities in which the program has purposefully engaged and the linkage between such activities and observed child progress. A key element in the analysis is a search for consistency — in differences and in perspectives between teacher and observer, and in the means-ends linkages.

This set of eleven questions does not exhaust all of the questions that could be addressed in establishing the causal theory of action for an individual child. However, this set does serve to illustrate several important features of the approach:

1. It defines three basic categories of information in developing the causal theory of action for an individual case: the diagnostic/needs assessment of the child, the description of the program as experienced by the child, and the assessment of child progress.
2. Since the phenomenon under study is dynamic and interactive, our research methodology is consistent with these qualities. The examination of the questions above is carried on in a prospective manner, beginning with the child's diagnostic assessment and following through the child's experiences during the academic year.
3. This approach has an analytic, or detective-like, logic similar to the modus operandi evaluation methodology suggested by Scriven (1976). The evaluator is constantly interacting with the evidence, drawing on past experiences, and searching the evidence for plausibility of the competing hypotheses.

4. As an evaluation strategy, it involves a combination of goal-directed and goal-free activities. While the educational plan for a child constitutes the starting point for the investigation, the specific content of questions asked and data collected may assume a much wider scope. Further, this scope may change over time in response to changes in program intentionality or observed child progress.

By now it should be clear that the primary purpose of the research strategy described above is to develop procedures for conducting an internally valid study of individual cases, i.e., did the intervention produce the observed results? Later in this chapter, issues of external validity will be raised, i.e., will the results of a particular intervention generalize to other similar cases? As will be noted, since external validity can rarely be ascertained from the study of a single case, to address these issues as a replication across cases is essential; but such replications depend upon the identity of diagnostic assessments, treatment approaches, and other variables that imply a level of controllability and predictability not found in open classrooms and rarely achieved in programs that give credence to individual differences. Such an individual educational program is described in the case study that follows.

AN APPLICATION OF THE CAUSAL THEORY
OF ACTION EVALUATION MODEL: BECKY

A. Program as Planned.
  1. *Child Objectives*   As noted in Case 1, Becky is a girl, who is almost 6 years old, who displayed unusual language usage, poor fine and gross motor skills, inappropriate social behavior, and a heightened sensitivity to distractions and details in her environment when she first entered Eliot-Pearson. In response to this set of assessed needs, the program objectives presented earlier in Table 1 were selected. In particular, several objectives were heavily emphasized with Becky throughout the entire year. These included the ability to express feelings, to develop a sense of independence and self-confidence, to increase the level of attention and involvement in activities, to improve the ability to make transitions, follow classroom routines, and make self-regulated choices, to increase positive interactions with peers, to acquire skills of group participation, to increase body awareness, to develop the ability to cut with scissors and use writing and drawing implements, to increase the ability to dif-

ferentiate between fantasy and reality, to acquire readiness skills, to acquire auditory memory skills, and to stimulate expressive language usage.

2. *Expected Outcomes*   Becky was expected to make progress during the year, particularly in the personal/social domain. Progress would be noted in sustained attentional ability, increased independence with appropriate reliance on teachers, increased ability to share materials and space with other children, greater proficiency in making transitions, and increased ability to participate appropriately with other children during group activities.

3. *Classroom strategies*   A variety of strategies might be utilized in helping to effect change for Becky in the personal/social domain. Since Becky preferred the dramatic play area of the classroom where she could become self-absorbed in doll play, her doll could be utilized as a transition object to introduce her to other areas of the room. For example, with doll in hand, the teachers might direct Becky to the fine motor area and structure an experience for her from which she could derive success, such as an open-ended activity using one-inch cubes. As the year progresses, the tasks can become more structured and longer in duration. The teachers should expect to maintain proximity to Becky but to decrease their immediate presence with her. However, they will probably continue to be required to assist her in making transitions. Peers, using teacher-directed modeling of shared behavior, should be encouraged to use the same area of the classroom that Becky occupies. Eventually, it is hoped that Becky will be able to participate in small group experience with minimal teacher intervention and generally appropriate behavior.

B.   Assessment of Child Progress

4. *Evidence of Progress*   At the end of the year, Becky's progress was tabulated by individual objectives on the following chart. This chart reflects the totality of the program objectives; however, only certain objectives and data points are particularly relevant for Becky.

The chart includes seven categories in which data are collected throughout the year. Relevant objectives for Becky are those that have more than two recorded independent sources of data. A description of the major data sources follows.

The MSCA, or *McCarthy Scales of Children's Abilities* (McCarthy, 1972), is a formal assessment instrument specifically selected to evaluate cognitive functioning in young children. It was administered in a pre/post format in the fall and spring.

A formal *classroom observational instrument* was also utilized in a pre/post format coincident with the MSCA. This particular procedure counted the frequencies of social interaction between Becky and her classmates and teachers, as well as frequencies of levels of play (Parton, 1932), during a twelve minute period of time. Becky was observed four times in the fall and spring. Reliabilities were achieved between two observers for all categories.

Tutorial was included in Becky's program twice a week to further reinforce her general skill development. Specific objectives were chosen that were appropriate for a one-to-one setting; a variety of teaching strategies was utilized throughout the year. The tutor assessed Becky's change on specific objectives at the end of the year. An independent observer completed open-ended *clinical observations* on Becky four times during the year while Becky was participating in class activities. These observations yielded descriptive information about Becky's social interactions, her involvement with materials, her play activities, her interactions with teachers, the quality of group participation, and her general affective tone. Judgments were made from the descriptive data to be included on the matrix.

At the conclusion of the school year, teachers completed a *final report* concerning Becky. This constituted a descriptive narrative that assessed her development in all major domains.

A *developmental checklist* was completed by the teachers twice during the year. It included a delineation of specific objectives in a criterion-referenced format, with comments about a child's progress or development on relevant objectives.

Finally, *time samples* were developed on an individualized basis for a few objectives that required more extensive documentation. This procedure was administered monthly to assess the ongoing progress in a specific area. For example, Becky's ability to sustain attention during a manipulative activity was monitored on a regular basis.

Table 4 summarizes Becky's evidence of progress on each of the individual program objectives that were selected for her. An assessment of the degree of change by objective is indicated for each instrument with relevant data on that objective. Change is shown by means of a four-point scale ranging from "0" (i.e., no change) through "†" (i.e., better than average change). Blank cells in the matrix appear if a particular instrument contains no data relevant for that objective. The last column in the table provides a summary assessment of all the evidence that is available for assessing progress on each individual objective. It should be noted that rules for assessing each data point were developed in the context of each case. Greater attention must still be devoted to standardizing and more clearly articulating these decision rules.

5. *Consistency of Expectations and Progress*   Consistency of progress expected and progress recorded was evident at several points. For example, with the objective "Becky is to increase her level of attention and involvement in activities" (Objective 5 — Personal/Social), the *formal observation* indicated that Becky engaged less in unoccupied play and more in solitary and parallel play. *Tutoring* noted that Becky was able to attend and focus on an activity for as long as fifty minutes; this was also confirmed by the *clinical observer*. The *final report* showed that Becky had increased her attention span during structured activities. Becky displayed less distractibility and more ability to sustain her attention, as noted significantly in her on-task behavior. All of these data suggest a high degree of change; thus, Becky was judged to have increased in her attentional abilities, an area of need for her.

In contrast, Becky made minimal progress in "improving her ability to make transitions independently" (Objective 6 — Personal/Social). The *tutorial* report noted Becky's continued difficulty in making the initial transition from the classroom to the tutoring room adjacent to the classroom. The *clinical observer* reported Becky's repeated need for teacher support during transitions. The *final report* and the *developmental checklist* corroborated the earlier observations. All four data sources reported a minimal change score, indicating little or no progress for Becky on this objective, although this was considered an important objective for her.

Progress was consistent for Becky on 9 of the 11 Personal/Social objectives initially selected for her. From the two previous examples it can be concluded that Becky's attentional ability increased across all categories, while the evidence indicated that Becky was not able to show gains in making transitions this year.

6. *Other Explanations for Progress*   Becky was not enrolled in programs other than those that she experienced at Eliot-Pearson. Thus, change that was perceived in Becky could not

Table 4. Evidence of progress: Becky

	MSCA	Observ. instrument	Tutorial	Clinical observ.	Final report	Develop. checklist	Time Sample	Summary assessment of change
Personal/Social								
1. Feelings			++		+	++		++
2. Separation			++		++	++		++
3. Independence			+	++	+	+		++
4. Impulse-control			+	++	+	+		++
5. Attention		+	+	+	+	+	+	+
6. Transitions			0	+	+	0		0
7. Feeding								
8. Toileting								
9. Self-image			+		++	+		++
10. Trust teachers			++		+	++		++
11. Make friends			+		+	+		+
12. Peer interactions		+	++		++	++	++	++
13. Group participation		++			+	+		++
Gross Motor								
1. Hop, skip, etc.	++		+		++	+		++
2. Body awareness								
3. Throw ball								
4. Coordination			++		++	++		++

Fine/Perceptual Motor

1. Cut and draw	++	+	++	++	†	++
2. Write and print	+	+	+	+	+	0
3. Shape discrimination						
4. Manipulatives	++	++	++	+	†	++
5. Button, zip, tie	0	0	0	+		0

Cognitive/Language

1. Exploration and mastery	++	++	†	++	++	++
2. Reality and Fantasy	+	+		+	+	+
3. Readiness	++	0	†	++	0	++
4. Match, classify						
5. Pre-reading						
6. Understand number						
7. Follow directions	++	+	++	++	+	++
8. Auditory memory	0	0	+	+	0	0
9. Expressive language	++	++	++	++	++	++
10. Clarity of speech	++	+	†	++	+	++
11. Name objects	++	++	†	++	++	++
12. Use pronouns	+	+	+	+	+	+
13. Proper syntax	++	+	†	†	+	+

Key: Degree of Change
++ Better than average change
+ Average change/developed appropriately
0 No change
† Little change/not as much as average child

be attributed to inputs from other programs. Her parents reported that, with rare exceptions, her only exposure to other children occurred during the school program. There is no doubt that maturation played an important role in Becky's development. However, the fact that she was able to keep pace with her nonhandicapped peers in nearly all areas of development is indicative of the effectiveness of the program, given Becky's needs and abilities at the outset of the school year.

C.   Program as Experienced.

   7.   *Program Intentionality*   In addition to assessing change on individual objectives, it is critical to examine the role of the program in actually effecting the changes noted in Table 4. The first component in this assessment requires gathering information on teachers' perspectives concerning individual program activities. At Eliot-Pearson, teachers were interviewed at the end of the year to ascertain their impressions of the involvement of the program, or the program intentionality, in actually bringing about change in children on particular objectives.

   Teachers were interviewed concerning the interaction of five variables with each child on each objective. The variables were as follows:

   a.   Adults — the role directly played by teachers and other professionals in bringing about change.

   b.   Peers — the role played by interaction with or observation of peers in bringing about change.

   c.   Physical Environment — the role played by the physical arrangement of the classroom space in bringing about change.

   d.   Instructional Materials — the role of direct use or manipulation of learning materials in bringing about change.

   e.   Other — the role of other program-based inputs, such as tutoring, speech therapy, physical therapy, etc., in bringing about change.

   These particular variables were selected because they are salient features of the open educational framework to which the program at Eliot-Pearson adheres. Teachers were asked to assign an intentionality score to each of these variables based on a 1 to 4 scale in which 1 indicates "was not responsible for perceived change" and 4 indicates "was critical in bringing about change." The "intentionality scores" for Becky are shown in Table 5.

Table 5. Program Intentionality: Becky

	Teacher emphasis	Adults	Peers	Physical environment	Materials	Other (tutor)
Personal/Social						
1. Feelings	yes	4	3	2	3	3
2. Separation	yes	3	2	2	2	3
3. Independence	yes	4	2	3	2	3
4. Impulse-control	yes	4	2	2	2	2
5. Attention	yes	4	2	2	4	4
6. Transitions	yes	4	2	3	3	3
7. Feeding	no					
8. Toileting	no					
9. Self-image	yes	4	2	3	3	3
10. Trust teachers	yes	4	1	3	3	3
11. Make friends	yes	4	3	3	3	3
12. Peer interactions	yes	4	3	3	2	2
13. Group participation	yes	4	2	3	3	
Gross Motor						
1. Hop, skip, etc.	yes	3	2	3	3	2
2. Body awareness	yes	4	2	2	3	3
3. Throw ball	no					
4. Coordination	yes	3	2	3	3	2
Fine/Perceptual Motor						
1. Cut and draw	yes	3	2	4	4	4
2. Write and print	yes	3	2	4	4	4
3. Shape discrimination	no					
4. Manipulatives	yes	3	2	4	4	4
5. Button, zip, tie	yes	3	2	2	2	3
Cognitive/Language						
1. Exploration and mastery	yes	4	2	3	3	3
2. Reality and fantasy	yes	4	2	4	4	

continued

Table 5 — continued.

		Teacher emphasis	Adults	Peers	Physical environment	Materials	Other (tutor)
3.	Readiness	yes	3	2	3	4	3
4.	Match, classify	no					
5.	Pre-reading	no					
6.	Understand number	no					
7.	Follow directions	yes	3	3	3	2	3
8.	Auditory memory	yes	3	2	2	2	
9.	Expressive language	yes	4	2	4	3	4
10.	Clarity of speech	no					
11.	Name objects	no					
12.	Use pronouns	no					
13.	Proper syntax	no					

This table can be used to summarize the program from the teacher's perspective. It graphically represents the teacher's theory of action, or the teacher's account of what took place, in the classroom during the course of the year. The format for displaying this information is consistent with the major features of the Eliot-Pearson program. A different educational approach, or a different evaluation audience, might entail a different format. The format shown in Table 5 was adopted as a means of examining the teacher's judgments concerning the program's accomplishments. For example, the objective "to increase the level of attention and involvement in activities" was highly emphasized for Becky. *Adults* (rating = 4) were an integral part of helping Becky sustain her attentional level, while *peers* (rating = 2) were not an essential component in achieving this objective for Becky. *Physical environment* (rating = 3) was less important than *materials* (rating = 4), although both of these variables were considered by Becky's teacher to be critical to the acquisition of her increased attentional abilities. Specific materials were utilized to help her learn to focus, while the arrangement of the physical environment into small, contained learning areas facilitated the teacher's work with Becky.

It should be noted that in developing their report on program intentionality, Becky's teachers drew heavily on their memories, case notes, and anecdotal records. In future efforts, the quality of the data would be enhanced if teachers were interviewed periodically throughout the year, rather than simply at the end of the year. Information gathered from several time points would provide valuable data concerning changes in teacher perspectives over time. In addition, such a strategy could serve as an ongoing mechanism for resolving apparent inconsistencies (see question 9 below) between the theory of action as articulated by the teacher and the theory of action as viewed by outside observers attempting to characterize the program's effects as experienced by the child.

8. *Outside Observers*   The information described above forms the basis for a retrospective clinical case study. Taken alone, it constitutes a limited data base for conducting applied research (see Hersen and Barlow, 1976). It provides only one perspective concerning a highly interactive phenomenon. Thus, information from an outside observer attempting to view the program, as experienced by the child, represents a critical comparison standard. When these data — collected by observers "blind" to reported program intentionality — agree with teacher reports, the validity of the description of the program is greatly enhanced. When inconsistencies appear, they suggest possible weaknesses in the program's intended theory of action and could thus prove valuable in informing future program efforts.

Since only four observations of Becky were conducted during the course of the year, only limited information was obtained. Nevertheless, when combined with the data from the formal observational instrument, some interesting conclusions could be drawn. For example, the structured observations of Becky showed, with the attention objective, that she increased significantly in solitary and parallel play by the end of the year. The informal open-ended clinical observation yielded a trend toward longer sustained involvement in activities.

In short, the observational data are critical to the successful implementation of the naturalistic single-case strategy. In planning future evaluation efforts, greater attention should be focused on developing procedures for gathering data on the program as experienced by the child.

9. *The Program as Intended and as Experienced*   Due to the limited observational data noted above, judgments concerning the congruence between the program as described by the teacher

(program intentionality) and as viewed by outside observers (program as experienced by the child) was also quite restricted. Where observational data did exist for Becky, congruence was obtained in most instances. For example, Becky was encouraged to devote a great deal of time and attention to utilizing the manipulative materials in the classroom. On virtually all measures of progress she displayed increased competence, flexibility and ingenuity in using blocks, rods, counting cubes, chips, interlocking puzzles, etc. The clinical observer frequently recorded Becky's successful experiences with manipulatives, whereas her teacher indicated that increasing Becky's feeling of comfort and competence with these materials was a critical objective during the school year.

10. *Intended Effects Versus Chance Effects*   An overall review of Becky's status when she entered Eliot-Pearson, of the program that was planned and presented, and of the observable changes that she demonstrated indicate a high level of intended effects. Specifically, Becky entered the program at Eliot-Pearson with problems in her language usage, social behavior, skill development, and attentional skills. Coincident with her assessed needs, specific objectives were selected for her, and evaluative information was collected across a number of data points. At the end of the year, progress was evident across all major domains. Becky made progress in the personal/social area, as indicated by increased attentional level, increased independence, increased ability to join other children in play and in sharing the same space, and she increased her ability to participate in small group activities. Gains were not evident in making transitions in the classroom.

In the motor area, Becky was more aware of her body in space and better able to plan her body movements. She showed more facility in manipulating small objects and in using scissors and writing tools. However, she did not show change in buttoning her own clothing.

Becky's cognitive and language skills were the least emphasized this year. Nonetheless, progress was indicated on a few objectives. Becky used more areas of the classroom, learned color and shape names, followed two-step directions, and was more appropriate in her conversations. She showed little or no change in differentiating reality and fantasy and in her auditory memory skills.

The program that was planned for Becky this year was intentional in its attempt to effect change on specific objectives. Progress was evident for many objectives, while others were more resistant to change. A reassessment of Becky's needs is in order, as well as a scrutiny of teaching strategies that were effective with her this year. In this manner, the parameters of the program that were effective for her will become more apparent.

11. *Theoretical Position*   The program implemented for Becky reveals an assessment of her needs; it also yields an insight into the basic orientation of the Eliot-Pearson approach. Personal/social objectives are afforded great care and great attention. Becky is assisted in learning how to interact with her social environment — both peer and adult. She is also encouraged to interact with and explore the physical environment of the classroom. Indeed, in many instances cognitive objectives are utilized as means to affective ends, and actual implementational strategies are developed in the teaching-learning process. Therefore, this approach reflects an emphasis on interactivity at all levels of performance and learning, as well as a deliberate attempt to enhance development through increasing every child's ability to adapt to a continually challenging learning environment.

PLACING A VALUE ON THE EFFECTIVENESS DATA

The Standards of Comparison Issue

We have related in some detail a causal theory of action model for evaluating the impact of open classrooms on individual children with special needs. From our pilot experiences with this approach, we are convinced that it is quite possible to make statements, with a high degree of certainty, about program impact on an individual child. Nevertheless, we still must confront the standards of comparison issue. That is, "Are the results that are obtained with a particular child at Eliot-Pearson better than the results that could be obtained in some alternative program?"

Ideally, it would be desirable to have data on how the child in question would have progressed under each of the alternative treatments that were possible. The treatment control group paradigm approximates the standards of comparison ideal by forming groups at random to receive alternative services. Because of ethical considerations and recent legal and procedural mandates that provide an appropriate education for all children (e.g., Public Law 94-142), it is impossible, however, to propose a "no services" group as the standard, since, in principle, every handicapped child should receive some services somewhere.

Thus, given the highly individualized nature of the program at Eliot-Pearson, the only reasonable standard for judging the progress of an Eliot-Pearson child is to judge it against the progress of children with similar needs and a similar educational plan in other eligible service placements. Extensive logistical difficulties arise when attempting to establish valid comparison bases of this kind. For example, at Eliot-Pearson the group of special needs children represents a diverse array of diagnostic assessments and handicapping conditions, including Down's syndrome, hearing impairment, cerebral palsy, blindness, learning disability, developmental delay, emotional disturbance, etc. Essentially, the program is delivering 18 highly individualized programs, each with its own goals, objectives, and implementational strategies. Even where objectives are the same across children, they may still require a different comparison standard since the developmental restrictions and expectations imposed by various handicapping conditions may be quite different.

In short, this situation implies a need for different standards of comparison for each child, where the choice of an appropriate standard is based on an identification of important developmental features concerning that child. These developmental standards do not currently exist, and it is likely that numerous difficulties would be encountered in any effort of this kind. Developing such quantitative standards requires the establishment of an extensive data bank of special needs cases. Diagnostic assessment, program description, and child progress data would have to be included. The data bank requires a standardized reporting of information. Taxonomic procedures for accumulating similar cases would also have to be developed. In addition, new strategies utilizing combinations of cross-sectional and longitudinal methods similar to those being developed by Strenio, Weisburg, and Bryk (1978) would be required. It is not clear that such standards will ever be developed.

The problems are further compounded by the fact that different programs and approaches may value very different short-term goals and objectives. For example, an open classroom program might have short-term goals for a specific handicapped child that could be quite different from the goals of a program with a more behavioral persuasion. These alternative programs simply define progress differently in the short term. Comparisons across these kinds of programs cannot be reduced to an empirical decision rule since the issue in question is either a theory, or in the absence of theory, a set of values. Lacking the theoretical base to resolve such questions, this type of comparison question becomes a matter of personal choice. The best that can be achieved is a careful description of the differences across programs in terms of their causal theories of action in similar cases. The differential patterns of progress that emerge from each of these programs would also have to be articulated. Such analyses could prove very useful to individual teachers and parents confronting child placement and personal value decisions. However, such information cannot be used by evaluators to decide that a particular program type is better or worse than some other program.

At the core of the standards of comparison issue is the question of whether the observed child progress is educationally *meaningful*. The traditional treatment control group approach, even when perfectly implemented, does not directly provide information of this sort. Rather, this approach substitutes the statistical significance (e.g., a significant *t* statistic associated with a mean difference between two groups) of an estimated effect for the educational significance of any measured program effect. When such studies attempt to assess the educational significance of the intervention, they invoke essentially arbitrary standards (see Carver, 1978). For example, in the recently completed Follow Through evaluation, the evaluators defined a mean difference between groups of one-quarter of a standard deviation on a normed test as educationally significant (Stebbins et al., 1977). This is an arbitrary criterion with no established theoretical base.

Thus, in the absence of a theoretically grounded longitudinal data bank of the type suggested above, decisions about the meaningfulness of individual progress should be based on individual clinical judgment. Clearly, in some cases there will be overwhelming agreement. However, in other cases there may be substantial disagreements stemming largely from very different individual value frameworks. It is important to realize that this situation is not greatly different from that of the well-implemented treatment control group study. The continuing debates and the persistence of different points of view, regardless of the results reported in a particular study or the quality of the methodology utilized, attest to this inherent ambiguity. In proposing a naturalistic single-case methodology, we have focused the meaningfulness question. The treatment control group approach, with all of its quantitative machinations, simply sidesteps the important question — "Does it really matter *enough* to act on the information?" This is the key policy or action issue.

Usefulness of Program Effectiveness Data

The results of a naturalistic inquiry such as the causal theory of action model have a variety of uses. Teachers in open classrooms can utilize the program effectiveness data to manage the classroom experiences of individual children. Open classrooms based on developmental principles require a form of ongoing evaluation that assists teachers in making sense of what their pupils are working on, and that informs them of some of the effects of their own behavior. The method commonly used in open classrooms to achieve these purposes is that of informal description. The open classroom teacher, as reported in the literature (see, for example, Brown and Precious, 1968), constantly jots down pertinent information about the child and his activities. These informal records presumably comprise the child's evaluation. There are several problems with this method that might conceivably be eliminated by the approach presented in this chapter.

The first problem is information overload. Naturalistic-phenomenological records are descriptions of behavior unbiased with respect to content: everything the child does is included in the records. Of course, it is impossible for a teacher to mark down or remember more than a fraction of what each of his students does every day, but this fraction mounts up. The records of 25 or 30 children can become immense within a few months. As the records grow in length, the information that they contain becomes increasingly difficult to use and to assimilate. Therefore, as the information accumulates, teachers' perceptions become more rigid and inflexible. Their categories for assimilating this information cannot keep pace with the increase in information, therefore, their view of their pupils is one of gradually reconciling new behavior to old patterns of perception. Their behavior becomes stereotyped, loses its diagnostic and interpretive function, and instead of evaluating on-going changes in learning, their informal reports begin to resemble lists of behavioral outcomes.

As the teacher's records of informal observations concerning each child grow, it becomes increasingly difficult to follow the effects of the complex of previous interventions and explorations. The resulting lists of behaviors are low on information. Given the interactive qualities of teacher decision-making in open classrooms and the requirements of individualization for children with special needs, as the teachers' information about their pupils becomes limited, the learning experience for those children correspondingly narrows. The single case causal theory of action model outlined in this chapter can be utilized as an information management system to guide the implementation of the diagnostic-prescriptive process in open classrooms. Such a system should not encounter the problems of information overload because it is designed to integrate and organize large quantities of disparate data concerning teacher intentions and children's experiences. Whether this potential use is realized is principally a matter of whether or not teachers and program directors find the data generated by this strategy useful enough to warrant the required contribution of their time to data collection efforts.

A second use of the effectiveness data, generated by the naturalistic single case studies, affects the parents of special needs children. If descriptions of educational programs of other children similar to their own were made available to parents, it could help to make concrete the meaning of the different causal theories of action of various programs and to present more clearly the likely outcomes associated with each alternative. This should lead parents to a more informed choice concerning program placements for their special needs children.

Third, as cases are accumulated over time, they provide an opportunity for building a knowledge base concerning the effectiveness of special education programming and educational alternatives in general. Although it is not possible to make direct inferences for future practice from any single individual case report, replication across similar cases would certainly provide such a basis. In order to accomplish this task, it is necessary to develop procedures for systematically accumulating the cases and for summarizing the descriptive evidence. It would be desirable to utilize a methodology that combines the concreteness of the individual cases with efforts aimed at building general program theories of action. The qualitative data analytic method (see, for example, Denzin, 1970; Schatzman and Strauss, 1973) seems best suited for this purpose.

SUMMARY AND CONCLUSIONS

Traditionally, the treatment control group paradigm has been utilized in the evaluation of program impact. However, in this chapter we have argued that this approach does not address the fundamental tenets of an open classroom that embodies a developmental perspective. An alternative to standard experimental design is presented, and its application and relevance to open classroom settings is discussed.

This chapter identifies several key features of the open classroom to which such an evaluation approach must be responsive. First, the dynamic characteristics of the developmental perspective and the interactive nature of open classrooms create a context characterized by only limited predictability. This characteristic presents problems for any goal-based evaluation model. Second, the basic decision making in open classrooms reflects shared control between teachers and children. This control cannot be transferred to the evaluator without seriously distorting the basic nature of the intervention. This feature of open classrooms is very important since it implies that experimental research strategies, which require evaluator control, are not feasible in this context. Third, the highly individualized nature of programming for special needs children within the open classroom can create very complex, short-term implementational structures. Such structures can only be understood by examining individual child progress in the full context of that case.

In response to these perceptions, we have pursued a naturalistic single-case methodology. Our approach requires the development of a causal theory of action for each case. It is based on the logic of an analytic investigation (see Scriven, 1976) in which every piece of information constitutes evidence concerning child progress or the alternative causes of that progress.

The mixed multiple measurement strategy represents a critical feature of this process. This approach permits the use of both quantitative and qualitative data, teacher reports and observers' records, and normative scores and criterion referenced milestones. *It involves an examination of all of the evidence that it is possible to collect.* Although statistical methods can play an important role in helping to evaluate the evidence, they do not dictate a rigid research sequence that must be pursued.

We have sketched and illustrated an approach to implementing these ideas. This framework was developed in an attempt to assess the effectiveness of the developmentally oriented program at the Eliot-Pearson Children's School. It is offered as a tentative first step. We hope that by presenting it here we might stimulate further thought on the basic issues raised by this model of evaluation and encourage the continued use and refinement of this approach.

In our experience this approach provided an accurate perspective concerning the impact on special needs children of the developmentally oriented open educational program at Eliot-Pearson. It helped us to identify some successful teaching strategies, as well as aspects of the children's development that required greater attention, consideration, and planning. Finally, it was useful in generating information that enabled each potential user — teachers, program directors, parents, and other professionals — to address the real valuation question, "has the program made a meaningful contribution to the lives of children?"

ACKNOWLEDGMENTS

We would like to acknowledge the assistance of Dr. Herbert Weisberg, co-principal investigator with Dr. Bryk in the Bureau of Education for the Handicapped grant to develop strategies for evaluating early childhood special education programs. Many of the ideas expressed here are outgrowths of this collaborative effort.

We would also like to express our gratitude to the teachers and staff at the Eliot-Pearson Children's School who devoted a great deal of time, energy, and imagination to the development of the program described in this chapter.

REFERENCES

Baer, D. M., Wolf, M. M. and Risly, T. R. 1968. Some current dimensions of applied behavior analysis. J. Appl. Behav. Anal. 1:91–97.

Bennett, N. 1976. Teaching Styles and Pupil Progress. Harvard University Press, Cambridge.

Blackman, L. D. 1972. Research and the classroom: Mahomet and the mountain revisited. Except. Child. 39:181–190.

Brown, M., and Precious, N. 1968. The Integrated Day in the Primary School. Ward Lock Educational, London.

Bryk, A. S. 1978. Evaluating program impact: A time to cast away stones, a time to gather stones together. New Directions for Program Evaluation 1:31–58.

Bussis, A. M., and Chittenden, E. A. 1970. Analysis of an Approach to Open Education. Educational Testing Service, Princeton.

Bussis, A. M., Chittenden, E. A., and Amarel, M. 1976. Beyond Surface Curriculum. Westview Press, Boulder, Col.

Carver, R. P. 1978. The case against statistical significance testing. Harvard Educ. Rev. 48:378–399.

Cronbach, L. J. 1975. Beyond the two disciplines of scientific psychology. Am. Psychol. 30:116–127.

Denzin, N. K. 1970. The Research Act: A Theoretical Introduction to Sociological Methods. Aldine Publishing Company, Chicago.

Dukes, W. F. 1965. N = 1. Psychol. Bull. 64:74–79.

Edgar, E., and Billingsley, F. 1974. Believability when N = 1. Psychol. Rec. 24:47–160.

Guralnick, M. J. 1973. A research-service model for support of handicapped children. Except. Child. 39:277–282.

Hawkins, D. 1974. I, thou, and it. In: D. Hawkins (ed.), The Informed Vision. Agathon Press, Inc., New York.

Hein, G. 1975. An Open Education Perspective on Evaluation. North Dakota Study Group on Evaluation, Grand Forks, N. D.

Hersen, M., and Barlow, D. H. 1976. Single-Case Experimental Designs: Strategies for Studying Behavioral Change. Pergamon Press, Inc., New York.

Johnson, G. O. 1962. Special education for the mentally handicapped — a paradox. Except. Child. 29:62–69.

Kamii, C., and Derman, L. 1971. The Engelmann approach to teaching logical thinking: Findings from the administration of some Piagetian tasks. In: D. R. Green, M. P. Ford, and G. B. Flamer (eds.), Measurement and Piaget. McGraw-Hill Book Company, New York.

Kamii, C., and DeVries, R. 1977. Piaget for early education. In: M. C. Day, and R. K. Parker (eds.), The Preschool in Action. Allyn and Bacon, Boston.

Kazdin, A. E. 1975. Methodology and assessment in evaluating reinforcement programs in applied settings. J. Appl. Behav. Anal. 6:517–539.

Kohlberg, L. 1968. Early education: A cognitive-developmental view. Child Develop. 39:1013–1063.

Kohlberg, L. 1972. The concepts of developmental psychology as the central guide to education. In: M. C. Reynolds (ed.), Proceedings of the Conference on Psychology and the Process of Schooling in the Next Decade. Leadership Training Institute, Minneapolis.

Kohlberg, L., and Mayer, R. 1972. Development as the aim of education. Harvard Educ. Rev. 42:449–498.

Kratochwill, T. R. 1978. Single Subject Research: Strategies for Measuring Change. Academic Press, Inc., New York.

McCarthy, D. 1972. The McCarthy Scales of Children's Abilities. The Psychological Corporation, New York.

Meisels, S. J. 1976. A personal-social theory for the cognitive-developmental classroom. Viewpoints (Bulletin of the School of Education, Indiana University) 52:15–21.

Meisels, S. J. 1978. Open education and the integration of children with special needs. In: M. J. Guralnick (ed.), Early Intervention and the Integration of Handicapped and Nonhandicapped Children. University Park Press, Baltimore.

Parton, M. B. 1932. Social participation among preschool children. J. Abnorm. and Soc. Psychol. 27:243–269.

Patton, M. Q. 1975. Alternative evaluation research paradigm. North Dakota Study Group on Evaluation, Grand Forks, N. D.

Patton, M. Q. 1978. Utilization-Focused Evaluation. Sage Publications, Beverly Hills, Cal.

Riecken, H., and Boruch R. (eds.) 1974. Social Experimentation: A Method for Planning and Evaluating Social Intervention. Academic Press, Inc., New York.

Schatzman, L., and Strauss, A. L. 1973. Field Research: Strategies for a Natural Sociology. Prentice-Hall, Englewood Cliffs, N. J.

Scriven, M. 1972. Prose and cons about goal-free evaluation. Evaluation Comment. J. Educ. Eval. 3:1–7.

Scriven, M. 1976. Maximizing the power of causal investigations: The modus operandi method. In: G. V. Glass (ed.), Evaluation Studies Review Annual. Vol. I. Sage Publications, Beverly Hills, Cal.

Stebbins, L. B., St. Pierre, R. B., Proper, E. C., Anderson, R. B., and Cerva, R. T. 1977. Education as Experimentation: A Planned Variation Model, Vol. IV-A. Abt Associates, Cambridge.

Stodolsky, S. 1972. Defining treatment and outcome in early childhood education. In: H. Walberg and A. Kaplan (eds.), Rethinking Urban Education. Jossey-Boss Publishing Company, San Francisco.

Stodolsky, S. 1975. Identifying and evaluating open education. Phi Delta Kappan 57:113–117.

Strenio, J., Weisberg, H. I., and Bryk, A. S. 1978. Combining longitudinal and cross-sectional information. Paper presented at Annual Meetings of the American Statistical Association, August 14–18, San Diego.

Sutherland, J. 1973. A General Systems Philosophy for the Social and Behavioral Sciences. George Braziller, New York.

White, O. R. 1977. Behaviorism in special education. In: R. D. Kneedler, and S. G. Travers (eds.), Changing Perspectives in Special Education. Charles E. Merrill Publishing Company, Columbus, Ohio.

Wynne, S., Ulfeder, L. S. and Dakof, G. 1975. Mainstreaming and Early Childhood Education for Handicapped Children. Wynne Associates, Washington, D. C.

Yates, A. J. 1970. Behavior Therapy. John Wiley & Sons, Inc., New York.

Open Education and Young Children with Special Needs
An Annotated Bibliography

Rebecca Brown Corwin

Open education represents a response on the part of teachers to a complex array of factors that are involved in classroom life. The most important element in this response seems to be an awareness of children's individual needs for creating meaning in the world. Open classroom teachers, particularly those who work with handicapped children, must be alert to a variety of classroom options and ways of teaching and learning.

The books and articles that have been included in this bibliography are particularly useful illustrations of various aspects of open education. The selections are intended to assist teachers and administrators who wish to learn more about open education and its view of teaching and learning. The selections are arranged by major topics that roughly parallel the growth in awareness among educators about open education in the United States during the past decade.

CURRICULUM REFORM:
THE FAILURE OF THE SCHOOLS TO MEET CHILDREN'S NEEDS

In the 1960s all aspects of society underwent extensive criticism. Many voices were raised against the schools. These selections are representative of the strongest and most frequently read critiques and polemics.

Holt, J. 1964. *How Children Fail.* Dell Publishing Company, New York.

This book is a powerful indictment of the "usual," or traditional, methods of education. Holt spent a year observing children's strategies, both for learning

---

The section "Practical Books for Teachers" was prepared by the staff of the Evelyn G. Pitcher Curriculum Resource Laboratory, Department of Child Study, Tufts University.

and nonlearning. Few classroom teachers can read the book without recognizing its message — children attempt to *appear* to know what the teacher is trying to teach. Holt is important to read or re-read. This book emphasizes the nonthinking approach, which many of the more traditional approaches to teaching unwittingly foster.

Herndon, J. 1968. *The Way It Spozed To Be.* Simon and Schuster, Inc., New York.

Documenting the struggle engaged in by teachers who know that what they are "spozed to do" is wrong, Herndon writes superbly and vividly about his own teaching experiences. Herndon describes classroom incidents brilliantly. His ideas persist because he sees through specific incidents to the patterns and principles that constitute the structures of children's learning. His observations provide many insights for teachers and serve to raise questions concerning the teaching-learning process.

Dennison, G. 1969. *The Lives of Children.* Random House, New York.

This is Dennison's history of an urban free school. Although his approach differs in some ways from that of open educators, he brilliantly documents the process of beginning to work with high-risk children in a free environment. The children's lives are the focus of the book, and the vividness of the descriptions helps make Dennison's portraits of "disturbed" or "learning disabled" children clear and compelling.

Silberman, C. 1970. *Crisis in the Classroom.* Random House, New York.

Silberman's book is the single most comprehensive coverage of American schools in the late 1960s. Silberman is not an alarmist; he simply observes, draws conclusions, and writes clearly about those conclusions. He appeals to British open schools as a source of ideas and reform. The scope and power of the book make it extremely valuable; many of the criticisms are still valid today.

BRITAIN: THE VISION OF ANOTHER WAY

The educational ideas realized in many of the British infant schools began to achieve popularity in the United States during the mid to late 1960s. At that time they were proposed as one way of solving some of the problems in the schools. Responsible spokespersons never proposed adoption of a "model" of British education. Rather, many went to great lengths to indicate that there was not a totally set way in which these teachers worked. Yet, the fact that within a compulsory school system teachers experienced freedom to help meet children's needs was enough to establish British informal education as a vision of a better way of teaching children.

Featherstone, J. 1971. *Schools Where Children Learn.* Liveright, New York.

Many of these essays first appeared in the *New Republic,* where they provoked enormous interest in British informal education. Featherstone's descriptions of school practice stress the involvement of classroom teachers in the reform and reshaping of school curriculum. He continually notes the high standards that are set in British schools and the fact that the British are willing to let children take their own time in fulfilling required skills work. The essays are highly descriptive both of classrooms and of the underlying theories of child development and curricula.

Blackie, J. 1971. *Inside the Primary School.* Schocken, New York.

This is one of the clearest descriptions of the practice of education in the informal British schools. Blackie includes information on the major subject matter areas, as well as the rationale underlying the integrated day, vertical grouping, and other features of informal classrooms.

Children and Their Primary Schools: A Report of the Central Advisory Council for Education (England). Volumes I and II. 1967. Her Majesty's Stationery Office. London.

The Plowden report (so-called) served to present a comprehensive review of the philosophy, practice, and focus of the informal education schools in England. The report is rich with information concerning every aspect of the schools. It also includes material on handicapped children and the reasons for keeping them with their nonhandicapped peers.

Weber, L. 1971. *The English Infant School and Informal Education.* Prentice-Hall, Englewood Cliffs, N.J.

This is one of the most comprehensive treatments of English schools that is available. Weber writes vividly of infant school classrooms that she visited. She describes curriculum and theory, and she identifies a number of guiding principles, which she suggests may be helpful for American schools, as well. Weber proposes guidelines for moving toward open education in America and includes an extremely helpful list of films and books.

Murrow, C., and Murrow, L. 1971. *Children Come First.* American Heritage Press, New York.

The Murrows' description of children and teachers at work in British schools is clear, and it includes extensive background information concerning ways in which the movement toward informality in England was begun and continued. The book contains a wealth of information useful to classroom practitioners, as well as more general information about organizing the delivery of services to schools and within schools. The Murrows draw conclusions about the needs of particular kinds of services and priorities in American schools.

Brown, M., and Precious, N. 1968. *The Integrated Day in the Primary School.* Agathon Press, Inc., New York.

The authors of this book were serving as head teachers upon its publication. They intended the work to serve as an explanation of the integrated day and, in particular, of the teacher's role. The book is especially useful in its descriptions of record-keeping systems and in its presentation of children's case studies. Two of the cases give insight into the educational processes by which the child with special needs is integrated into the regular informal classroom.

Ridgway, L., and Lawton, I. 1969. *Family Grouping in the Primary School.* Agathon Press, Inc., New York.

In this work Ridgway and Lawton cover all aspects of heterogeneous, vertical age-grouping as an organizational pattern, including children's social, emotional, and intellectual development. They include concrete examples of ways of grouping and sample schedules.

Featherstone, J. 1971. *An Introduction.* Citation Press, New York.

This book is the introductory work in the series *Informal Schools in Britain Today,* edited by Maurice Kogan. Featherstone summarizes the background history of the informal schools movement and identifies the major features of British informal classrooms. He provides an excellent historical overview of changes in the British primary schools. He touches on curriculum, school organization, evaluation, and the school context. Featherstone also draws some conclusions concerning the relevance of informal education for American schools. The entire series of twenty-two books is an excellent resource.

Garry, M. T. 1972. *Internship in a Primary School.* National Association of Independent Schools, Boston.

Garry provides a vivid account of her experiences in teaching in an inner London school. She describes her work with language-deprived urban children and includes longitudinal records of an acting-out 5-year-old, as well as an entire chapter on difficult children.

Richardson, E. 1964. *In the Early World.* Pantheon Books, New York.

Richardson establishes, as the central goal of his work, the development of valid artistic statements by children. He approaches all of learning through the arts. He shows that children express their ideas through the medium of the arts. The remaining subject areas become integrated into this expression. He includes numerous examples of children's work and longitudinal descriptions of children and their written work. The classroom environment is clearly established to promote and develop high standards, and Richardson describes many of the ways in which those standards were achieved.

Barth, R. 1970. When children enjoy school: Some lessons from Britain. *Childhood Education,* 46:195–200.

Barth investigates the topic of enjoyment in education and relates it to options, significant choices, collaboration with peers, trust of adults, consistent order in the school climate, and minimal comparisons with others. Barth carefully differentiates between the enjoyment that arises as a byproduct of school experience and the enjoyment that is aimed at as an end in itself. This represents a useful distinction between "fun" and a deeper, more satisfying kind of engagement with learning.

AMERICAN ATTEMPTS AND EXPERIENCES WITH OPEN EDUCATION

This section includes books and articles that describe American schools that have implemented the concept of informal education. The value of the writings lies in their descriptions of classrooms, as well as in assessment of the processes by which changes were implemented. A variety of approaches to informal education is documented here, and they help to clarify questions about classroom practice.

Barth, R. 1972. *Open Education and the American School.* Agathon Press, Inc., New York.

This book contains Barth's often-quoted list of assumptions about open education; many practitioners have had occasion to discuss and debate them. It is important that this list serve as a catalyst, rather than as a credo for believers. Barth chronicles the rather dismal history of one attempt at implementing open education within a system that was not, ultimately, supportive of its goals. He also devotes one chapter to the role of the principal in implementing new programs in the schools. The annotated bibliography is very helpful.

Devaney, K. 1974. *Developing Open Education in America.* National Association for the Education of Young Children, Washington, D.C.

Devaney provides a useful review of the changes taking place in some American schools. She extensively describes various supports, including principals, advisors, teacher centers, parents, and curriculum planners, that are necessary for the teachers involved in change. In each case, Devaney gives examples of programs that are already developed or currently developing in this country.

Sargent, B. 1970. *The Integrated Day in an American School.* National Association of Independent Schools, Boston.

This book documents the changes and growth that Sargent witnessed during a year of teaching 5-, 6-, and 7-year-old children. Floor plans demonstrate the changing use of space; records of materials and activities are included to show how various areas within the classroom were used. Extensive discussion of the flow of activities from children's interests illustrates how learning can be extended and supported in an open classroom. Because the descriptions of materials and space are placed within a chronological sequence, the context for learning is clearly developed. This is one of the most specific and helpful books for the classroom teacher.

Langstaff, N. 1975. *Teaching in an Open Classroom: Informal Checks, Diagnoses, and Learning Strategies for Beginning Reading and Math.* National Association of Independent Schools, Boston.

In this book Langstaff describes beginning reading and math in her classroom along with the checks that she used to diagnose children's learning strategies. She includes case studies of five children over two years' time, her predictions based on observation and informal assessment, strategies to be followed with each child, and analyses of the results.

Manolakes, T. 1972. Introduction: The open education movement. *National Elementary Principal* 52:10–15.

Manolakes gives some history of the open education movement in America and reinforces the notion that it is not, nor can it be, a British transplant. He proposes that as interest in open education grows, there must be an increase in the availability of support systems for teachers. He suggests that principals become educational leaders or, as their British counterparts, head teachers.

Hapgood, M. 1972. The open classroom: Protect it from its friends. *National Elementary Principal* 52:43–48.

Hapgood critiques the romantic notions held by some open classroom advocates and differentiates between a "free" open classroom and a "transitional" open classroom. She advocates moving toward open structures slowly, and she gives suggestions concerning how to initiate an open classroom. The article also draws important distinctions between laissez-faire classrooms and open classrooms.

Kohn, S. 1972. The observer: Vito Perrone and North Dakota's quiet Revolution. *National Elementary Principal* 52:49–57.

The history of North Dakota's New School of Behavioral Studies in Education and its link to the history of change in that state's schools is presented in this article. Kohn includes a description of a British teacher center and presents a strong argument for creating an analogous institution in the United States. He includes an interesting list of parameters for an open school.

Rathbone, C. H. 1972. Examining the open education classroom. *School Review* 80:521–539.

Rathbone identifies and discusses four key organizational features of open education: space, time, grouping, and organization of instruction. His analysis includes a delineation of the goals of open education and a discussion of their appropriateness and their suitability for evaluation. He makes a useful distinction between fact (what *is* happening), expectation (what we *think* will happen), and intent (what we *want* to have happen). These differences are critical to the interpretation of any classroom model.

Rogers, V. R., and Church, B. (eds.) 1975. *Open Education: Critique and Assessment.* Association of Superintendents and Curriculum Developers, Washington, D.C.

This collection of essays about open education makes a significant contribution to the exploration of the concept of openness and its relation to American values. The editors include one successful case study and one that is less successful. A chapter that reviews the research on open education is particularly helpful for those who wish an overview of the research findings.

Elofson, T. H. 1973. Open Education in the Elementary School: Six Teachers Who Were Expected to Change. Center for Instructional Research and Curriculum Education. Illinois University, Urbana, Ill. In: Educational Research Information Clearinghouse. ERIC number ED 084 023.

Elofson provides an eloquent state-of-the-art statement and a history of open education. Her study of six teachers in Washington, D.C. suggests conclusions concerning the conditions that are necessary for teacher support and growth, and presents a clear picture of the process of change and personal/professional growth.

Perrone, V., and others. 1977. *Two Elementary Classrooms: Views of the Teachers, Children and Parents*. Kendall/Hunt. Dubuque, Iowa.

The authors include excerpts from extensive interviews with teachers, children, and parents who are involved in two classrooms that are beginning to implement informal education. Detailed transcripts allow the reader to develop a strong sense of the reality of the classrooms and their environments, routines, and expectations.

COLLECTIONS OF ESSAYS ON OPEN EDUCATION

These books stand apart from the descriptions of open education practices either in Britain or America. In all three, the authors intend to give some sense of the definition of open education, its basis in various theories, and its implications for areas such as curriculum, teachers' roles, and school organization. All three collections are comprehensive in their scope.

Rathbone, C. (ed.) 1971. *Open Education: the Informal Classroom*. Citation Press, New York.

This is the first of the major collections of essays on open education. It includes many original and pioneering ideas. Two of David Hawkins' essays, entitled "I-Thou-It" and "Messing About in Science," are included. These are extremely important philosophical essays concerning the relationship between teachers, curriculum materials, and children in the process of learning. Anthony Kallett's "Two Classrooms," a vivid contrast of a good traditional classroom and a good open classroom, is important. Rathbone's essays on teacher education and the rationale for the open classroom are also extremely useful.

Nyquist, E. B., and Hawes, G. R. (eds.) 1972. *Open Education: A Sourcebook for Parents and Teachers*. Bantam Books, Inc., New York.

Nyquist and Hawes have selected a large number of important essays, including those that deal with the basic differences and advantages of open education, articles concerning ways in which open education functions, how to introduce open education to the schools (a collection of case studies), basic philosophy and research findings, and an excellent annotated bibliography. They have collected significant essays by many of the pioneers in the field, and the case studies are extremely helpful.

Silberman, C. (ed.) 1973. *The Open Classroom Reader*. Vintage Press, New York.

Silberman's selections are divided into four major categories: descriptions of how classrooms are organized and what they look like, the rationale for open education in terms of the aims of education and the nature of childhood, aspects of the teacher's role, and descriptions of curriculum practices. He includes excerpts from the Plowden Report, psychological theorists, educational philosophers, practicing teachers, teacher advisors, and others with practical knowledge of applications. This is a thorough, comprehensive collection and may be the best one-volume overview that is available. Silberman's selections are excellent, and his introductory essays provide a very useful context.

CURRICULUM REFORM AND CLASSROOM PROVISIONING

Curriculum decisions have always been of primary importance; they can be viewed as the backbone of a teacher's efforts. Many of the most important decisions in teaching have to strike a balance between children's interests and needs and the surface curriculum demands. To achieve this end, teachers must learn to be excellent observers of children and resourceful experimenters; the environment must be structured to facilitate the maximum amount of independence; and balance between the group and the individual, as well as between social and academic work, must be sought.

A tremendous amount of energy in open education has been directed to reforming the curriculum of the schools or in focusing attention on the places in which reform is needed.

Educational Development Center, Inc. 1970. *The E.S.S. Reader.* Newton, Mass.

This collection of essays forms a framework for planning curriculum based on observations of children working with materials and engaging in problem solving. David Hawkins' introduction to the essays summarizes much of the process of discovery and experimentation that marks the open education attitude toward children and learning.

Hawkins, D. 1974. *The Informed Vision.* Agathon Press, Inc., New York.

Hawkins' essays highlight the importance of allowing children to engage in real tasks so that their interests may be expressed and developed. This collection of essays is a philosophical exploration of many of the ideas that are critically important in curriculum planning. Their impact on open education has been strong, and their power lies in their thoughtful exploration of key issues and concepts.

Chittenden, E. A. 1969. What is learned and what is taught. *Young Children* 25:12–19.

Chittenden explores Piaget's developmental perspective and extracts those notions that are most important in planning for children's learning. He contends that action, repetition, variation of task, and real situations or objects are the keys to providing for maximal learning. Chittenden explores the balance needed between learning and teaching. The essay is a good, short survey of the major issues in curriculum planning.

Bussis, A. M., Chittenden, E. A., and Amarel, M. 1976. *Beyond Surface Curriculum: An Interview Study of Teachers' Understanding.* Westview Press, Boulder, Col.

This book represents an extremely important investigation of the levels upon which curriculum can be planned for children. The authors interviewed teachers in order to determine their patterns of planning curriculum for children. The teachers differentiate between two levels of content: surface content (the "what" to teach) and organizing content (the "what for" of learning). Within each of those categories the authors investigate teachers' constructs of the fusion between learning, child development, and instruction.

Corwin, R. B., Hein, G. E., and Levin, D. 1976. Weaving curriculum webs: The structure of nonlinear curriculum. *Childhood Education* 52:248–251.

This article presents a short description of the complexities of open education curriculum, contrasting it with the traditional linear model. The authors use a flowchart to aid in record keeping and planning. The interrelationship of subject matter areas, children's learning, and real-world experiences is clearly described.

Taylor, J. 1971. *Organizing and Integrating the Infant Day.* Allen and Unwin, Limited, London.

Taylor provides an excellent overview of the practical aspects of the integrated day for classroom practitioners. She illustrates her suggestions with a rich array of specific examples. This is one of the best books that promises to help teachers in the daily classroom implementation of many open education ideas.

Engel, B. 1973. *Arranging the Informal Classroom.* Education Development Center, Inc., Newton, Mass.

This book focuses on provisioning the open classroom. It clearly illustrates a wide variety of classroom equipment and furniture that can be made by teachers for their classrooms. The book will be useful to teachers trying to implement an informal classroom without the support of a large school budget.

Kogan, M. (ed.) 1971. *Informal Schools in Britain Today.* Vol. I: Curriculum. Citation Press, New York.

This is the first volume in an Anglo-American collaborative effort. The series consists of a collection of twenty-two small volumes, each of which treats a different aspect of curriculum in depth. The individual volumes include illustrations of children's work, as well as helpful concrete examples of classroom materials and activities.

Yardley, A. 1974. *Structure in Early Learning.* Citation Press, New York.

Yardley explores ways to balance a theoretical framework of conceptual development with concrete ideas and situations. She differentiates between structure that is presented only in academic areas and a deeper level of structure that is based on children's cognitive processes. She includes very helpful chapters in each of the academic subject areas, as well as socialization, emotional growth, cognitive development, record keeping, and relationships with parents.

Biggs, E. 1970. *Freedom to Learn.* Addison-Wesley Publishing Company, Inc., Reading, Mass.

Biggs' volume includes theoretical information, as well as practical methods of implementing a problem-solving, materials-based approach in mathematics, both for teacher education and for children. Throughout the volume useful connections are drawn between theory and practice; the illustrations are clear and extremely helpful.

Schwebel, M. and Raph, J. (eds.) 1973. *Piaget in the Classroom.* Basic Books, New York.

This collection of essays focuses upon the connections of Piaget's cognitive developmental theories with classroom practice. It represents an extremely thoughtful and challenging collection of essays on curriculum. The authors do not make superficial connections between Piaget and classrooms, but consider relationships between deep levels of planning, implementing, and provisioning the learning environment.

Biber, B., Shapiro, E., and Wickens, D. 1971. *Promoting Cognitive Growth: A Developmental-Interaction Point of View.* National Association for the Education of Young Children, Washington, D. C.

This monograph succinctly presents goals for a preschool program based upon developing competence, interpersonal relatedness, individuality, and creativity. The authors include sequences of learning and vignettes of classroom interactions, analyzed in terms of these goals. This is a significant contribution to the literature for teachers of young children.

Elkind, D. 1970. *Children and Adolescents: Interpretive Essays on Jean Piaget.* Oxford University Press, New York.

Elkind's essays connect Piaget's theories to a variety of issues that teachers face daily. He writes specifically about children's notions of time, their egocentrism, and the difficult questions that they ask. These essays clarify the relationship between cognitive aspects of development and the social/affective areas that are often considered separately.

Weikart, D., Rogers, L., Adcock, C., and McClelland, D. 1971. *The Cognitively Oriented Curriculum: A Framework for Preschool Teachers.* National Association for the Education of Young Children, Washington, D.C.

The authors include both structure and principles of a cognitively oriented curriculum program for preschool-age children. The book is very clear and the activities that are suggested are appropriately described and set into a cognitive framework. Record-keeping methods and specific teaching ideas are included.

Dropkin, R. (ed.) 1976. *Teachers with Children: Curriculum in Open Classrooms.* Workshop Center for Open Education, New York.

Teachers describe their classroom curricula in a variety of subject areas. Lillian Weber's essay "On Curriculum" helps to clarify the open classroom practitioner's view of curriculum and classroom implementation issues. Catherine Molony contributes a helpful section on documentation.

PRACTICAL BOOKS FOR TEACHERS

"What to do tomorrow with the children?" or "How do I facilitate one child's interests or instructional needs?" These are questions that teachers constantly ask as they strive to create a balance between the group and the individual referred to at the beginning of the previous section.

For some teachers there seems to be too many resource books of curriculum ideas or activities, yet for others there are never enough. Many of the activity books that are available attempt to exploit a current craze or reform movement. They quickly outrun their usefulness. Other books live on and are cherished by teachers representing all philosophical dispositions. What is unique about most of these lasting, practical books is that they have a sound, conceptual structure — a sense, a feeling, and a knowledge of what is developmentally appropriate for young children. They define and exemplify child growth and development concepts. They also acknowledge the material realities of today's classroom by suggesting activities that require commonly available materials or scrounged or recycled materials.

The following books were selected because they qualify as unique and enduring in the ways that were just described. They were also chosen because of the appeal that the activities have for young children and teachers of young children.

For the most part, each book presents activities that are not so didactic that the adaptation of the activity and its materials for special needs children is impossible. In fact, there may be no such thing as curriculum or activites *solely* for special needs children. Instead, what is required is a constant matching of individual objectives expressed as needs, and instructional treatments expressed in relevant, appropriate activities. The following books contain such activities, and often the needs that they fill are suggested or at least implied.

This book list is short and incomplete compared to what is available on the curricular marketplace. Some of the many books that have not been included stress the importance of children producing products, rather than the encouragement of individual variation and experimentation during the process of product creation.

Although this list is not exhaustive, it is presented with the expectation that interested teachers will pursue the bibliographic references in them, as well as in other sections of this chapter.

Nuffield Foundation, 1970. *Nuffield Mathematics Project Teacher's Guides.* John Wiley and Sons, Inc., New York

This set of guides is one of the most significant Piagetian-based collections of curriculum units ever produced. It presents concrete, relevant mathematical experiences for children 5- to 7-years-old. Concept attainment and activities for building skills in computation are based in activities requiring no special apparatus or environmental changes.

Titles include:

Mathematics Begins	Checking Up 1
Beginnings	Shapes and Sizes
Pictorial Representations	Computation and Structure
Environmental Geometry	Mathematics: The First 3 Years
I Do and I Understand	Mathematics: The Later Primary Years

The Schools Council (Great Britain). 1972. *Science 5/13 Series.* McDonald Educational, London.

This set of guides is for teachers who are interested in the integration of science and mathematics through children's first-hand experiences in the material world. Developmentally oriented, these carefully developed teacher's guides present concrete activities that require the use of commonly available materials and no special apparatus.

Titles include:

Early Experiences	Time
Structure and Forces	Like and Unlike
Working with Wood	Using the Environment
Science from Toys	Change
Trees	

These guides are for the teacher who is seeking innovative ways of integrating science and math.

Barratta-Lorton, M. 1972. *Workjobs.* Addison-Wesley Publishing Company, Inc., Reading, Mass.

Barratta-Lorton has written this book for teachers who prefer treating curriculum skills by having children play instructional games and use instructional manipulatives. Instructions for using commonly available materials for constructing these materials are included.

Baratta-Lorton, M. 1975. *Workjobs for Parents.* Addison-Wesley Publishing Company, Inc., Reading, Mass.

Similar to the book described above, this book for parents shares examples of games that can be made at home by parents who attempt to extend school learning into the home environment.

Farrow, E., and Hill, C. 1975. *Montessori on a Limited Budget: Almanac for the Amateur Craftsman.* Montessori Workshop, Ithaca, N. Y.

Farrow and Hill wrote this book for the teacher who is handy with tools and woodcraft and wants to make the classic Montessori manipulatives. Although these materials are very structured in intended use, they are important materials for treating the mathematical/spatial concepts of one-to-one correspondence, grouping, and seriation. The theory behind the materials and the special concepts and teaching practices are well explained.

Wiseman, A. 1973, 1975. *Making Things.* Books 1 and 2. Little, Brown & Company, Boston, Mass.

Both books are written for teachers who prefer project/product-making experiences for children. Kite making, musical instrument making, classroom furniture, cooking projects, and rubber stamp making exemplify the activities that are found in these books.

Caney, S. 1975. *Play Book.* Workman Publishing Company, New York.

A project/product booklet for teachers who prefer such activities for young children. Projects, constructions, games, puzzles, and other activities for children are organized according to the spaces in which they play. Discards and inexpensive materials are used to create unique products.

Caney, S. 1975. *Toy Book.* Workman Publishing Company, New York.

Similar in format to the above book by the same author, this book, again for teachers who prefer project/product activities, shows how to make toys and provides suggestions of ways in which toys can be many different things to a child. The toy designs are simple and can be built by children themselves from everyday objects.

Ault, R. 1972. *Kids are Natural Cooks.* Parents Nursery School, Cambridge, Mass.

Written for teachers and parents who want to cook with young children, this book provides a collection of recipes that are fun to make, taste good, and are good for you. Children of all ages will be helped to understand the natural processes involved in growing, preparing, eating, and digesting foods of many different kinds through cooking in the classroom.

Skelsey, A., and Huckaby, G. 1976. *Growing Green.* Workman Publishing Company, New York.

This book was written especially for teachers, parents, and children who want to garden together both indoors and outdoors. The book is refreshing, since it includes activities beyond, but including, the tried and true in growing things with children.

Shrank, J. 1974. *The Seed Catalog: A Guide to Teaching-learning Materials.* Beacon Press, Boston.

Shrank has created a comprehensive guide to books, films, tapes, records, publications, games, video tapes, and other instructional materials that teachers can choose from to add ideas to their instructional practices.

Simons, R. 1976. *Recyclopedia: Games, Science Equipment, and Crafts from Recycled Materials.* Houghton Mifflin Company, Boston.

Simons, with her long experience at the Children's Museum of Boston, has compiled an excellent book of games, crafts, and scientific equipment that can be made from recycled materials. Each idea or project is described fully with directions for its construction. The aim of the book is to provide the reader with the basic conceptual tools necessary for improvising and exploring beyond the scope of the suggestions in the book.

Blake, J., and Ernst, B. 1976. *The Great Perpetual Learning Machine.* Little, Brown & Company, Boston.

Blake and Ernst have written a most popular resource book that appeals to teachers of many dispositions. The sections on organizing space, math, science, nature and ecology, arts and crafts, music and movement, ourselves, and language are dealt with fully and creatively. Most ideas for activities are multimedia in nature, but use commonly available resources.

Pitcher, E., Lasher, M., Feinburg, S., and Braun, L. 1979. *Helping Young Children Learn.* (3rd Edition). Charles E. Merrill Publishing Company, Columbus.

This book, written for teachers and future teachers, is unique in its field in the way in which it weaves excellent activities with sound understanding of children's learning. Music and art for young children, children's literature, understanding the physical world, integrating curriculum, and learning problems in the classroom are among the topics that exemplify the content of this most complete and well-conceived book.

National Association for the Education of Young Children. 1978. Washington, D. C.

NAEYC is the national organization for teachers of young children and the voice that speaks nationally on behalf of young children. NAEYC's books and pamphlets are valuable resources on a wide range of curriculum topics appropriate for young children. Titles listed as "Ideas for Teaching" include: *Block Book, Cognitively Oriented Curriculum, Idea Book, Ideas That Work with Young Children, Mud, Sand, and Water, Piaget, Children, and Number, Science with Young Children,* and *What is Music for Young Children?* Modestly priced, these books represent the finest example of the confluence of theory and practice.

Harbin, G., and Cross, L. 1976. *Early Childhood Materials*. Walker and Company, New York.

For teachers interested in commercially available curriculum programs in early childhood education, this book with its annotated bibliography provides an overview of the purposes and content of significant early childhood programs. Particular attention is devoted to young children with special needs.

Stephens, S. C. 1975. *A Curriculum Guide for Early Childhood Education*. Developmental Learning Materials, Niles, Ill.

This little booklet not only suggests activities that utilize D. L. M.'s well-conceived materials, but goes well beyond that to present activities that are appropriate to each in the suggested curriculum areas. Kinds of activities, goals for each activity, and teaching attributes appropriate to each curriculum area are carefully outlined in this handy booklet for all teachers of young children.

Eliason, C. F., and Jenkins, L. T. 1977. *A Practical Guide to Early Childhood Curriculum*. C. V. Mosby Company, St. Louis.

Eliason and Jenkins have written this excellent book for those in the process of preparing to teach young children, as well as for inservice teachers. Their concern for the quality of young children's school experiences is expressed in their ideas for generating thematic curriculum experiences. Lesson plans for a variety of curriculum ideas, including color, numbers, transportation, animals, and weight, are presented in such a way that they spark teachers' imaginations, while providing sufficient structure to get one started.

Education Development Center, Inc. 1971. *A Working Guide to the Elementary Science Study*. Newton, Mass.

A comprehensive guide to the more than 50 science curriculum units developed by this National Science Foundation-funded curriculum development project. Considered by many to have been on the cutting edge of curriculum innovation in this country, the Elementary Science Study developed 10 units that are appropriate for early childhood. The titles include: *Light and Shadows, Gerbils, Sinking and Floating, Mobiles, The Life of Beans and Peas, Geo Blocks, Pattern Blocks, Attribute Blocks, Mirror Cards,* and *Sand.* Developed with a Piagetian orientation, these units are best for teachers looking beyond the traditional conceptualizations of science education.

Edco Reading and Learning Center. 1976. *A Practical Guide to Creating Reading Games*. Educational Collaborative of Greater Boston, Brookline, Mass.

Compiled for teachers of both preschool and early primary grades, this book is probably the most comprehensive, detailed, usable booklet available on this subject.

Cataldo, J. 1969. *Words and Calligraphy for Children*. Reinhold Book Corporation, New York.

Cataldo has collected examples of children's artwork and shared them as ideas of how children can be encouraged to approach lettering and writing with a free, exploratory attitude. Included are ideas of how to use letters, words, prose, and poetry as expressive elements in painting and drawings.

Eberhart, A. 1975. *Swinging on a Tune: Songs for the Very Small and Very Tall.* Emporia State Press, Emporia, Kan.

Eberhart has successfully written this book with an eye to creating a book that is useful to both adults and children. Some of the tried and true songs, plus many new songs, are found in this book. The introduction suggests that these are special songs to be used in special ways: "to capture the mood of the moment, calm ruffled feelings, travel through transition periods...to enjoy any time any place." The book is a practical guide for teachers who want to use music in these and other ways.

DOCUMENTATION AND EVALUATION

The issue of accountability has increased the pressure on professionals in all areas. In education, most methods of evaluation measure only a small portion of children's behaviors. The effort to document and evaluate the effects of informal classrooms has led to a focus on developing alternative methods of evaluation. The critical issue is that of matching the means of evaluation to the ends of education. Since children in open classrooms are considered as total individuals, means of recording and documenting their progress must include a great deal more than the standard measures of cognitive gain. This focus on alternative forms of evaluation methodology pervades the selections in this section.

McDonald, J. B. 1974. An evaluation of evaluation. *Urban Review* 7:3-15.

This article focuses on the problems inherent in relying on standard methods of evaluation that are used in schools. McDonald argues that since knowledge is uncertain, personal, and constantly evolving, goals for school programs should not be dependent on our ability to measure only performance acts.

Eisner, E. W. 1972. Emerging models for educational evaluation. *School Review* 80:573-590.

Eisner reviews earlier efforts at curriculum reform and suggests the need for more work in the field of evaluation. He identifies several basic problems with the standard experimental evaluation paradigm. Eisner posits three types of objectives that require appropriate evaluation methodologies: instructional objectives, expressive objectives, and a third category which he describes as similar to a problem in architecture, in which a tightly structured problem may lead to a range of solutions. It is evident that standard paradigms are not adequate for the full task of evaluation.

Patton, M. Q. 1975. *Alternative Evaluation Research Paradigm.* North Dakota Study Group on Evaluation, Grand Forks, N. D.

Patton deliberately heightens the contrast between quantitative and qualitative research methodology. He proposes that different types of questions require different types of research methods. The issues involved in research are considered carefully. Patton proposes that neither method meets all the needs of educational research, but that aspects of both methods can be productively combined.

Hein, G. 1975. *An Open Education Perspective on Evaluation.* North Dakota Study Group on Evaluation, Grand Forks, N. D.

Hein reviews open education issues that are relevant to evaluation and explains the characteristics of a number of evaluation paradigms. He reviews evaluation alternatives and he urges that their scope be broadened. Hein suggests the political structure of education and society must be altered as well, since evaluation reflects their biases and expectations.

Carini, P. F. 1975. *Observing and Describing: An Alternative Methodology for the Investigation of Human Phenomena.* North Dakota Study Group on Evaluation, Grand Forks, N. D.

This monograph presents a strongly reasoned argument for phenomenological observation in contrast to the technological observation that is generally used to investigate behavior and activity in the schools. Four levels of observations within the classroom are suggested, and examples of ways in which such observations might be recorded are presented through concrete examples of real situations. The book is carefully written and is rich with information concerning the "how-to" as well as the "why-to" of descriptive research.

Perrone, V. (ed.) 1975. *Testing and Evaluation: New Views.* Association for Childhood Education International, Washington, D.C.

This small volume is an excellent collection of essays concerning a number of aspects of testing. Deborah Meier reviews most of the problems and issues of reading tests succinctly and vividly. George Hein presents an important essay that describes tests as reflecting a sorting mechanism in our society. Bussis, Chittenden, and Amarel point out the pressure that educational models put on teachers to ignore the fact that standards of quality develop over time and that reassessment of our basic assumptions about treatment and behavioral outcomes is necessary. Brenda Engel contributes a helpful annotated bibliography on evaluation. This is an extremely useful book, and the references will help readers to follow lines of interest further.

Tobier, A. (ed.) 1973. *Evaluation Reconsidered.* Workshop Center for Open Education, New York.

This collection includes a series of articles on issues and perspectives concerning evaluation, alternative approaches to evaluation (including concrete examples in three different case studies), samples of forms and documents used in schools, and an account of how the ESEA documentation program failed because of difficulties inherent in evaluation methodology and implementation. This collection contains some extremely important essays and is of value to those who are trying to develop different forms of evaluation and documentation.

Horwitz, R. A. 1976. *Psychological Effects of Open Classroom Teaching on Primary School Children: A Review of the Research.* North Dakota Study Group on Evaluation, Grand Forks, N. D.

Horwitz reviews all of the major studies concerning open education. He also examines what he calls "progressive" practice (1930–1950) and reviews the recent evaluative research on open schools. His approach to both achievement and self-image is careful and systematic and includes suggestions of alternative ways of keeping track of children's progress.

Stodolsky, S. S. 1975. Identifying and evaluating open education. *Phi Delta Kappan* 57:113–117.

Stodolsky reviews a number of approaches to defining and identifying open education and then describes program evaluation issues. She takes the classic view of evaluation as an attempt to study outcomes of learning and suggests that it is critically important to measure open education's intended outcomes in different ways.

Hawes, G. R. 1974. Special report: Managing open education. *Nation's Schools* 93:33–47.

This article summarizes the issues that arise from the applications of standard evaluation methods to open classroom environments. Hawes includes examples of record-keeping methods and observations concerning diagnosis, evaluation, record keeping, and alternatives to testing.

Roderick, S. A., and Weed, E. S. 1976. How shall we evaluate the open classroom? *Elementary School Journal* 77:25–30.

The authors study 30 classrooms to measure differential achievement of children in conventional and open classrooms. They conclude that the broader dimensions of education must also be evaluated, not for open classrooms alone, but for all classrooms.

Spodek, B., and Walberg, H. J. (eds.) 1975. *Studies in Open Education.* Agathon Press, Inc., New York.

This collection of essays seeks to assist open educators in the development of a more systematic approach to theorizing about and directly studying open classrooms. Many of the selections include rating scales or observational frameworks, and Walberg and Thomas present an analytic review of the literature.

Engel, B. 1977. *Informal Evaluation*. North Dakota Study Group on Evaluation, Grand Forks, N. D.

This public school case study focuses on documentation and evaluation at three levels: the child, the classroom, and the institution or program. Informal record-keeping techniques are used to document the school program, and the wealth of information that is included illustrates the richness of data that can be gathered in informal ways. The monograph includes a list of basic principles of evaluation in open education.

Engel, B. 1975. *A Handbook of Documentation*. North Dakota Study Group on Evaluation. Grand Forks, N. D.

In this volume Engel presents the reader with a variety of ways of documenting classroom activities for a number of purposes. Her examples are concrete, and she includes comments about the utility of each type of record-keeping method. This is an extremely helpful book for the professional who is looking for methods to document a range of experiences in nonstandard ways.

Carini, P. F. 1973. The Prospect School: Taking account of process. *Childhood Education* 49:350–356.

Carini presents a portrait of an informal school and describes extremely careful ways that are used to document and record children's work and growth along a variety of dimensions. This is a concrete example of the successful use of informal, structured record-keeping techniques.

TEACHER CENTERS: SUPPORT FOR TEACHERS IN NEW ROLES

One of the major components in the development of informal classrooms in Britain has been the availability of support services. Support for teachers has come in three major ways: from the head teacher, or principal, from educational advisors, and from teacher centers. When each of these supports is available, teachers are able to rely upon them for help in thinking about and reacting to new challenges in planning for children's learning.

Although Americans have been somewhat slower to implement support services, there is now a national trend toward supporting teachers through a variety of inservice models and in a variety of different ways.

This section includes books and articles that deal with issues on a practical and theoretical basis, as well as some research on the effects of the advisory model on teachers and children.

Thornbury, R. (ed.) 1974. *Teachers' Centres*. Agathon Press, Inc., New York.

This collection focuses on aspects of teacher centers in England. The history of teacher centers reveals much debate concerning the degree to which they should

316   Corwin

remain locally controlled and to what extent they should become increasingly "professional." The essays consider regional curriculum development, support for urban teachers, and problems with centralism. Many essays are resonant of the problems facing developers of teacher centers in the United States.

Hapgood, M. (ed.) 1975. *Supporting the Learning Teacher: A Sourcebook for Teacher Centers.* Agathon Press, Inc., New York.

Hapgood includes many essays from a wide variety of sources. Many of the major teacher centers in the United States are represented in this collection, as well as a section linking teacher centers to teacher-training institutions. Among the authors are those who have begun centers, those who have attended workshops, those who sponsor workshops, and those who hope to develop other models of teacher support.

Rogers, V. (ed.) 1976. Special Issue: Teacher centers. *Educational Leadership* 33:403–480.

These essays cover a range of aspects of teacher centers, including case studies of three centers in action. Rogers' introductory article, "An Idea Whose Time Has Come?" is a helpful overview. Lickona and Hasch contribute a useful review of the research on teacher centers.

Devaney, K. 1978. *Essays on Teacher Centers.* Far West Laboratory for Educational Research and Development, San Francisco.

This collection of 12 essays focuses upon inservice experiences that engage teachers' talents and energies while supporting them intellectually and emotionally. The writings were gathered from those who have direct teacher center experiences in both the United States and England. In-classroom advisory work, teacher-designed curricula, and fundamental principles are treated. Contributors represent a wide range of advisors, teacher center staff members, and consumers of services. An annotated bibliography is included.

Lance, J., and Kreitzman, R. 1977. *Teachers' Centers Exchange Directory.* Far West Laboratory for Educational Research and Development, San Francisco.

This is an update of the 1975 book, *Exploring Teacher Centers,* which is available in the ERIC files as ED 107 601. It is extremely comprehensive, including the addresses, hours, aims, phone numbers, and other operational details of the major teacher centers in the United States. The authors include a good bibliography of books and materials, as well as the directory of centers and inservice programs. This volume is very helpful for those interested in teacher centers and teacher-training models.

Yarger, S. J., and others. 1974. *A Descriptive Study of the Teacher Center Movement in American Education.* In: Educational Research Information Clearinghouse. ERIC number ED 098 159.

This study presents a great deal of specific information concerning teacher centers in America. The authors include a history of centers in America, and they analyze 203 teacher centers in order to develop a typology of centers. All of the instruments and analytical tools that were used in the study are included. The authors conclude that centers should be active, aiming toward professional development, and that children should be considered the primary focus of the centers.

Cook, A., and Mack, H. 1975. *The Word and the Thing: Ways of Seeing the Teacher.* North Dakota Study Group on Evaluation, Grand Fords, N. D.

The authors suggest a variety of ways in which teachers can be helped to gain planning, evaluation, and assessment skills and can be aided in becoming researchers in their own classrooms. An extremely clear example of this kind of support is given, as teachers begin to gather information concerning the issue of dependency in children in their classrooms. The monograph proposes that question-focused discussion groups have excellent potential for assisting teachers in becoming agents in their own learning.

Alberty, B., and Dropkin, R. (eds.) 1975. *The Open Education Advisor.* Workshop Center for Open Education, New York.

This collection focuses on how advisors can be educated to their jobs, ways in which they might work with teachers, and the future of the advisory role. It includes useful narrative information from advisors concerning their perceptions of their roles and ways of proceeding. An extensive description of the Open Corridor program shows the ability of a community within a school to support an emotionally disturbed child. Another article presents an excellent description of a teacher's work with a disturbed child in an open classroom. Material on bilingualism is also included.

Weber, L. 1972. Developments in open corridor organization. *National Elementary Principal* 52:58–67.

Weber describes the Open Corridor Program in New York City as a support program for teachers. She describes the rationale for teacher centers, for change in education, and the need for advisors as external agents of change in the school.

Muskopf, A., and Moss, J. 1973. Open education: An in-service model. *Elementary School Journal* 73:117–124.

The authors describe a 4-week summer workshop in a teacher center, including the activities that teachers participated in and their relationship to the demonstration classroom of children being conducted concurrently. They analyze the dimensions that made the workshop successful as a learning and change experience. The authors see that many regular teachers can function as specialists and suggest some inspection of the implications of specialist roles as they currently tend to be defined.

SPECIAL EDUCATION AND OPEN EDUCATION

A variety of models exist for working with special needs children; many of the most successful models share a great deal in common with informal classroom structures. Many of the citations included in this section recommend an open classroom environment as the most appropriate and least restrictive environment possible for young children with special needs. It has become increasingly apparent that traditional classroom structures do not always meet the special needs of some children; more variety is indicated.

Hawkins, F. 1975. *The Logic of Action.* Pantheon Books, New York.

Hawkins documents her work with 6 preschool-age deaf children, in which she introduced the children to experiences and materials that enabled them to connect their classroom experiences with the world outside and around them. The book illustrates the type of diagnostic sensitivity that a careful observer of children can develop by watching children come to grips with real problems and real materials. Hawkins shares with us her process of planning and diagnosis. The book is one of the most useful and important in education. Through her eyes, one sees the inner dynamics of an open classroom at work.

Miller-Jacobs, S. 1975. *Mainstreaming Special Needs Children Into Open Settings.* In: Educational Research Information Clearinghouse. ERIC number ED 117 898.

Miller-Jacobs reviews assumptions about open education and identifies themes in both open and special education. She describes six programs for special needs children and evaluates one of them. She concludes that special needs children can use open settings in much more productive ways than generally believed.

Miller-Jacobs, S. 1976. *Open Education for Preschool Special Needs Children.* In: Educational Research Information Clearinghouse. ERIC number ED 135 451.

Miller-Jacobs defines open education, preschool education, and special education in order to explore common goals and themes: development of the total child, fostering of independence, use of multiple adults, and forms of individualization. All three themes focus on experiential learning and emphasize the processes of learning rather than only the products. Miller-Jacobs indicates ways in which preschool teachers can begin the process of implementing an open classroom, and she gives concrete examples.

Meisels, S. 1978. Open Education and Children with Special Needs. In: M. J. Guralnick (ed.) *Early Intervention and the Integration of Handicapped and Nonhandicapped Children.* University Park Press, Baltimore.

Meisels sees clearly the need to resolve issues that arise in the mainstreaming of handicapped children into nondeficit oriented settings. He proposes that the open classroom structure allows teachers to make extensive use of expressive materials and to individualize their programs in the most helpful way. He describes in detail a program that integrates handicapped children into regular preschool open classrooms.

Meisels, S. 1976. A personal-social theory for the cognitive-developmental classroom. *Viewpoints* (Bulletin of the School of Education, Indiana University.) 52:15–22.

Meisels discusses and explains the cognitive-developmental classroom with particular emphasis on implications for social development and for the handicapped child. He proposes that the affective and cognitive approaches can be integrated in open classrooms. He illustrates this model by describing a preschool mainstreamed program. The article represents a plea for developmental approaches to education that will focus on the needs of the whole child.

Binder, G. 1976. Open and special. Notes from Workshop Center for Open Education 5:17–20.

Binder reviews the open education attitude toward fitting programs to children, rather than children to programs. He makes a plea for viewing all children's needs as worth meeting, and he reminds the reader that the early special education classrooms were more similar to open classrooms than to traditional approaches.

Harlow, S. D. 1975. *Special Education: The Meeting of Differences.* North Dakota Study Group on Evaluation, Grand Forks, N. D.

In this monograph Harlow explores some of the issues concerning labeling and diagnosing children with special needs. He argues that due to our narrow framework of normality, schools may be creating handicaps where none exist. Harlow urges that children be evaluated differently and that school programs be adjusted to provide for them carefully. He proposes that the specialist teachers should support classroom teachers in their work with all children, rather than focus their services on only a few children.

Harman, S. G. 1975. All children are special. Notes from Workshop Center for Open Education 4:15–27.

The author carefully examines the Massachusetts state law that has served as a model for national legislation on special needs children. Her analysis reveals that the legislation has the potential to serve as a mandate to change all classrooms to provide better responses to the needs of all children. This is an interesting, provocative view of the legislation.

Knoblock, P. 1973. Open education for emotionally disturbed children. *Exceptional Children* 39:358–365.

Knoblock itemizes many characteristics of disturbed children and matches them with the supports that open education provides for them. He contends that open education is the extension of the self-actualization model of psychology to children. Knoblock views open education as a highly appropriate environment for disturbed children.

Index